**Teaching Expertise
in Three Countries**

Teaching Expertise in Three Countries

Japan, China, and the United States

Akiko Hayashi

The University of Chicago Press
Chicago and London

The University of Chicago Press, Chicago 60637
The University of Chicago Press, Ltd., London
© 2022 by The University of Chicago
All rights reserved. No part of this book may be
used or reproduced in any manner whatsoever
without written permission, except in the case of brief
quotations in critical articles and reviews. For more
information, contact the University of Chicago Press,
1427 E. 60th St., Chicago, IL 60637.
Published 2022
Printed in the United States of America

31 30 29 28 27 26 25 24 23 22   1 2 3 4 5

ISBN-13: 978-0-226-81865-8 (cloth)
ISBN-13: 978-0-226-81867-2 (paper)
ISBN-13: 978-0-226-81866-5 (e-book)
DOI: https://doi.org/10.7208/chicago/9780226818665
.001.0001

Library of Congress Cataloging-in-Publication Data

Names: Hayashi, Akiko, 1979– author.
Title: Teaching expertise in three countries : Japan,
    China, and the United States / Akiko Hayashi.
Description: Chicago : University of Chicago, 2022. |
    Includes bibliographical references and index.
Identifiers: LCCN 2021041544 | ISBN 9780226818658
    (cloth) | ISBN 9780226818672 (paperback) | I
    SBN 9780226818665 (ebook)
Subjects: LCSH: Preschool teachers—Japan—
    Longitudinal studies. | Preschool teachers—
    United States—Longitudinal studies. | Preschool
    teachers—China—Longitudinal studies. | Education,
    Preschool—Japan—Cross-cultural studies. |
    Education, Preschool—United States—Cross-cultural
    studies. | Education, Preschool—China—
    Cross-cultural studies.
Classification: LCC LB1775.5.H39 2022 | DDC 372.11—dc23
LC record available at https://lccn.loc.gov/2021041544

Contents

Preface

While finishing my postdoc at the University of Georgia in the United States in 2012, I applied for a faculty position in Japan, the application for which required a long-term research plan. As the job was in a department of comparative education, I thought it would be a good idea to submit a multisited international project. That spring I had conversations with preschool teachers and directors whom I have known since 2002, when we were all in our early twenties. We talked about how we had changed over the previous ten years. With those informal conversations in my head, I got the idea to explore how those teachers had *changed* over the years. A new research topic had emerged—an international comparative study in Japan, China, and the US! I didn't get the job, but I got a research project, which led to this book, *Teaching Expertise in Three Countries.*

In this book, I present and analyze how preschool teachers in Japan, China, and the US changed between their earlier and later years in the classroom and what helped them change. I use the word *expertise* in the title not in the neoliberal policy makers' meaning, which is used to evaluate, regulate, and control practitioners, but instead to describe how experienced early childhood practitioners come to view their own practice as a craft that they learn mostly on the job and become increasingly skilled at. I view *expertise* as the aspects of their work that experienced practitioners can do better than they could when they were less experienced.

This research became possible because I have had the tremendous good fortune of having a long engagement with research sites and key participants in three countries. In 2002, I became a member of a study that eventually became the book *Preschool in Three Cultures Revisited: China, Japan, and the United States.* Since then, I have visited the research sites in Japan every summer. I started my PhD program at Arizona State University in 2005, which made it possible for me to keep in touch with the research sites in the US, especially with Alhambra Preschool in Phoenix. Over the past eighteen years, I have had multiple opportunities to see key participants in China, including preschool teachers and directors at Daguan Kindergarten in Kunming and

Sinan Road Kindergarten in Shanghai. I visited them in China three times, and I also met them when they visited our research sites in the US and Japan. This study, which looks at how practitioners change over the years, is supported by my long engagement with these research sites and with these participants. I deeply appreciate their willingness to participate in research alongside their busy everyday lives at preschool.

At the research sites in Japan, I was fortunate to witness the process of apprenticeship learning and transitions of responsibility. As I am completing the writing of this book, Director Ritsuko Kumagai of Senzan Yōchien in Kyoto is completing the process of transferring the leadership of the kindergarten to her daughter Tomoko, who has begun participating in the research interviews as an interviewee alongside her mother. The other two main research sites in Japan are, coincidentally, in the same situation: at Madoka Yōchien in Tokyo, Yoshio Machiyama has transferred the role of director to his son Taro, and at Komatsudani Hoikuen in Kyoto, Hidenori Yoshizawa has transferred leadership to his son Hironori. Now, all three preschools have new directors, but the previous directors are always on-site—physically, emotionally, and philosophically. Seeing them pass their responsibilities down to a new generation of emerging leaders gave me ideas for how to structure this study.

In the past few years, I have also experienced a transfer of responsibility and leadership. After years of my own apprenticeship to him, my advisor Joseph Tobin, the lead author of *Preschool in Three Cultures Revisited* (2009) and my coauthor on *Teaching Embodied* (2015), passed these research sites down to me, assisted in the research from an early stage, and has supported me along the way. We started this project together at a time when he was gradually stepping back, just as the Japanese preschool directors did as they turned responsibility over to their new directors. Joe supported my work throughout the project. He allowed me to use data that his research team collected in 2002 for the *Preschool in Three Cultures Revisited* study, accompanied me when I videotaped classrooms and conducted interviews with teachers and directors, and gave me advice on intellectual ideas when I needed stimulus during the long journey of writing this book. This book would never have existed without him.

Preschool in Three Cultures Revisited (Tobin, Hsueh, and Karasawa 2009) focused on continuity and change in systems of early childhood education in three countries over a period of twenty years. This book, *Teaching Expertise in Three Countries*, focuses on continuity and change in preschool teachers over a period of a dozen years. The six featured teachers in this book are the classroom teachers videotaped in 2002 for the *Preschool in Three Cultures Revisited* study. To those familiar with the *Preschool in Three Cultures Revisited* study, you will see these preschool educators again and get to see how they have grown up. To new readers, I hope you enjoy a story of teachers maturing and gaining wisdom, as we all hope to do as time goes by.

Akiko Hayashi
Tokyo, Japan, 2021

Foreword

As Akiko Hayashi explains in the preface, there is a parallel between this book's story of how preschool teachers in three countries gain expertise with experience and her professional journey and maturation as a scholar. This book is based on a study that is a continuation of a line of work I began in the early 1980s, which led to the publication in 1989 of *Preschool in Three Cultures: Japan, China, and the United States*. Twenty years later, I launched a sequel to that project, which led to the publication in 2009 of *Preschool in Three Cultures Revisited*. In 2002, when I met her, Akiko Hayashi was one of the young graduate research assistants on that project. She is now a mature scholar, with great expertise in conducting comparative international research. It is comforting to be able to turn the leadership of this multidecade research venture over to a former apprentice who has become such a capable researcher.

This line of research, featuring video-cued studies of preschools and preschool teachers in Japan, China, and the United States, has a life of its own. It began with one set of researchers, David Wu, Dana Davidson, and me, and then twenty years later, Yeh Hsueh and Mayumi Karasawa took the places of Wu and Davidson. It now continues under Akiko Hayashi's stewardship. I have no doubt that as the world changes and preschools evolve, this comparative international project will continue, enlisting new collaborators, taking on new forms, addressing new research questions, and providing new insights.

Teaching expertise, the focus of this new book, is a critical topic in this era of early childhood education standardization, de-professionalization, globalization, and reform. If, as the old saying goes and this book demonstrates, experience is the best teacher, one implication is that we should do what we can to promote the job longevity of preschool teachers and directors. Policy makers and teacher educators in all three countries are trying to improve the early childhood education sector by introducing curricular reforms, providing in-service workshops, and raising job qualifications. Alongside such efforts, this book suggests the most efficacious way to improve early childhood education quality would be to improve the conditions of teaching so that more teachers will stay in the field long enough to become accomplished, like the six teachers featured in this study.

The great strength of this book is the prominence given to the voices of the experienced Chinese, Japanese, and US early childhood educators interviewed for this study. Despite working in very different early childhood education systems, these practitioners from three countries present a surprisingly consistent narrative of what it means to learn to teach well with experience. The combination of cross-national and diachronic analysis makes this study a unique contribution to our understanding of the practice of teaching.

Joseph J. Tobin
Athens, Georgia, 2021

1   Introduction

In 2015, I went to Komatsudani Hoikuen in Kyoto and showed Chisato Morita a video our research team shot in her classroom in 2002, when she was in her third year of teaching. As she watched a scene in the video in which she leads her students through an origami activity, Morita commented, "Yoyū ga nakatta" (I lacked composure). At another of the old field sites in 2015, Sinan Road Kindergarten in Shanghai, I showed Jian Wang a video shot in her classroom thirteen years earlier. When the video ended, Wang commented, "When I was young, my focus was on teaching lessons. But I came to understand that the caring part of the job is much more important." In 2015, at St. Timothy's Child Center in Honolulu, after watching a video made in her classroom in 2002, a video in which we see her repeatedly intervening in children's disputes, Jannie Umeda summarized how she has changed with experience: "Now I let things go more than I used to."

In this book, I analyze these and other statements made by experienced teachers interviewed in Japan, China, and the United States about how they have changed between their earlier and later years in the classroom. At the center of this book are video-cued interviews conducted in 2015 with Chisato Morita, Jian Wang, Jannie Umeda, and three other preschool teachers (Mariko Kaizuka, Jingxiu Cheng, and Fran Smith) who were videotaped in 2002 for the study that became the book *Preschool in Three Cultures Revisited: China, Japan, and the United States* (Tobin, Hsueh, and Karasawa 2009). In 2002, these six teachers (two each from China, Japan, and the US) were early in their careers. In 2015, when we interviewed them again, they were veterans. At the core of this book are the reflections of these six teachers on how they changed with experience and what helped them change. I combine these teachers' self-reflections with comments from colleagues who have known them since the beginning of their careers and with video-cued interviews we conducted with other experienced early childhood educators in all three countries, whom we asked to reflect on differences between early-career and veteran teachers and on what helps teachers change.

Looking beyond Induction

In an interview for an earlier study on embodied teaching (Hayashi and Tobin 2015), Director Ritsuko Kumagai of Senzan Yōchien in Kyoto emphasized the importance of *mimamoru*, a pedagogical approach of holding back and not giving children who are struggling more help than they need. She then added, "For a teacher to be able to really do *mimamoru*, it takes at least five years." This comment by Kumagai gave me the idea for the research project that became this book: Why does it take so long to become good at *mimamoru* and other skills for preschool teaching? What is it that happens during these (at least) five years that allows teachers to improve?

There is a large literature on induction into teaching, but there has been less research on the development of expertise after this initial stage. Most induction studies focus on how effectively beginning teachers employ content-area and pedagogical knowledge and the impact on their teaching of in-service professional development opportunities (for example, Feiman-Nemser et al. 1999; Ingersoll and Strong 2011; Wang, Odell, and Schwille 2008; Luft, Roehrig, and Patterson 2003; Tatto and Senk 2011). My approach to studying expertise differs from induction studies in terms of time frame, as I focus not on the first one to three years of teaching but instead on change that occurs after the first five years. It also differs from most studies of teaching expertise in being internationally comparative and in focusing on early childhood rather than on primary or secondary education.

Experience and Expertise

In the three examples with which I began this book, experienced teachers described how they have changed over time. Chisato Morita reports that now, in contrast to when she began, she is in less of a rush and more composed. Jannie Umeda says that whereas she worked to direct children when she was an inexperienced teacher, she now focuses on being more present. Jian Wang summarizes the change over the years in her priorities from instructing children to caring for them.

Why did it take these teachers five or more years of experience before they could make these changes in their practice? Why couldn't they do this kind of teaching earlier? I suggest that even if a more experienced colleague had urged Morita to slow down, Jannie to be less directive, or Wang to be less instrumental, the teachers could not yet have done so, because doing so required not just a different conscious understanding of good teaching but an ability they did not yet have to know when and how to be composed, present, and responsive to the needs of their students. In other words, the expertise of these veteran teachers could only be acquired through years of experience in the classroom.

In this book, I refer to the abilities of an experienced teacher as *expertise*, which I conceptualize as a combination of a teacher's professional knowledge, skills, and disposition. While few interviewees were comfortable being called experts, all described themselves as having, with experience, become more capable practitioners. As one Japanese preschool director commented, "Some teachers, even after many years, don't become all that great at their jobs, but they become better than they were at the beginning. They become better versions of themselves." I would add that there are some teachers who are very capable even at the beginning of their careers, but that such teachers are rare and that they, too, change with experience.

Scholars in a range of disciplines use different terms to describe what I suggest are similar conceptualizations of expertise. The philosopher of science Eric Polanyi (1962) uses the term *tacit knowledge*; the philosopher Gilbert Ryle (1949) *know-how* (as opposed to *know-that*); the sociologist Pierre Bourdieu (2000) *professional habitus*; the philosopher of education Max van Manen (1991) *pedagogical tact*; and the cognitive anthropologist Maurice Bloch (1991) *non-linguistically processed practical skills*. The educational psychologist David Berliner describes experienced teachers as "arational":

> If novices, advanced beginners, and competent performers are rational, and proficient performers are intuitive, we might categorize experts as "arational." They have an intuitive grasp of a situation and seem to sense in nonanalytic, nondeliberative ways the appropriate response to make. They show fluid performance, as we all do when we no longer have to choose our words when speaking or think about where to place our feet when walking. (1988, 5)

The cognitive psychologist Rand J. Spiro and his colleagues Brian P. Collins and Aparna R. Ramchandran refer to skilled practitioners as having the "complex, open, and flexible habits of mind" needed to negotiate "ill-structured domains":

> In complex and more ill-structured arenas of knowledge—counters the tendencies just described with approaches that foster the building of knowledge characterized by multiple representation, interconnectedness, and contingency (context-dependence, a tendency to recognize when it is

appropriate to say "it depends" and to acknowledge that many situations are not "either/or," but rather shades of gray in between). (2007, 20)

I find each of these conceptualizations helpful, but as an educational anthropologist, I set them aside as I entered into this study, and I do so once again now, as I write this book, to make room for the Chinese, Japanese, and US teachers' emic constructs. In my interviews with experienced early childhood educators, I generally did not use the terms *expertise* or *expert* (or their Japanese and Chinese equivalents). Instead, I asked "How have you changed with experience?" "How are experienced teachers generally different from beginners?" and "What helped you change?" In this book, I use the word *expertise* to connect with concepts from other domains of professional practice, while keeping in mind that my goal is not to apply a priori concepts to ethnographic data but instead to discover our participants' conceptualizations of how they change with experience.

What Helps

Malcolm Gladwell, in his 2008 book *Outliers*, made famous the "ten-thousand-hour rule," which suggests that it takes at least ten thousand hours of practice to become an expert at anything. Ten thousand hours at forty hours a week comes out to about Director Kumagai's five years. Gladwell's book was based largely on the work of the psychologists Anders Ericsson, Ralf Krampe, and Clemens Tesch-Römer (1993). In a book published in 2016, Ericsson and Robert Pool argued that Gladwell had misrepresented the findings, and that while ten thousand hours may be enough to make one competent, the number of hours required to become an hour is closer to twenty thousand, and these hours need to be spent in focused, "deliberative practice."

The Ericsson study was of violinists and pianists. I suggest that preschool teaching is a very different sort of domain of practice. For such ill-structured domains as emergency room medicine, police work, and—I would add—preschool teaching, deliberative practice is not practical. You can practice scales on the violin and repeatedly go over the sections of a Bartok concerto, but you cannot practice preschool teaching alone, and this professional field is not easily broken down into isolated parts that can be mastered one at a time through deliberative practice.

What, then, most helps preschool teachers improve? Possible answers include structured professional development activities, mentoring, and on-the-job learning. There is a robust literature on teachers' professional development, including studies on the impact of workshops, advanced coursework, and lesson study. Most of my interviewees mentioned having participated in one or more of these forms of structured professional development.

Few, however, cited such formal activities as having played a large part in their growth. Many of my interviewees told me that mentoring had played a key role in their development. While none reported having had a formal mentor, most described having learned from one or more experienced teachers they had the good fortune to work alongside. When I asked them to reflect on how they learned from their more experienced colleagues, they mentioned observing, asking for help, being offered unsolicited advice and feedback, and reflecting on events that had transpired and planning for the days to come.

The most common answer to our question "What helped you change between your early years in the classroom and now?" was, in a word, "experience." This response prompts the following questions: What kinds of experiences? With what kinds of reflection? And with what kinds of scaffolding from others? The scaffolding of experience can take many forms, including reflection guided by a mentor, informal discussions with colleagues, and a preschool providing an atmosphere that encourages young teachers to take chances and not be afraid to fail. One of the biggest areas of difference I found across the three countries was the ways in which mentors scaffolded younger teachers' experience along a continuum that runs from frequent direct advice and critique to minimal feedback. In the chapters that follow, I present what experienced early childhood educators in Japan, China, and the US reported as having been most impactful in their own professional growth.

How to Study Expertise

The most common approaches to studying expertise rely on cross-sectional comparisons of novice and expert teachers, based on observations of beginning and experienced teachers in their classrooms, questionnaires or interviews administered to beginning and experienced teachers, or quasi-experimental studies. For example, Schempp et al. (1998) asked novice and more experienced teachers to explain the logic behind hypothetical lessons. They found that more experienced teachers teach less by the book and more by improvisation. David Berliner (1986, 1987, 1988) and his colleagues showed beginning and experienced teachers photos of classrooms and then asked them to recall what they had seen. They found that expert, experienced teachers are more intuitive and more skilled at reading students and contexts. A limitation of these studies is that the comparisons are of different cohorts of teachers rather than of the same teachers over time.

I have used several original methods to tackle the question of how teachers change with experience, each a version of a video-cued ethnographic interview (Tobin, Wu, and Davidson 1989[1]; Tobin 2019). The participants are the two Japanese, two Chinese, and two US preschool teachers who were videotaped in 2002 for the *Preschool in Three Cultures Revisited* study. These teachers were near the beginning of their careers in 2002 and were veterans when interviewed in 2015 (table 1).

We began by showing these teachers the videos the research team had made of them teaching when they were younger and asked them, each in the company of a more senior teacher or administrator they identified as a mentor, to reflect on how they have changed and what has helped them change in the intervening years. We interviewed each teacher alongside a colleague because our pilot interviews suggested that even with the help of a video that shows them teaching years earlier, it can be difficult for practitioners to pinpoint the ways they have changed. This task becomes easier when someone who has worked closely with the teacher over the years was also present, to help them remember what they were like when they got started, and to reflect on how they have changed and what helped them change.

Without a cue to structure their reflections, it would have been difficult for interviewees to identify how they have changed with experience. The videos functioned as a memory stimulus, a mnemonic that brought these six veteran teachers back, cognitively and emotionally, to versions of themselves they only dimly remembered. As they watched these videos alongside their old colleagues, the six teachers would invariably make comments such as "I was

Table 1. Participants over the years

Country	Institutions	Teachers and directors
Japan	Komatsudani Hoikuen (daycare center) in Kyoto	Chisato Morita, Takaya Nogami, Hironori Yoshizawa, Hidenori Yoshizawa
	Madoka Yōchien (kindergarten) in Tokyo	Mariko Kaizuka, Yoshio Machiyama, Taro Machiyama
China	Sinan Road Kindergarten in Shanghai	Jian Wang, Jingxiu Cheng, Zongli Guo
US	St. Timothy's Child Center in Hawaii	Jannie Umeda, Linda Rios, Lori Onaga, Cheryl Cudiamat
	Alhambra Preschool in Arizona	Fran Smith

so young!" and "I didn't remember that I had set my room up like that" before moving on to more self-critical comments such as "I was trying hard, but I really didn't know what I was doing." We then asked questions that shifted the conversations to more specific ways in which their pedagogy had evolved with experience. For example, we paused the video at a point when a teacher was using a particular pedagogical technique, such as mediating a dispute among children, and asked the teacher whether she would handle the situation differently now.

Expanding beyond the six core teachers and their mentors, we also conducted video-cued focus group interviews with experienced teachers and directors who did not know the teachers in the videos; in these cases, the videos were used to start as conversation starters. We began these video-cued interviews by asking "How many years would you guess this teacher has been teaching?" and "How can you tell?" We then shifted the discussion away from the videos by asking these experienced educators about their own growth over time as teachers and then to a more general discussion of what they see as the main differences between beginning and experienced teachers and what they believe most helps teachers to change.

We also conducted video-cued interviews with professors of early childhood education. I see these professors as experienced early childhood specialists. Most of the professors we interviewed have long been involved with preschool teacher training programs, though many do not have extensive practical experience. They provide important insights into the characteristics of preschool teaching expertise.

While the focus of the interviews was on how teachers had changed over time in their professional lives, the discussions often included references to their lives outside of school. For example, some of the interviewees discussed how having had children of their own changed their pedagogy. And while the focus of the study was on change over time in teachers' individual pedagogical beliefs and practices, not on policy or educational reform, teachers often could not disentangle the personal from the political, as they related stories of disruptions to their careers caused by school closings and unbearable supervisors and described how the evolution of their pedagogical beliefs was sometimes in tension with top-down educational reforms and paradigm shifts in notions of best practices in early childhood education.

In total, across the three countries, we conducted video-cued interviews with 112 experienced early childhood educators. Some of these interviews we did with individuals, some with pairs, and some in focus groups of four to six participants. I recorded, transcribed, and coded each discussion and then conducted textual and interpretive analyses of the interviews, tracing out central themes and points of similarities and differences across the three countries. I have used many quotes throughout the book, and most of these come from different participants rather than drawing on only a small portion of the 112 participants. There are some repeated quotes that are used with different emphases in different places.

Studying Teaching Expertise in Three Countries

My comparative design has allowed me to identify both commonalities and differences in the development of expertise among preschool teachers in these three countries, as well as to ask the question of whether there are shared notions of expertise and shared pathways of professional growth across preschool teachers that transcend nation. A three-country comparative design has the advantage over a two-country design of helping to avoid binary thinking and producing one-dimensional differences, such as an East-West divide (Tobin, Wu, and Davidson 1989). While I found some similarities between Japanese and Chinese educators' conceptions of, for example, the "empty-minded" presence of skilled educators, their conceptions of the role of mentors were very different, with the Chinese emphasizing the need for mentors to continually provide advice and criticism and the Japanese emphasizing a much more hands-off, less critical approach. US teachers described finding their own mentors, in contrast to reports by our Chinese participants of more systematic assignments of mentors and by our Japanese participants of a more collective mentoring of younger teachers by their seniors.

The veteran Chinese and Japanese early childhood educators made points about the nature of teaching experience and professional development that connect with, extend and, in some cases, challenge the Anglophone literature. For example, the concept of *thoughtful thoughtlessness* (*wuwei* 无为), which a Chinese preschool director told us was characteristic of experienced teachers, is both like and unlike David Berliner's concept of experienced teachers' *arationality*. Japanese participants' descriptions of the state of mind of experienced teachers being *blank slates* (*hakushi*) allowing them to react spontaneously to the children in front of them can be compared with van Manen's concept of pedagogical tact. In the chapters that follow, I read these and other Japanese and Chinese emic concepts alongside their US counterparts.

Chinese participants often responded to questions by citing Taoist and Confucian concepts, while Japanese participants cited Zen notions. I argue that such citations do not so much reflect these educators' systematic engagement with these philosophical and religious traditions as they do their turning to familiar tropes and metaphors to explain something that is usually implicit. They cite culturally familiar discourses to describe things that, as Polanyi suggests, "one knows but can't easily say." In the concluding chapter, I turn to the question of whether my participants are using different words to describe the same thing or whether these different words reflect different conceptions of learning to teach well.

About This Book

There are three chapters by country and a concluding chapter. Each of the three country chapters that follow has a different structure, reflecting the nature of ethnography; I use participants' definitions and categorizations, and the three chapters do not use the same headings. A portion of the Japan chapter appeared, in a different form, in Chapter 5 of *Teaching Embodied* (Hayashi and Tobin 2015), for which I took the lead in writing. My project of looking at changes in teachers got started then and has now matured into this book. I refer to teachers' names using the form most commonly used in each teacher's culture: In Japan and China, educators generally refer to each other using family names while at work. On the other hand, most of the teachers interviewed in the US referred to their colleagues by their given names. Japanese interviewees usually added "sensei" after a teacher's name,[2] and Chinese interviewees similarly added "laoshi."

2 Japan

When I went back to the Japanese preschools in 2015, Chisato Morita was still working at Komatsudani Hoikuen in Kyoto and Mariko Kaizuka was still working at Madoka Yōchien in Tokyo. During the intervening years, Morita had worked continuously at Komatsudani, rotating among the infant, toddler, and the older children's classrooms. Kaizuka took a nine-year break from teaching, from when her twins were born in 2005 until the twins began elementary school in 2014. In 2015, both teachers were about forty years old and were again working with four-year-olds in the same classrooms they had been teaching in when the research team recorded them in 2002. This allowed me to pursue a research strategy with Morita and Kaizuka unavailable to me in China or the US: making new videos in Morita and Kaizuka's same classrooms. Like the China and US chapters, this chapter begins with the reflections of two teachers, cued by watching their 2002 videos, on how they have changed and stayed the same over the thirteen intervening years. Next, I present the central themes that emerged from interviews in Japan with Morita and Kaizuka as well as other experienced Japanese teachers, directors, and early childhood education experts. I conclude this chapter with an analysis of the videos of the two teachers teaching four-year-olds from both 2002 and 2015.

Morita: "I Used to Be in a Rush"

Chisato Morita has spent her entire career working for the same program. Komatsudani is a private *hoikuen* (daycare center) located in a 280-year-old Buddhist temple on a hillside overlooking Kyoto. The director, Hironori Yoshizawa, is also the temple's priest. His father, Hidenori Yoshizawa, was the director and head priest of the temple in the 1980s, when Komatsudani was the key Japanese site for the original *Preschool in Three Cultures* study. Morita joined the staff in 1999, at the age of twenty-two, after graduating with a degree in childcare from a local university. As is the custom at Komatsudani and

Hmmm, what color fish should I make?

Figure 1. "What color fish should I make?"

other *hoikuen,* she has rotated through the age groups over her twenty years of working at the school, from the infants to the six-year-olds. In 2002, she was in her third year of teaching and was working with the *nenchū-gumi* (middle class) of four-year-olds. In the video shot that year, we see Morita holding up a stack of brightly colored origami paper as she says (figure 1):

> "I wonder, what color fish should I make? Who wants to use blue? Raise your hands. Okay, now who wants yellow? Here you go. Hold on, I'll bring it over to you." [Once each of the children has a sheet of square paper, Morita folds her paper in half.] "First we make a triangle. That's right. Our fish are now triangles. And then fold in both sides, right, like that, just like when you make a tulip. Then fold the two corners in, like this. And one more fold, like this. Got it? Good. No? Here, I'll help you."

For the next ten minutes or so, Morita circulates from table to table, helping first one child and then another with their folding. Once the children have folded their papers into fish shapes, Morita says, "It seems so sad without a mouth or eyes. What should we do? I'll take a marker, and draw an eye on my fish, like this." As she again moves around the classroom, checking on the children's progress, she stops at a table where one girl is crying because she has drawn eyes on the wrong side of her fish. Morita consoles her, "That's okay. All of our faces are different, right?" The crying child does not seem totally convinced by this explanation, but she stops crying, turns her folded origami creation over, and draws eyes on the other side of her fish.

When we returned to Komatsudani Hoikuen in 2015, Morita was in her sixteenth year of teaching. We sat down with Morita, her former co-teacher and the school's present head teacher Takaya Nogami, and Director Hironori Yoshizawa. All three commented on the origami scene, all pointing out her tendency, as a young teacher, to always seem to be in a rush[1]:

TOBIN: What are your reactions to watching the video?

MORITA: There's a lack here of calmness and composure (*yoyū ga nakatta*). I used to be in a rush. It's like I felt I had to explain everything. I talked and talked, and lacked the composure to wait for the children's reactions, and I kept up this kind of one-way talking, right through the origami activity, and then into lunch, talking and talking like this, from one activity to the next, throughout the day.

NOGAMI: Yeah, right. It seems like you continually were focused on what *you* had to do next. Therefore, we can say that you hadn't yet reached the point as a teacher that you could really *see* each child. Your focus was on keeping the attention of the group.

MORITA: I talked too much. I was frantic! I felt compelled to keep filling the space with my talking. It's like I was following a script. There was no time or space for the children's reactions. I was too preoccupied with my own thoughts (*jibun de ippai*). It was a fun activity, but . . .

NOGAMI: You have changed. You now are able to explain things by showing, not by talking. And when you do talk, you talk to each child, and not to the whole class.

YOSHIZAWA: It seems like ten years ago you tried to do everything in the proper way. It's like you were following all the rules, like according to the way you were taught at the university. With experience, and especially having experiences of failure, you have gradually changed.

TOBIN: Is there any tendency to help when you see a child struggling?

MORITA: Well, yeah, I want to help them, but I know they are happy when they discover they can do it on their own. But yes, it is really tough to wait.

HAYASHI: How about when you just started teaching? Your first year of teaching?

MORITA: No, I couldn't. I did everything for them. I didn't wait at all. We have to have *yoyū* (patience) in order to accept children's *amae* (dependency needs) and know when to encourage them to do something on their own, and when to give them help and one-to-one attention.

HAYASHI: What is the difference between new teachers and experienced teachers?

NOGAMI: The ability to see children—not only see them but also to be able to judge what kind of children they are—or the ability to predict what this child might do in various situations.

MORITA: For example, if I know that two children aren't going to act aggressively, then I can watch them fighting as a competition of who is stronger. But if I know that one or both of these children have a potential to be aggressive, then, I might say to them, "Hey, hold on there!"

NOGAMI: Right, like, in one situation, it's fine to hold back and keep an eye on them, while in the other situation, you have to say, "Oh, this is not okay."

HAYASHI: How do teachers get to the point of being able to make such distinctions?

MORITA: Experience, maybe?

YOSHIZAWA: Maybe only experience?

NOGAMI: By experience, maybe?

In conversation, Japanese interlocutors often add *kana* (maybe) to the end of a sentence to soften their statement and to seek their listeners' confirmation of the reasonableness of what they are saying. In this case, I see something additional going on. I believe that by adding "maybe" to the end of their answers, these participants are suggesting doubt—not doubt that experience is necessary for the development of expertise but doubt that experience alone can be an adequate explanation.

Morita suggested that for experience to be beneficial, it needs to be coupled with mentoring:

HAYASHI: Do you remember what helped you change?

MORITA: It's hard to say, but when I see new teachers who don't know some things that I know, then I feel like I've grown. I learned from watching *senpai* (my seniors) things like "I could have waited longer" and some useful expressions to use with children. I was watching Nogami-sensei all the time when I first had my own class in the room next to his. This was helpful, but we need to figure things out on our own. It's not something that somebody could teach me to do.

Morita also emphasized the importance of learning by a process of trial and error, although the metaphor she picked was an odd one:

New teachers lack experience, so they haven't yet developed that kind of sense experienced teachers have. As we get more experience, the sense emerges in us. It's like picking mushrooms: "Oh, we can eat this mushroom, but this one is poisonous." People come to know which mushroom is okay to eat through experience.

I did not point out that expert mushroom hunters must have learned to avoid the deadliest of mushrooms by a process other than trial and error.

Kaizuka: "I Thought I Had to Behave the Same Way with Everyone!"

Madoka is a private *yōchien* (kindergarten) located in a middle-class neighborhood in Tokyo. The program serves three-, four-, and five-year-old children from the local community, from about nine in the morning until two thirty in the afternoon.[2] In 2002, when the research team shot the video in her classroom, Mariko Kaizuka was in her early stage of teaching. When we visited Madoka in 2012 to interview her again, Kaizuka was not there, having taken a leave in 2005 to start a family after nine years of teaching. Her twin sons, born in 2005, were students at Madoka from 2008 to 2011, which kept her in contact with the school and gave her the opportunity to see the school from a parent's as well as a teacher's perspective. She returned to teaching at Madoka in 2014.

We watched the video shot at Madoka in 2002 with Kaizuka and her former and current directors, Yoshio Machiyama and his son, Taro, respectively. Much of the discussion of the video focused on Kaizuka's handling of a dispute between two boys, Nobu and Yusuke. In the video, as the children are preparing to go home, we see Nobu, in tears, approach Kaizuka (figure 2):

NOBU: Yusuke pulled my hair.
KAIZUKA: Why did you do that, Yusuke?
YUSUKE: 'Cause Nobu-kun pinched me.
KAIZUKA: You say he pinched you first? Is that true?
YUSUKE: No.
KAIZUKA: That's strange.
NOBU: He walked by and pulled my hair.
KAIZUKA: And then you pinched him? Nobu, did you pinch him or not? You pinched him, right? I don't like this. God, too, is watching. Do you understand? Think about it. And when you are ready to tell the truth, come talk

Figure 2. "Is that true?"

to me. Think about it. I am more bothered by your lying than by what you
did. Think about it [as Kaizuka turns her attention momentarily to a girl
asking for help with a button, Yusuke wanders away]. Yusuke, come back,
we're not done.

YUSUKE [with tears in his eyes, whimpering]: I did it first.

KAIZUKA: It's really important to say you're sorry when you do bad things.
I've done bad things to friends, but then I realized I was wrong and apolo-
gized. If you apologize, you feel much better. Do you understand? Do you
have something to say?

YUSUKE: I'm sorry.

NOBU: That's okay.

KAIZUKA [to Nobu]: You, also, have to say "sorry."

NOBU: I'm sorry.

YUSUKE: That's okay.

KAIZUKA: You'll have to change your clothes quickly. Everyone is waiting for
you.

After watching this scene, Kaizuka stopped the video and commented:

KAIZUKA: When I was dealing with those two boys, I wish I had been able
to pay more attention to the other children.

MACHIYAMA: I totally understand what you mean. By your later stage of
teaching, you would be paying attention to the other children. That's the
difference. This was your early stage of teaching.

KAIZUKA: It seems like I lacked calmness and composure (*yoyū ga nakatta no kana*).

MACHIYAMA: I agree. I think we have the same feeling. She focused on only these two boys. If she had more *yoyū*, she could've said "Please wait" or "I am still talking with them," something like that to the other children. She would do these things now.

KAIZUKA: I totally agree. I really think so.

MACHIYAMA: We have almost the same impression. We had the same understanding even before we said it.

HAYASHI: When you are faced with this kind of situation in your classroom, what are you thinking?

KAIZUKA: To be honest, once the classroom day begins, it's not always conscious. I just think, "How am I going to deal with the children in front of me?" Of course, at the same time, I'm thinking about managing the class. But if something unexpected happens, like a fight, then the tendency is just to focus on that one incident. It's difficult!

Kaizuka and Machiyama agree here that what Kaizuka lacked early in her career was the ability to balance her attention to individual children with her attention to the group. Lacking composure, she had tunnel vision and a single-minded determination to deal with the problem right in front of her, at the cost of being less attentive to children on the periphery and to the larger classroom context.

Kaizuka and Machiyama also emphasized how, with experience, Kaizuka became better able not only to balance attention to individual children and the group but also to treat different children differently:

HAYASHI: Did your way of dealing with children change between your fourth and ninth years of teaching?

KAIZUKA: Yes, I changed over the years. At the beginning of my teaching career, I thought I had to behave the same way with everyone—for example, to scold everyone the same way and get their attention the same way. But with experience, I gradually changed and learned to scold and get attention in different ways with different children.

TOBIN: Would you say that such change over time is typical in teachers?

MACHIYAMA: It *should* be. Teachers *should* change how they deal with children depending on each child. But not everyone does.

Kaizuka and Machiyama suggest not only that Kaizuka got better at being able to adjust her teaching to the needs and abilities of individual children but also that with time and experience she developed a wider repertoire of teaching strategies. Kaizuka told me:

> Probably, to be honest with you, it just doesn't work if we use the same way with everyone. If we do things the same way with this kid and with that kid, the same way won't work to reach everybody's heart. One child might get this, but not the other one. So we ask ourselves, what can I do? Which approach should I use with this child? It takes time to figure out.

Introducing this thought with "to be honest" communicates trust in me and the sincerity she is bringing to the interview, on the one hand, but on the other, it communicates a sense that she is about to say something that goes against the official or commonly accepted position. Similarly, in another passage quoted above, Kaizuka used the phrase "to be honest" to introduce the counterintuitive idea that much about her (and other teachers') pedagogy is intuitive and done without conscious thought. In this second case of introducing a point with "to be honest," Kaizuka may be challenging a guiding assumption of Japanese early childhood education that one should treat children equally (Tobin, Wu, and Davidson 1989). She also may be subtly arguing against the assumption that adjusting teaching to individual differences among children is a skill that can be learned from textbooks, guidelines, or workshops. We can say she is arguing against what Bakhtin would call an "authoritative discourse" (1981) of Japanese preschool pedagogy, and voicing an "internally persuasive discourse" of experienced preschool teachers, who know that the ability to work effectively with a heterogeneous group of young children can only be learned the hard way, through experience. Because speaking in front of one's director is a context that for many teachers calls for a degree of indirectness and circumspection, Kaizuka's use of the phrase "to be honest" suggests trust not only in me but also in her boss. Agreeing with Kaizuka, Machiyama emphasized that experienced teachers are able to communicate well with children: "The difference between beginners and veterans is that tenth-year teachers have skills for scolding and saying things to children in a way they will understand. This is probably related to Kaizuka-sensei's point about changing the way she teaches depending on children."

While Machiyama reciprocated Kaizuka's trust with consistent expressions of agreement and support, he also distanced himself a bit from the way she dealt with the children's fight:

MACHIYAMA: You spoke to them strongly!
KAIZUKA: Yes, I spoke strongly. It's a question of *kejime* (adjusting tactics to

the context). It's not good for a teacher to be authoritative *all the time*, but there should be moments to be strict, and this was one of them. There are other times teachers can be more alongside children. Here I spoke strongly to the two boys because they hurt each other and then lied, so I felt that this was a situation where I couldn't compromise.

MACHIYAMA: It's interesting that you used "I" (*watashi*). That suggests that not everybody would handle this situation the same way, and this is just *one* of the ways to deal with this incident.

Machiyama picked up on Kaizuka's use of "I" here because pronouns are not required or even typically used in Japanese conversation. Japanese preschools teachers, compared with their counterparts in the US and China, intervene in children's disputes less often and less aggressively (Lewis 1988; Tobin, Wu, and Davidson 1989; Tobin, Hsueh, and Karasawa 2009). Without criticizing her, Machiyama acknowledged Kaizuka as being a bit of an outlier in her approach to dealing with children's disputes by referring to her strategy as "just one way" to deal with such incidents. As we will see in the last section of this chapter, after thirteen years of teaching Kaizuka, eventually came around to seeing her 2002 intervention as being too intense.

When I asked her what had most helped her to improve as a teacher, Kaizuka suggested that the biggest factor had been becoming a parent. She told me that after years of dealing with disputes between her twin sons, she had become more relaxed as a parent and a teacher:

HAYASHI: If you were to face the same situation now, how would you deal with children?

KAIZUKA: I am not sure if it is good or bad, but I still want children to tell me the truth and not to tell a lie. But I've learned with my own children that if I didn't see it happen, I can't say, for instance, "You did it," or, "That's bad." So now I would tend to be less strong in my interventions.

Conceptualizing Differences between Novices and Experts

TIME, SPACE, AND COMPOSURE

Many Japanese participants used the word *yoyū* in describing the difference between teachers earlier and later in their careers. As we have seen, both Morita and Kaizuka described their teaching in their 2002 videos using the phrase *yoyū ga nakatta* (I lacked composure). This phrase can refer either to situations in which one has a lack of time or space to maneuver, or to a lack of *awareness* of the time and space that could have been used, as in such statements as "I rushed too much because I didn't realize that I had more time than I thought I had." For a situation in which objective pressures demanded quick action, *yoyū ga nakatta* can be translated as "I had to hurry." For a situation in which a person acted more quickly and frantically than they needed to, a more apt translation would be "I rushed it." It is this second meaning of the phrase, the sense of retrospectively realizing that one acted with more haste and less composure and calm than one should have, that I take as a key difference between early-career and more experienced teachers. In describing their teaching from twelve years before with the phrase *yoyū ga nakatta*, Morita and Kaizuka, as well as other experienced Japanese teachers we interviewed, are not saying "I didn't have enough time" but rather "I acted *as if* I didn't have time, when in reality I did." Another translation of this phrase in this context could be "I lacked composure."

Yoyū can also refer to anxiety experienced when a task feels overwhelming, versus the pleasure and flow experienced when one feels up to the demands of a complex task (Csikszentmihalyi 1975). This came out in a focus group we conducted with four preschool directors and a head teacher, in which connections were made between *yoyū* and enjoyment in teaching:

RITSUKO KUMAGAI: When the teachers in your videos watch themselves teaching and say, "I lacked *yoyū*," I think they are implying that because they felt rushed, they couldn't enjoy their *hoiku* (work with young children). This is important because when the teacher isn't enjoying what she's doing, then children won't enjoy it. If I ask new teachers, "Did you enjoy being with the children today?" The answer is that of course they didn't, because they didn't have a sense of *yoyū*. Because they don't know how to develop or implement a good lesson plan, don't know how to read a situation, and don't know how to deal with unexpected interruptions, when they are with children, they feel frantic. Teachers can mark their progress based on how much they are enjoying their teaching. On our playground, I can see clearly from their facial expression whether teachers enjoy *hoiku* or not. Teachers can't enjoy their teaching if they are being chased by a lesson plan.

NOGAMI: Yes, now that Morita and Kaizuka have reached a point when they enjoy teaching, they can see their progress.

RITSUKO KUMAGAI: Education is fun! We should be enjoying the work.

TOMOKO KUMAGAI: First-year teachers can't enjoy themselves because they lack *yoyū*, so we leaders need to keep them from feeling overwhelmed. We can do this by giving them a sense of realistic goals, and protecting their emotional and physical health. For example, we can make sure they head home by 6:30 p.m. so they can come to school the next day refreshed.

NOGAMI: Once they start staying late, it becomes a habit that's hard to break.

The participants in this dialogue, two directors and a head teacher, seem to be suggesting that young teachers, because they often feel overwhelmed by their engagements with children and have a sense that there isn't enough time or space in the day to accomplish what they have planned, compensate by staying at school longer than they need to. Why stay late at school? Perhaps to demonstrate to themselves and their colleagues and directors that while they are clearly struggling, they remain committed to their jobs. Perhaps because they are seeking opportunities to chat about events of the day with their more experienced colleagues and get their advice. Perhaps to make exacting preparations for activities that can fill every moment of the next day. And perhaps just to have some moments of peace and quiet (*yoyū*) before heading home.

SCRIPTED PEDAGOGY

In a passage quoted above, Director Ritsuko Kumagai used the metaphor of young teachers "being chased by their lesson plans." Japanese early childhood education teachers typically follow daily, weekly, and monthly schedules of activities, but most preschools do not require or expect teachers to write or follow formal lesson plans of the type that include goals, standards, initiating events, and outcomes. Therefore, Kumagai's comment can be interpreted as suggesting that younger teachers tend to become subject to their own over-planning and their over-reliance on planned and anticipated aspects of teaching at the expense of being more spontaneous, relaxed, and present. An example of this trade-off would be Morita's origami activity, in which the lesson plan drove her mode of interacting with the children. The activity became more about her determination to get twenty young children to each make a fish than children being engaged in a creative activity. This concern with getting through her lesson led Morita to intervene more often and more strongly to help children with their paper folding than she would if the activity were less procedure- and outcome-focused. Looking back twelve years later, Morita viewed her teaching as performative and unnatural.

Director Kumagai's reference to young teachers being chased by their lesson plans resonates with Morita's comment when watching her 2002 video:

"It's like I was following a script." Some US interviewees complained that they were being compelled to follow a "scripted curriculum" and to teach by literally reading from a script composed by a textbook company and mandated by a school district. I believe Morita is here suggesting that as a young teacher she went into activities like her origami lesson with a rigid plan in her head for the procedures she would follow and how she would guide the children's progress through the lesson. Relatedly, another interpretation of her comment would be that the version of herself she watched and critiqued in the 2002 video was scripted like a character in a play, suggesting that as a young teacher lacking calm, composure, and confidence, she was playing the part of a teacher instead of being a teacher.

Morita's colleague Director Hironori Yoshizawa suggested the script Morita was following as a young teacher was made up of the authoritative voices she carried in her head:

> YOSHIZAWA: It seems that ten years ago that you tried to do everything in the proper way. It's like you were following all the rules, like according to the way you were taught at the university. With experience, especially having experiences of failure, you have gradually changed.

A group of experienced teachers at Makomanai Yōchien in Sapporo described their early teaching as being too governed by the schedule:

> SASAKI: I was focused on myself (*jibun de ippai*). It's like, we have a daily schedule, so I have to put myself into that schedule. In my first year, I was always thinking that I shouldn't fall behind in the schedule. Gradually, I started being able to handle things that I hadn't planned or anticipated, because I started having an understanding of children.
>
> WATANABE: Yeah, me too! I couldn't be flexible. And I also felt that I had to follow a plan. Now, when something unanticipated happens, I can adjust. It was very difficult to be flexible. I think I didn't have *yoyū*. I think that if you could see me then, you would see that I was trying to smile in front of children, but my facial expression was not natural. When I talked to children, I was preoccupied with my own thoughts (*jibun de ippai ippai*). I felt like I have to give them answers, and as a result I talked too much. But with experience—of course I have to keep working on my *hoiku*—I have become more able to listen to children with calmness, receive children's feelings, and share with them my opinions and feelings. As I started to have *yoyū* with children, I think my facial expression became more natural.

Sasaki and Watanabe, like Morita, described their teaching early in their careers as *"jibun de ippai."* This phrase is tricky to translate into English, as *jibun* means "oneself" and *ippai* means "full of." Together, these words can be translated as "preoccupied by my own thoughts" or "too much in my head." However, these English phrases do not seem like explanations for the tendency of young teachers to be dominated by scripts and schedules. Watanabe attributes her lack of flexibility and her inability to depart from her daily plan to her lack of composure (*yoyū*), a phrase also used by Morita and Kaizuka. I take these comments to mean that, as young teachers, they rigidly adhered to and depended on scripts and daily schedules to help them in making it through each day without losing their composure or control of their classes. The inexperienced versions of these teachers were governed by scripts, fixed notions of children and good teaching, and worries they carried around in their heads. A consequence was a loss of spontaneity, an inability to respond to the unexpected, and a lack of responsiveness to children.

BLANK SLATES

Professor Hiroshi Usui of Hokkaido Education University described the difference between veteran and novice teachers this way:

> Experienced teachers, although they may have some first impression or intuition about each of the children in their class, can free their minds of bias or prejudice by deleting the impression, like a white sheet of paper (*hakushi*).

Usui's meaning here is not that experienced teachers approach children without prior knowledge, but rather that, like a good psychotherapist or detective, they need to develop the ability to put aside their preconceptions. Freeing their minds from assumptions, they can then be present to the child in front of them. As Usui commented, "Experienced teachers can anticipate children's behavior because they are skilled at reading children's moods and movements." In his book on teaching and parenting, Hiroshi Azuma (1994) described the key to reading children as achieving a stance of "empty mindedness." He argued that true understanding is impossible if one does not make one's mind clean and empty when listening to others. Zen emphasizes the notion of *satoru* (emptying one's mind) as a key to becoming a mature person. A related Zen term, *mushin*, means "making one' mind empty."

A group of veteran preschool directors at Ochanomizu University made similar points:

KAMISAKAMOTO: First there are children, then there are teachers. It's crucial to face the aspect of ourselves that faces children. When we are young, we tend to be full of ourselves (*jibun de ippai*). Ears that don't catch children's whispers. Eyes that don't see children. I wonder why, when I was a young teacher, I couldn't hear what children were saying. I only gradually became able to see and hear children.

HAYASHI: *Jibun de ippai* is an interesting concept.

KAMISAKAMOTO: It's like, "My focus isn't on the children, but me."

MIYASATO: It seems like we are thinking about children, when actually we're thinking about ourselves. Or to put it more precisely, it's that "we are only thinking about those children who follow what the teacher wants."

KAMISAKAMOTO: Isn't that perhaps a bit too harsh?

Director Eri Kamisakamoto of Ochanomizu University Kindergarten explicitly connected young teachers' preoccupation with their tendency to miss the meanings of what children say and do, speaking poetically of ears that "miss children's whispers." "Whispers" here suggests not just that young children often speak softly but also that their words are often too nuanced and seemingly inconsequential for inexperienced teachers to attend to.

Directors Kamisakamoto and Miyasato used the phrase *jibun de ippai* to describe a kind of self-absorption that prevents the young teacher from being attentive and responsive to children.

In a similar vein, Professor Usui also suggested that it takes many years for teachers to attend to children's whispers (*tsubuyaki*):

It's interesting that in their early years of teaching, their focus is very narrow, and they only gradually widen their perspective. This is typical of the developmental trajectory of teachers. Let's think about children's whispers. Being able to hear whispers takes experience. It may take seven years before they can feel children. Early in their career, they tend to see only the whole class; they cannot see differences between each child's emotions and needs. Only gradually they come to be able to see each child's feeling and thinking. Veteran teachers have the composure (*yoyū*) to pay attention to each of the children in their class, but younger ones can't. This means that although the Japanese system is based on the assumption that there is uniform quality across classrooms, it isn't possible for a young teacher's class to reach the same level as the class of a veteran.

A group of teachers at the Sapporo School for the Deaf had a similar take on the relationship between *jibun de ippai* and being present to children:

HAYASHI: Can you say a little bit about *jibun de ippai*?

IWAKURA: It means not really being able to see children. It's always thinking, "What can I do? What shall I do?" But with experience, we start to be able to see children.

MAKI: It's like the children aren't there.

TANAKA: I think it means having a narrow focus. Like focusing on only one thing, or one child, and not focusing on other children.

HAYASHI: It sounds like a kind of selfishness: "I am thinking about only myself." But it's not that exactly, is it?

TANAKA: No, It's not.

MAKI: It's not so much that we are thinking about ourselves. It's that we are preoccupied with thinking what we should do next. We are thinking about children, but not adjusting to them. It's like, "Whatever the children say, I'm going full speed ahead with my plan."

IWAKURA: At that moment, we are thinking about doing something for the children, but in actually it's about me. There are some things that we can see only with maturity. We are not able to see children. For example, Kaizuka-sensei, ten years ago, in the video she's like, "What can I do, what can I do?" She didn't have much to go by yet.

TANAKA: They're just trying not to make mistakes.

IWAKURA: Less experienced teachers' selves are small (*jibun ga chīsai*). Kind of small. Experience is rich. With experience, the self becomes full with children.

HAYASHI: So, what's the opposite of *jibun de ippai*?

MAKI: It's like we have a lot of hands!

TANAKA: It's like, "Whatever happens, we can handle it."

SEEING CHILDREN

Experienced Japanese educators used several related terms to describe the differences between novice and veteran teachers' ability to "see" children. Professor Usui, as quoted above, spoke of experienced teachers being "skilled at *reading* children's moods and movement." Other participants described experienced teachers using variations of verbs for seeing, including *miru* (see), *mikiru* (see everything), *mitousu* (foresee, anticipate), *mikiwameru* (see with judgment), and *mimamoru* (see and protect). Several of these terms were used by a group of experienced teachers at Makomanai Yōchien as they discussed Morita's nonintervention in a dispute among children over a teddy bear:

WATANABE: With four-year-olds, I think it's better to intervene a bit more when there's trouble. I couldn't tell from the part of the video you showed us whether the teacher couldn't see (*mikiru*) what was happening or she was seeing and holding back (*mimamoru*).

OTANI: The key is to be able to anticipate (*mitōsu*) children's behavior. My first few years, I was frantic. I thought I was seeing children, but in retrospect I can say that I didn't understand what children would do next. Gradually, I become able to anticipate children's actions, and therefore able to deal with things before something bad would happen, like I could guess that an activity might run long, and therefore I could adjust. Being able to anticipate made a big difference in my teaching.

SASAKI: At the beginning, I felt so frantic that I couldn't see (*miru*) the children around me. Frantic! A feeling of ease (*yutori*) only came to me gradually. The answer came from seeing children's facial expression, children's attitude. I did a lot of self-reflection about this, which led to improvement. I am still in that situation.

Nogami used another *mi* (see) verb to define the core of early education teaching expertise:

HAYASHI: What is the difference between new teachers and experienced teachers?

NOGAMI: The ability to see children and have the judgment to know what each child might do in various situations.

Nogami's response here was actually only three words long (*mikiwameru chikara kana*), but one of these words, *mikiwameru*, is so rich in meaning in this context that it took me sixteen words to translate it into English. Dictionaries define *mikiwameru* as "ascertain," "get to the bottom of," or "see through." However, Nogami here is saying much more—namely, that an experienced teacher has the wisdom and judgment to be able to, at a glance, anticipate what sort of intervention, if any, is needed in a particular situation. *Mikiwameru* comes as close as any single word can to encapsulating the essential strength of an experienced Japanese preschool teacher.

The ability to see and read children and predict their actions is challenging for novice Japanese teachers who must be able not only to see, judge, and predict the behavior of individual children but to do so with a class of twenty or more. This requires a sophisticated ability to balance attention. Several of my participants told me that young teachers have particular difficulty balancing their attention between individual children and the class as a whole. Nogami, for example, said to Morita about her teaching in 2002, "You have changed. You now are able to explain things by showing, not by talking. And when you do talk, you talk to each child, and not to the whole class." Professor Usui commented, "Younger teachers put a lot of their efforts into getting children's attention, dealing with discipline problems, and calming children down. They struggle with distributing their attention."

Professor Takako Kawabe of the University of the Sacred Heart (Seishin Joshi University) appreciated Kaizuka's ability to distribute her attention during the lunch period: "I can see that she is looking at each child, as well as paying attention to the whole group. And she has control of the daily routines, which allows her to avoid future trouble." Teachers at Makomanai Yōchien made similar points:

> WATANABE: The first few years, there's a tendency to see the whole class, but not see the small things, like an injury or a fight. Seeing the whole comes before seeing the details. With experience, teachers become able to see both the whole and the details, and become aware of how to deal with each child differently, one by one.
>
> OTANI: My point is similar. Our preschool has some floating teachers, who help out by moving from room to room. I still often have those teachers tell me afterwards, "So and so was like this," "So and so was like that," which means that I can't yet see all that goes on (*mikiru*) with children. At these times, I feel I still can't see the whole. Sometimes I want to talk to an individual kid before talking to the whole group, but so far I can't. My challenge is to see (*mikiru*) the whole (*zentai*).

Zentai can be translated as "whole" or, in this context, as "whole class." However, as used by these teachers, this term is more encompassing than the English word *everyone* or the Japanese *minna* (everybody). *Zentai*, as used by these teachers, implies knowing how each child interacts with his or her twenty-some classmates, the character of the class as a group (which varies from year to year and month to month), and how the behavior of this group changes across contexts.

Japanese early childhood educators' discussions of these terms for seeing, evaluating, and predicting suggest a developmental trajectory of teachers' attention, from initially being too much in one's own head (*jibun de ippai*)—and therefore unable to attend to children—to seeing and knowing children well enough to get through daily routines, to attending to the interaction patterns of the class as a complex whole, and to being able to attend simultaneously to the group and to individual children. For example, Nogami said about Morita in responses to her 2002 video, "It seems like you continually were focused on what you had to do next. Therefore, we can say that you hadn't yet reached the point as a teacher that you could really see each child. Your focus was on keeping the attention of the group." Nogami's comment suggests that the tendency of younger teachers to attend to the group is closely connected with their struggles to get and hold the attention of the children. Or to put it another way, insecurity about their ability to command the attention of the class as a whole makes it hard for a younger teacher to attend to the needs and actions of individual children.

As Otani explained, young teachers also struggle with balancing being responsive to children with the need to keep on schedule:

> When I was younger, clean-up time was all about cleaning up. For me, even if some kids still wanted to play, it was clean-up time. Sure, I could understand their feelings, but nevertheless I was like, "It's clean-up time now, so clean up!" Now, I think about their feelings, like "How can I respond to these feelings given what is coming next?" I am still learning, but I think I am getting better at this, at least compared to when I was young.

Once a teacher reaches the stage when they can begin to attend to children as individuals, they become aware of children's differences, and therefore of the need to take these differences into account. Morita explained how, with experience, she became able to individualize her way of interacting with children:

> MORITA: It depends on many factors. For example, a child who was born in April (the beginning of the Japanese school year) tends to be able to do many things on her own. Therefore, we teachers will spend more time with a child who was born in March (the youngest in the class). It's not only age. There are days when a child who usually can do something by herself is feeling a need for me to care for her. I let a child *amaeru* (express dependency needs) when she is struggling and having a hard time. But we have to have *yoyū* in order to do this.
>
> YOSHIZAWA: Around June each year, Nogami-sensei comes to tell me, "We are getting to know the children." What he means is we now know each child's personality and habits, how each child might act in certain situations, and how the children in the class interact. Therefore, we tell teachers, including new teachers, to observe children as much as possible.

Sawasaki acknowledged, bravely, that in addition to knowing each child as an individual, she has to be able to take into account her own emotional reactions to children, including children she may not like very much:

> There are children I can easily interact with, and there are children who are difficult for me to deal with. I think I've reached the point where I can interact even with those children who are not easy for me. I now can take into account things like that child's family environment. Another factor is that I now have my own children, which gives me a longer perspective on the children I teach, and leads me to think, "What kind of people do I want them to be in the future?"

HOLDING BACK AND GIVING CHILDREN SPACE

After watching sequences (with the sound off) from both Morita's and Kaizuka's 2002 videos, Professor Kawabe commented, "So full!" (*ippai ippai*). She was referring specifically to how Kaizuka dominated the discussions with the two boys in their hair-pulling dispute and the way she directed how the daily monitors should serve lunch boxes:

> She leaves no empty space (*yohaku*). I couldn't tell exactly what she was saying, but it's clear that those two boys had no space to talk. It's the same thing in the scene at lunch. She handled it okay. But instead of her doing all the talking, she could have said things like "Let's think about the best way to serve the lunch boxes." She's in a constant rush, full speed ahead without pause.

The term Kawabe used here for lack of space, *yohaku*, contains the same *yo* as does *yoyū ga nai*, which I have translated as "lacking time and space" or "a lack of composure." The term *hakushi* (literally, white paper) also shares with *yohaku* the kanji *haku* (white). *Yohaku* can be translated literally as "white space," or more figuratively as "the unfilled space in the margins." I take Kawabe's meaning here to be akin to the English-language concept of "leaving some room to maneuver" or "wiggle room." The idea here is that inexperienced teachers, in their anxiety and tendency to be "full speed ahead," fill the time and space of the classroom with their talking, actions, and directives, leaving neither the children nor themselves latitude in which to act freely and spontaneously. This is consistent with Morita's description of her early teaching as "too crammed with words." Across my interviews, Japanese participants contrasted novice and experienced teachers using a binary of "full" and "empty," as in the phrases *ippai* (full), *yohaku* (empty space), and *hakushi* (blank slate). In Western discourse, "fullness" is a trope associated with maturity and "emptiness" with immaturity, but these concepts have the opposite associations in Japanese pedagogy, philosophy, and aesthetics, where austerity is valued over complexity and sparseness over abundance (Hayashi and Tobin 2015).

Hakushi and *yohaku* share both the character for "white" and a meaning of emptiness. However, in Japanese preschool pedagogy, they refer to two very different concepts. Japanese interviewees used *hakushi* to describe the ideal state of awareness and perception of the experienced teacher. In contrast, they used *yohaku* to refer to the way an experienced teacher will refrain from talking, directing, and mediating in the classroom in order to give more freedom and room to act to the children. *Yohaku* is among a set of related terms that refer to a pedagogical strategy of teacherly restraint, terms that include *hanareru* (hold back) and *mimamoru* (watch and guard). For example, Professor Junko Hamaguchi of Ochanomizu University said:

HAMAGUCHI: Veteran teachers often say that when we teachers stop doing anything, children change. Then it becomes peaceful. Throw away all preoccupations with routines, and then see what happens. By the next day, children will have changed. It's difficult to hold back like this, but it's worthwhile.

HAYASHI: Is this connected with *mimamoru*?

MIYASATO: *Mimamoru* is a bit more like "withdrawing myself from a situation." When there are problems among children, it's like, "I'm taking my existence away from here." The word *mimamoru* is difficult!

Morita gave the example of how she has changed over time in something as simple-seeming as deciding whether to help a child with her shoes:

Of course, it's quicker if I help a child put her shoes on, especially when we are short on time. In my second year of teaching, I often made that kind of mistake. I helped them too often and too quickly, which means I took away from children the chance to grow up on their own. It was like I thought my job was to put their shoes on, or my job was to take care of children. Student teachers tend to put shoes on children when they appeal for help. I tell them, "Wait." Then student teachers are like, "Then what am I supposed to do?" Then they just stand around, thinking they don't have anything to do. Actually, it is our job to wait and watch (*mimamoru*), but they haven't gotten that far yet. The first year of teaching, we think our job is to help.

Nogami related the ability to hold back with having trust in children:

> NOGAMI: New teachers intervene quickly in children's fights because they are afraid that children might do something wrong or terrible. Or new teachers try to keep their children inside the classroom because they get nervous if their children are out of their sight. Or for example, they stop children from playing in the mud. I won't stop children from doing that. I would just think, "It's no big deal; we can wash them off."
> TOBIN: Do you say this to new teachers?
> NOGAMI: Yes, I tell them, "Please don't act so strongly. Children won't do terrible things. They know what they can do and can't do."

Nogami also attributed the difficulty younger teachers have in holding back to misplaced *omoiyari* (empathy):

> In our early years of teaching, it made us feel good about ourselves to think that we were helping children. Or maybe we wanted to get credit from others for helping children. Or we thought the fact that we put their shoes on was evidence of our teaching ability. Over time, when children appealed for help (*amaeru*), we gradually got better at *mimamoru*.

Morita suggested that the art of teaching lies in knowing when to help a child and when to hold back, but that this knowing isn't necessarily conscious:

> HAYASHI: How do you know when to help a child and when to hold back?
> MORITA: It's a feeling, something I sense.

Across these comments there is an underlying theme: the more teachers gain the ability to hold back, the more space and time is made available to children. This idea comes from Sōzo Kurahashi, the founder of Ochanomizu University Kindergarten, who said that early childhood education should be "for children, from children, and with children." We can hear echoes of Kurahashi's ideas in comments made by the directors of the Ochanomizu University Center for Early Childhood Education and Care:

> MIYASATO: Very rarely, there are teachers who can do this kind of teaching from the beginning. I mean, have a kind of classroom where children can explore their abilities, children can say their opinions—in short, what Kurahashi was talking about. This way of teaching is very passive. Children are the protagonists. This takes time and requires skill. In the

context of early childhood education, often a lack of control over children is conflated with a lack of teaching ability. If teachers think that not having control is a bad thing, then they have no hope of becoming a peaceful teacher. I would tell them, "Not having control isn't a bad thing. We have to give up to control." Oh, that's a good phrase! I should use it when I have the chance!

KAMISAKAMOTO: If I conceived of teaching as seeking to have control, I don't think I could reap any sense of achievement from my work. By letting go of the goal to control children, we can focus on the essential qualities of teaching.

MIYASATO: It doesn't mean we encourage chaos. We mean that children make their own lives, on their own. Therefore, we can wait.

Sachiko Iwakura, a preschool teacher at the Sapporo School for the Deaf, made similar points about her work with deaf children:

IWAKURA: Of course, it depends on their developmental stage. After children develop some ability, they can solve their own problems. This is our hope. I want to intervene, but I am like, "You can do it!" Perseverance. Those experiences are what gives them their confidence. If we, as adults, intervene, then they would think that teachers will always help them. Therefore, I only intervene when it's really necessary.

HAYASHI: When teachers are young, do they know what is necessary?

IWAKURA: I often intervened when I was in my twenties and thirties. Especially in my twenties. I often intervened because I was thinking that I wanted to be a good teacher. In that sense, right now I might be a mean teacher! But I now think that's fine.

FLEXIBILITY AND AMBIGUITY

Japanese teachers and directors suggested that another aspect of teaching expertise is the ability to be flexible and to tolerate ambiguity. A teacher needs to become less in their head and more present, which requires them to be empty of fixed notions, preconceptions, and scripts. The opposite of novice teachers following scripts and lesson plans is teachers with experience becoming more spontaneous and present. Director Kumagai described this state of mind as the ability to recognize and tolerate ambiguity and complexity:

There's always some play in the steering wheel, some room for adjusting, and therefore, the car can run straight. To put it another way, it's not all black and white; there is always a gray zone. The only way to learn that gray zone is through watching. New teachers learn it from watching their senior teachers. That's the way humans grow.

A recognition of ambiguity and complexity requires flexibility and a repertoire of skills and strategies, as Professor Kawabe explained:

Teachers must take up various positions. Sometimes we have to be face to face with a child; the next time, side by side, to give us and the child the same line of sight, so we can see and feel the things. Sometimes we have to go ahead and be a model. And sometimes we have to be behind the children, to *mimamoru*. It takes time to recognize these four positions, and then another seven or eight years to be able to adjust positions unconsciously, depending on the situation.

Mastering this repertoire of positions and knowing when to use each allows a teacher to differentiate their ways of being with children, according to changing contexts and the unique personalities, needs, and abilities of each child.

Professor Usui suggested that aspects of Japanese culture make this shift to individuated treatment of children challenging for Japanese teachers:

Because Japan emphasizes homogeneity, and there is a general assumption of sameness, beginning teachers tend to treat all children the same way and believe that teachers should all teach the same way. With experience, teachers gradually get better at noticing differences among children, and then they can begin to treat different children differently, and also to feel freer to follow their own style of teaching.

EXPERTISE AS EMBODIED PRACTICE

The book *Teaching Embodied* (Hayashi and Tobin 2015) makes the case that with experience, a teacher's practice becomes more embodied in two related senses of the term: over time, they learn to communicate with children using their words less and their bodies more, and they can act and react without needing to stop to think, allowing their teaching to be more fluid, spontaneous.

Several participants emphasized the value of embodied action over talk. For example, Morita described her teaching thirteen years prior as "too full of words," and Nogami added, "You now are able to explain things by showing rather than talking." Director Machiyama suggested that this is a key differ-ence between new teachers and experienced teachers:

MACHIYAMA: First-year teachers have a tendency to say things, to tell the children something, like "That's bad!" Tenth-year teachers are like, uh, they keep quiet, create a sort of silent situation in the classroom, that they handle not with words, but with their body. Tenth-year teachers create an atmosphere and it becomes more of a dialogue and more reciprocal. It's not only the teacher telling things to children but also listening to children.

HAYASHI: You're saying that teachers create an atmosphere with their bodies. Could you explain more about how they do this?

MACHIYAMA: With everything, like facial expressions, including sadness, loneliness, anger, and happiness, or thoughtfulness. They try to show what's in their mind, like, "That's not clear," or, "Just a second, I'm think-ing," or "What do you think?" or, "Now I get it." They don't announce a conclusion.

Several participants made analogies between skilled teaching and playing sports, as in this discussion among directors:

RITSUKO KUMAGAI: Skilled soccer players don't reflect on their play with statements like: "I moved my leg this way then that way." They say, "It's not conscious, it's embedded in my body." We can't explain with words that I move this way if an opponent comes that way. It's not like conscious thinking or acquired skills. It's embedded in my body.

MACHIYAMA: With younger teachers, there is more unnecessary movement.

TOMOKO KUMAGAI: First-year teachers move around too much; they fly around everywhere!

MACHIYAMA: Right, it's totally different between a first-year and tenth-year teacher.

NOGAMI: They move around so much that they miss the moment that they should have watched. I am sorry that my examples are always related to soccer. But on television these days, there is a red or blue line showing each player's movement and at the end of the game it shows the total ki-lometers each player ran. It shows like, "This player ran only x kilometers today, so he didn't move that much." I sometimes hope that we could do the same on our playground with teachers.

In broadcasts of soccer in England and the US, players tend to be praised for how far they ran in a match, which is called their "work rate." But Nogami is suggesting here that he sees an inverse correlation between a high number of kilometers covered by a preschool teacher on the playground and the quality of her attention to children. This is another example of the value Japanese educators place on the "empty" side of the empty-full binary.

What Helps Japanese Teachers Develop Expertise

MENTORING

Directors expressed a great sense of responsibility for the collective well-being and professional growth of their staffs. For example, Noriaki Ishihara, the assistant director—and future director—of Makomanai Yōchien in Sapporo told us:

> I think the key is the degree to which we provide an environment in which teachers feel they can take risks. The first step is to give them the kind of emotional support that allows them to do whatever they want. The second is, if they do something wrong, we should have a system that allows for giving them feedback. I think both new and experienced teachers can keep making progress if we can create this kind of system.

In an interview, Professor Kawabe pointed to the interaction of various actors in scaffolding the development of teachers:

> KAWABE: When I think about how the teachers I know who have become good, I would say the first factor they have in common is that their preschool has a positive atmosphere. It's a climate that allows teachers to be open to themselves. To grow, they need to reflect and reflection requires opening themselves. They need to have the right kind of climate, good contemporaries, and good *senpai* (older colleagues), who provide models.
>
> HAYASHI: How do they learn from *senpai*? Observing? Talking?
>
> KAWABE: Some teachers can learn from watching, but others can't. Those teachers who can learn from watching tend to be open, and they learn from watching good teachers around them. But for teachers who lack openness and the ability to learn by watching, directors need to have a system for scaffolding their development.

The director of the Ochanomizu University Center for Early Childhood Education and Care, Akemi Miyasato, made a similar point:

Because direct feedback and critique don't work, administrators have to come up with tasks that are helpful to teachers who are struggling. We have to find ways to approach those teachers. The most difficult teachers are teachers who don't think that they have problems.

While directors see themselves as having responsibility for their staff's growth, most told us that they rarely offer criticism or direct advice to teachers, as we can see in this conversation with the administrators at Komatsudani:

HAYASHI: How do you help new teachers?

YOSHIZAWA: We tell teachers, including new teachers, to observe children as much as possible.

NOGAMI: The only thing I do when new teachers come to preschool is to give them advice about children, such as paying attention to children's feelings. I try to tell them about children. I think that's it.

HAYASHI: Do you ever tell a new teacher that it would be better to do something a certain way?

NOGAMI: I say that only when teachers don't focus on children, like when they do something because they want to show off to parents or other teachers.

In a free-flowing conversation, administrators from Komatsudani, Madoka, and Senzan expressed similar views on the value of being parsimonious in handing out criticism and advice to teachers:

HAYASHI: What's the role of the director in staff development: How much impact do you as a director have on teachers?

NOGAMI: Well, it's impossible not to have impact on teachers, so you try as much as possible *not* to impact teachers.

TOMOKO KUMAGAI: Wonderful!

NOGAMI: That's my job. That's the only thing I can do.

RITSUKO KUMAGAI: Wonderful.

NOGAMI: Is it wonderful?

TOMOKO KUMAGAI: Teachers want to get Tomoko's okay. Then they can do things with confidence. So I have a wide range of ways of giving them my okay.

RITSUKO KUMAGAI: It's a kind of security.

NOGAMI: They care about Tomoko's view of them.

TOMOKO KUMAGAI: I say, "Do whatever you want."

RITSUKO KUMAGAI: It's like they want some standards to go by.

TOMOKO KUMAGAI: I say "okay" sometimes even though it's not okay from the point of view of good practice. Sometimes they ask me, "Didn't you say this is okay?" So I say, "Right, go ahead."

MACHIYAMA: That's important.

HAYASHI: So do you try not to say "No"?

TOMOKO KUMAGAI: Right.

MACHIYAMA: Me, too. I try not to say anything! I say something only if it's obvious there will be trouble, such as if a teacher doesn't give a report on an injury. I do sometimes remind them of our school's overall approach, our philosophy. I think that's my job. Then a teacher can say she's following our approach, like she can say, "This isn't only my idea, but also something the director told us."

TOMOKO KUMAGAI: We have a lot of chances to talk about our Senzan approach, starting with general conversations, like asking our teachers, "What do you think of Senzan's approach?"

HAYASHI: When do you do this?

TOMOKO KUMAGAI: Perhaps over drinks.

NOGAMI: It's nice and helpful that a director keeps talking about the school's approach.

HAYASHI: I want to make sure I understand this. For example, if one teacher came to you with a new idea that you can see immediately is not going to work, you still would let her do it, even though you think she would fail?

MACHIYAMA: We hope that our system is set up so that this situation won't happen.

Machiyama makes an important distinction between a director giving direct advice about practice, which the other administrators agree is counterproductive, and a director projecting a consistent program philosophy, one that gives direction and provides security to teachers.

Later in the conversation, the four administrators expressed the need to acknowledge the dependency needs of their young teachers:

RITSUKO KUMAGAI: It's like children holding out their arms crying to be picked up. They need help, right? First-year teachers need someone who can give them help.

NOGAMI: Do you do that for them?

TOMOKO KUMAGAI: We do. It takes a lot of time. We are not an actual family, but we have to treat our young teachers with gentleness.

MACHIYAMA: In order to play that role of a *senpai* (mentor), it's better to say, "Hmm," rather than "That's bad." A *senpai* needs to hold back a little bit and give support to a classroom teacher from the back, not in front of the children. If she does so, the classroom teacher also becomes like, "Thank you so much for your support." Not everyone has that skill.

RITSUKO KUMAGAI: When teachers who earnestly want my advice come to me, and I can see that they are growing, that makes me feel good about what we're doing. I say, "Do whatever you want, everyone." And then they can do whatever they want, based on their capacity.

NOGAMI: But don't you have moments where you're thinking, "I told you this last year"?

RITSUKO KUMAGAI: Right. But in that case, we try to strengthen their good parts.

TOMOKO KUMAGAI: Because they are adults.

Not all directors and mentors are so gentle. Director Kamisakamoto said, "When I entered the field, my *senpai* were very strict! They were warm with children, but not with us young teachers! Such strictness creates tension and makes it difficult for young teachers to grow."

Nogami's hesitancy to give young teachers any advice beyond paying attention to the children, the Kumagais' comparison of the dependency needs of young teachers and young children, Machiyama's point that *senpai* should give support "from the back," and Director Kamisakamoto's observation that mentors are ineffective if they fail to be as warm with younger teachers as they are with young children all reflect a view of mentoring that recognizes the importance of creating and maintaining a close emotional bond between mentor and mentee as more important than any direct communication of advice or critique. Directors used the term *anshinkan* (security) to describe the atmosphere they feel allows for their young staff to take chances and grow professionally. An implication of this is that good directors and senior colleagues try to keep their assistance in the background. There is a parallel here with the pedagogical strategy of *mimamoru* Japanese teachers employ with children (Hayashi and Tobin 2011). In working with both young children and young teachers, there is a belief that the most constructive approach is to hold back and intervene as lightly as possible, and only when necessary. This gives young teachers, like young children, a greater feeling of self-efficacy and responsibility for finding their own solutions than they would have if their behavior were continually mediated and corrected. As Director Ritsuko Kumagai explained:

Whether we are talking about supporting young children, new teachers, or more generally building a community, the most important thing is to identify and accept each person's strengths and weaknesses. We bring this approach to understanding children as well as teachers. This is a key role of the director in leading a program. We create an atmosphere of teachers watching and supporting (*mimamoru*) each other.

The teachers made similar points from the perspective of those being supported and mentored. At the beginning of this chapter, I quoted Morita's answer to my question of what helped her change as a teacher: "I learned from watching *senpai* things like 'I could have waited longer' . . . I was watching Nogami-sensei all the time when I first had my own class in the room next to his. This was helpful, but we need to figure things out on our own." Iwakura described how she learned from *senpai* not by seeking their advice, but through observational learning: "When I became a teacher, I looked for the kind of teachers who I wanted to be and I shadowed them."

The mentoring is not only from *senpai* to *kōhai* (juniors) but also from peers to peers. For example, Iwakura said that after thirty-some years of teaching, she has become increasingly aware of the role colleagues play: "Recently I've been thinking about the strong influence of colleagues. I believe that we can't see ourselves if we don't have colleagues." Iwakura's comment here is consistent with Bakhtin's (1990) concept of answerability—that we cannot truly see ourselves objectively or evaluate the effects of our actions.

Ritsuko Kumagai and Nogami also emphasized the importance of teachers helping each other grow by sharing perspectives:

KUMAGAI: As humans, we have a desire to improve ourselves. If we don't lose this desire, with experience a veteran teacher emerges. In addition, we have to support each other with our many eyes. Not just one teacher evaluating a situation on her own, but rather one teacher getting help from everybody.

NOGAMI: Exactly. Isn't this Japanese culture? Even in soccer?

LEARNING THROUGH EXPERIENCE

What is the relationship of experience to expertise? Japanese teachers and directors gave no single answer to this question. Reading across their comments, we can infer that they see three pathways by which teachers learn from experience: trial-and-error learning; learning from children; and learning from reflection.

Participants in several interviews suggested that teachers learn through a process of trial and error, with an emphasis on error. For example, Director Yoshizawa said of Morita's development as a teacher, "With experience, especially having experiences of failure, she gradually changed." Morita responded, "Well, I made a lot of mistakes and had a lot of failures. Then gradually, I learned that this is a one-year-old and this is a four-year-old— therefore, we need to change the way we explain things to them." Taro Machiyama also emphasized the pedagogical value of failure:

> It's difficult to explain how teachers acquire expertise because these are things that are not taught. It's not like senior teachers tell new ones what to do. This is something that you have to work out on your own: "I tried something. It didn't work. What shall I do next?" This is the process. Teachers are reared on failure.

Director Ishihara spoke of creating a system for letting teachers experience failure:

> I often think about how to support young teachers. I want them not to worry about mistakes because we are here, experienced teachers and directors, in order to support their mistakes. We shouldn't be afraid of making mistakes. It's just that we need a system within our staff for supporting mistakes.

Many interviewees in the US and China also referred to novice teachers as learning through trial and error, but I see some subtle differences. In all three countries, experienced teachers recalled making many mistakes when they were younger, but only in Japan did my participants refer to their mistakes as "failures." In the US, my participants tended to put more emphasis on the value of trials (trying lots of things and seeing what works best) than on the value of errors. Among the three countries, it was only in China that my participants spoke about the value of experts pointing out novice teachers' errors, in contrast to Japan, where the emphasis, as I will discuss in a following section, was more on learning from self-critique than on critique from others.

Several of the Japanese interviewees emphasized that the most valuable types of teaching experiences are the experiences of being with children. You can learn *about* children in preservice university coursework, but it is not until teachers have had years of experience in classrooms that they reach the stage when they can truly see, listen to, understand, and therefore learn *from* children. For example, Director Miyasato told us:

> Young teachers say things like, "I can't wait to see the children tomorrow!" Of course, the children in every preschool are treasures. It's just a question

of whether we can see them or not. If we focus on this essential point, it doesn't matter if the preschool's curriculum is play-oriented or not. What matters is having teachers who understand children. I've taught for more than thirty years. Having reached this point, I want to say to teachers who are struggling right now that their possibilities for engaging with children will expand if they just keep being focused on seeing children. Curriculum and pedagogy are important. But whatever teaching methods we use, we need to remember that what we are doing is raising (*sodachi*) children. Caring for young children starts from understanding children correctly.

Miyasato went on to recount a particular experience from several years into her career in which the children in front of her suddenly came into focus, a moment that marked her shift from a struggling beginner to a confident professional. This was a moment when she had the opportunity to watch a video made of her students on the playground:

> This experience gave me a new sense of perspective and assurance about what it means to be a teacher. One scene that I can't forget in the video was a moment when a girl was excluded from a game of hide-and-seek, and she sat on a swing, lonely. Then another girl came close to her and, without saying anything, put a hat down next to her as if to tell her, "You can wear this whenever you want." I hadn't been aware of this incident when it happened. Seeing it on the video made me realize that children's lives are so rich and the things teachers see are only one small part of children's lives. There are so many other things happening! This is such a nice profession!

This anecdote suggests that such a moment of realizing that preschool children lead rich, complex lives apart from their interactions with teachers can be liberating for teachers. From such moments of truly seeing children, veteran teachers can come to decenter their notions of teaching and become free of the heavy burdens carried by younger teachers who feel that everything, good or bad, that students experience in preschool depends on them.

Given that from their first day on the job a teacher has abundant opportunities to see—and therefore opportunities to learn from—children, why does it take them years to have the sort of breakthrough that Director Miyasato describes? One explanation, as Morita and other Japanese participants, suggested, is that during their first few years of teaching they are in a rush, in their own head, focused on getting through activities, and worried about how they are being perceived by their director, other teachers, and parents. As a result, their level of anxiety and preoccupation makes it difficult for them to truly see, hear, and therefore learn from the children in front of them.

Director Miyasato described a moment of transformation, a moment when she became aware of children's character and capabilities and, therefore, of who she could be as their teacher/with them. Most of the teachers interviewed in Japan described their transformation as more gradual. And most described the process as nonlinear, with several years spent at the beginning of their careers struggling to get comfortable in the classroom and then breaking through to a new stage when they began to find themselves as teachers. An explanation for this trajectory could be that during this first stage of their career, teachers gain experience that gradually allow them to overcome their initial anxiety and, therefore, become open to learning from experience at a deeper level. Mizuho Tanaka, a teacher at the Sapporo School for the Deaf, made an insightful distinction between two different kinds of experience:

TANAKA: When I was younger I was competitive with other teachers. But then gradually I started to become more open-minded and open-hearted (*sunao*), which allowed me to accept and appreciate the strength of other teachers. Like I came to appreciate that Iwakura-sensei is a wonderful practitioner and that Maki-sensei is great at interacting with children.

HAYASHI: When you were young, what kept you from thinking in this way?

TANAKA: I had too much energy. I was too focused on my self-improvement. And that energy went not only toward me, but also toward others, who I perceived as rivals. I had a principal who told me a long time ago that "There is a difference between experiencing life and just passing time." He told us that as young teachers we needed do our best to become experienced and to learn to change with experience.

HAYASHI: Wow—you are raising a deep question about the meaning of experience.

TANAKA: There is a difference between a teacher who is just being in a classroom where things happen and a teacher who is having an experience. The key is whether or not there is *ishiki* (awareness), whether or not we turn the things that we experience into *chinikuka* (literally, to turn into blood and meat).

Chinikuka is defined in Japanese dictionaries as to "digest," "internalize," or "embody." It is most often used in ordinary conversation to describe a process of mastering a set of skills. Tanaka suggests that it takes years to reach the point in one's career where just struggling to be competent shifts into a process where one acquiring expertise.

Tanaka also said that this process requires a level of *ishiki*. This term can be translated into English as "awareness," "consciousness," "attentiveness," or "self-reflection." Her use of *ishiki* in this context invites the question of the role of reflection in the acquisition of expertise. Several of the participants offered nuanced views of the function of reflection, seeing some forms of reflection as honest and others as empty or even self-serving, and seeing reflection as useful in some situations and less so in others. Tanaka's admission that when she was younger too much of her reflecting took the form of comparing herself to her rivals is an example of unhelpful reflection. Nogami, in conversation with other experienced preschool directors, reported how, as a beginning teacher, he found sports festivals and musical performances for which the whole school gathered painful because his limitations as a teacher were on display both to others and to himself:

> NOGAMI: At the beginning, I didn't like those events because those were times when people could see my skills and I could see myself, and my skills. I don't know when it was that I began to realize that these events were actually good opportunities for self-reflection. I am curious when that was?
>
> RITSUKO KUMAGAI: You became yourself when you accepted 100% of yourself.
>
> NOGAMI: Well, I did? Good.
>
> TOMOKO KUMAGAI: When we give advice, teachers say, "Well . . . But . . . Because . . ."
>
> NOGAMI: Well, maybe when we can accept that kind of advice, this is what it means to be a veteran?

Ritsuko Kumagai defines a veteran teacher not as a teacher who is expert in all aspects of her craft but rather as a teacher who is able to acknowledge one's weaknesses as well as one's strengths. A crucial step in reaching this stage is being able to view oneself objectively, without defensiveness or ego. Tomoko Kumagai emphasized the difference between younger and veteran teachers' abilities to learn from feedback and Nogami concurred, suggesting that teachers become veterans when they reach the stage when they can accept feedback undefensively.

Yoshizawa, who is both the director of Komatsudani Hoikuen and head priest of the temple it is a part of, and Nogami offered comments on the difficulty of self-reflection:

YOSHIZAWA: People get panicked if they keep doing reflection every day. We work eight hours a day. We are told we should reflect each day on what we did that day and we should keep it in our mind. But if we did that, we'd go crazy. It's very difficult to honestly retain in our memory what we felt in the moment. We just can't.

NOGAMI: When people try too hard to self-reflect, they tend to focus on writing their reflections beautifully, or writing only about good things. When this happens, self-reflection gradually becomes a lie.

YOSHIZAWA: Well, I would say that it's not a lie. It's something that is just impossible to keep in our mind, and it's difficult to honestly think about what we felt in the moment.

NOGAMI: It's difficult.

Professor Kawabe suggested that self-reflection takes different forms at different stages in a teacher's career: in the first stage, things are so new and overwhelming that they cannot yet do meaningful self-reflection; in the second stage, they need to be encouraged to make their self-reflection conscious and share their self-reflections with others; in the third stage, their ability to self-reflect and to teach becomes more unconscious.

HAYASHI: What do you think most helps a teacher's growth?

KAWABE: As a professional, I think that it is about self-recognition of one's own actions.

HAYASHI: And it takes time?

KAWABE: Yes, it takes time. At most *yōchien*, teachers begin with three-year-olds, and then the next year they have the same group of children as four-year-olds, and then their third year with the children is when they turn five. Because for the first three years they've taught children of three different ages, these young teachers are a bit overwhelmed (*ippai*). In their fourth year, they have three-year-olds again, which gives them a chance to make comparisons with their earlier experience and reflect.

HAYASHI: Do you think this process is something that mostly happens unconsciously?

KAWABE: I think there are some teachers who can do it unconsciously because they have a sort of natural sense. But what I think is best for most teachers is initially to ask them to raise their reflections to the level of consciousness, and then gradually their thinking can drop down into their unconscious. The job of preschool teaching requires quick decision-making. To make this decision-making conscious, they need to do keep a journal or videotape themselves, and then reflect on their actions and discuss it.

HAYASHI: And then eventually their thinking becomes unconscious?
KAWABE: For the teachers we call veterans this must be so, right?

STRUCTURED PROFESSIONAL DEVELOPMENT

There is a large, enthusiastic literature in English on the virtues of Japanese lesson study (Lewis 2000; Lewis, Perry, and Murata 2006; Doig and Groves 2011; Lewis and Lee 2017; Hiebert and Stigler 2000). While lesson study is practiced widely in Japanese primary schools, it is less common in middle and high schools and rarely practiced in preschools. The version of structured professional development found in Japanese preschools is called *ennai kenshū*, (literally, inside-the-preschool learning study groups). In the context of early childhood education, the term *jugyō kenkyū* (lesson study) is not used because the preschool curriculum is conceptualized in terms of activities rather than lessons, and the curricular emphasis is on social-emotional development rather than academic learning.

The all-day schedule of the *hoikuen* makes it difficult to bring staff together for formal professional development activities, in contrast to the *yōchien*, where staff can gather after children go home in the early afternoon. And because they serve children of working parents, it is more difficult for *hoikuen* than it is for *yōchien* to be closed to children for professional development days. Survey data (e.g., Benesse 2009) suggest that while almost all Japanese preschools conduct some form of *ennai kenshū*, the frequency and types of these in-house professional development activities vary widely across programs. Some preschools conduct *ennai kenshū* by grade-level teams. Some focus on a particular topic or problem each year. Some bring in outside experts to introduce new perspectives and facilitate discussion. Some have teachers teach lessons in front of their colleagues with children present, some do simulated lessons without children, and some use videotaping.

One common form of *ennai kenshū* found in private *yōchien* is the gathering of the whole staff every few months to observe one teacher conducting an activity with children (live or on videotape), followed by feedback and discussion. The directors and teachers at Makomanai Yōchien in Sapporo described their approach to *ennai kenshū*:

ISHIHARA: We have *ennai kenshū* three times a year.
HAYASHI: Do the teachers visit each other's classrooms?
SAWASAKI: No, for each session, only one class is open, and all of the teachers come together to watch an activity in that class.

ISHIHARA: After the activity (*hoiku*), we each write down on a piece of paper the things we noticed, and we tape our papers on the wall. The teacher whose lesson we watched reads and then responds to all of these comments.

HAYASHI: Isn't this heavy for her? Emotionally difficult?

ISHIHARA: Is it bad to have heaviness? I think it's fine.

HAYASHI: Are you teachers at Makomanai used to getting feedback?

TODATE: There are so many things that I can't notice on my own. When my colleagues watch me, they can give me advice and act as a check on what I'm doing in my classroom.

OTA: Even though we may get hurt, we learn from getting a range of feedback.

ISHIHARA: The teachers know how to present their feedback. They don't do it in a harsh way. They kind of sugarcoat it.

INAFUNE: Director Ishihara is harsh! Well, when we are giving feedback, it's like one of us is harsh and the other one is generous.

TAKAHASHI: When we are young, receiving feedback from more senior colleagues can be painful, but I think *kenshū* can be even tougher on experienced teachers, because there is the expectation that experienced teachers should be better.

ISHIHARA: Emotions run deep at *kenshū* for all of our teachers. During these sessions, they all think about things sincerely. But bringing these ideas back into practice in their classrooms is another story. We have a proverb: "Easy to say, hard to do." The natural tendency is to forget things. No matter how much experience teachers have, they need to remain humble and open (*sunao*). Otherwise, they can't continue.

Professor Kawabe, who often runs professional development workshops for preschools, suggested to me that there is great variation in how teachers learn on the job, and that *ennai kenshū* is particularly helpful for those teachers who are not self-directed learners:

Some teachers can learn from watching, others can't. Those with the ability to learn from watching learn from observing the good teachers working next door to them. Teachers like this tend to be unguarded and open. But for those teachers who lack the ability to watch themselves and who are closed, we need to have systematic professional development. This can take the form of learning from going to workshops, or keeping a journal and having someone else read and respond to it, or *ennai kenshū*. *Ennai kenshū* is good because teachers can watch each other teach and then talk about it together: "What was good? What could have been done differently?"

Professor Kawabe emphasized the importance of the director establishing a positive atmosphere for her staff's professional growth:

> When I think about how the good preschool teachers I know became good, I would say the first factor that they have in common is their preschools have a positive atmosphere (*fūinki*). It's a climate (*fūdo*) that allows teachers to be open to themselves.

Unlike individual self-reflection, *ennai kenshū* is a group process that depends on the leadership, good will, and trust of the teachers as a community.

The other form of structured professional development for preschool teachers are workshops and conferences led by outside experts. *Yōchien* teachers are required to complete thirty hours of out-of-school professional development every ten years. These workshops for preschool teachers were mentioned as helpful by professors of early childhood education, but rarely by practitioners. Preschool directors acknowledge that their teachers tend to be reluctant to attend workshops and yet remain hopeful that their staff will come back from workshops with some new ideas. As Director Kamisakamoto of Ochanomizu University Kindergarten told us, "Of course there are teachers who go to workshops only to get the credit hours. But there are also teachers who think, 'I want to learn this because this is an area of weakness for me.'" Her colleague, Director Miyasato, from the Ochanomizu University Kindergarten, said:

> I know there is a criticism that these workshops required for license renewal don't mean anything. Teachers go because they have to. But I still hope that good workshops can be beneficial. Teachers may think after attending, "My boss forced me to go, but I have to admit, 'That was a good workshop.'" Our approach is to send two teachers at a time to outside workshops, around ten times a year. What makes it meaningful is that because they attended the workshop together, they can talk with each other about the workshop on the way back home and in the days that follow. Maybe those workshops don't help teachers with teaching the next day, but they help to strengthen their foundations.

Teachers' growth as professionals takes different forms in different types of Japanese preschools: between deaf and hearing preschools, between *yōchien* and *hoikuen*, between private and public programs, and between programs of high and low quality. Structural differences may impact careers and professional development. As explained above, formal professional development activities are harder to schedule and are thus rarer in *hoikuen* than in *yōchien*. Differences in employment practices make professional development very different in public than in private programs. And private programs that are motivated mostly by profit tend to have a much higher turnover rate and, thus, less emphasis on the professional growth of their staff than do more traditionally minded, well-run programs.

While, as Directors Kamisakamoto and Miyasato acknowledge, most preschool teachers are not motivated to attend workshops, two experienced preschool teachers who worked for many years at the Sapporo School for the Deaf explained to us how attending a workshop was a turning point in their professional lives:

TANAKA: We were having hard time with our teaching. We had lost confidence in the way we were teaching deaf children, which was mostly using oral methods. We knew that what we were doing just wasn't working well enough. We felt like we had hit a wall. Because we knew we were in trouble, we decided to go to a workshop in Tokyo on sign language education. We went together. I can't forget that moment at the workshop. "Wow! What is this we're seeing!" We saw young deaf children using their hands in unbelievably wonderful ways, far beyond what we had known was possible. This had a *huge* impact on us.

IWAKURA: It was a whole different take on deaf child development compared to what we'd known. They showed a dramatic video and it was like, "Oh, that's the way deaf children develop!"

HAYASHI: How long had you been teaching when you had that moment?

TANAKA: Probably twenty years? We had a deep and growing sense that something was wrong, which gave us the feeling that we couldn't keep going in the same way any longer.

The conference they attended in 2005 was run by Meisei Gakuen, a school that had been opened recently by proponents of Japanese Sign Language and JSL education. Once back in Sapporo, with their enthusiasm reignited by their experience at the conference, Tanaka and Iwakura initiated a new study group focused on learning everything they could about how deaf children can acquire fluency in signing. They eventually were instrumental in starting a JSL program at the Sapporo School for the Deaf. The workshop and the study group were critical for Tanaka and Iwakura's growth as teachers because they were working in a sector of early childhood education where there was a lack of clarity and confidence about what constituted effective practice and an ideological divide among educators, policy makers, and parents (Hayashi and Tobin 2014, 2015). By contrast, in most Japanese preschools, there is less of a need for formal professional development because there is general agreement about pedagogy and curriculum. Therefore, expertise in these settings can be passed down from more experienced to less experienced staff through informal mentoring and observation.

The majority of both *hoikuen* and *yōchien* teachers work in private programs, 79.8% as of May 2018 (MEXT 2019). The government has a policy of rotating teachers and directors working in the public sector from school to school every five years or so, while a teacher working in the private sector tends to spend their whole career working in one program. While the policy of requiring staff to rotate every five years is often not enforced, teachers at public preschools tend to see their expertise as less tied to the program where they are currently working than to their years of working in the public sector. They are also more likely than their private preschool counterparts to cite ongoing professional development as playing a significant role in their growth as teachers.

Perhaps the biggest divide in approaches to professional development is between programs of low and high quality. As Professor Hamaguchi explained, "There is a big difference between preschools that value making money and those that value the quality of their education. Many of these profit-oriented preschools keep salaries low by only employing young teachers." Professor Kawabe explained that some private preschools offer trendy curricula intended to attract parents who are anxious to get their young children off to a fast start academically:

KAWABE: These academic-oriented preschools are a growing movement. They want to teach everything, as early as possible. Some parents like this, like a program that teaches English as early as possible. There is no such movement in the public sector, and therefore their enrollments are declining. These academic and English-language programs have no time or interest in raising the level of their teachers. Public programs have a budget for professional development. There is no such expectation in the private system.

HAYASHI: So do you think public preschool teachers on average are stronger than those in the private sector?

KAWABE: It's not always the case. That's a very difficult question. I would say that in either case, what is important is that the program is open to improving their quality.

HAYASHI: Private preschools have one advantage. Their teachers don't move. Which means they can take a longer perspective on their teachers' growth, right?

KAWABE: That is a strength that can also be a problem. If teachers never move, they can become . . .

Director Miyasato also saw both strengths and weaknesses in the relative absence of turnover in private preschools:

The private preschools that are strong have experienced teachers. In those preschools, teachers tend to not leave, which keeps the quality high. Those experienced teachers play a crucial role. If they are resistant to change, or if they are authoritarian, it becomes a scary atmosphere for the younger teachers. On the other hand, if they welcome new ideas, and if they have an attitude of being open to learn from young teachers, then the mood at the preschool becomes lively.

LOCALIZED EXPERTISE

When asked if, after thirteen years of teaching, she considers herself to be an accomplished teacher, Morita replied, "I don't know if I would be good at another school. The way of being with children depends on each daycare center. This *hoikuen* and that *hoikuen* may have different points of view." I heard similar comments from other experienced teachers; some told me that they see their teaching skills as being so nested in their own schools that they have difficulty imagining them being transferable to other settings.

This reflects in part the strong influence in private *hoikuen* and *yōchien* of directors, who are often also the owners. As family businesses, they tend to have a very stable leadership, with the directorship only changing when it is passed down from one generation to the next, as it has at Komatsudani Hoikuen and Madoka Yōchien. Directors of these preschools emphasize the unique character of their programs, referring, for example, to "the Madoka way" or the "Senzan atmosphere." They see themselves as deeply embedded in their local communities, often serving children of alumni who want their children to have the same kind of preschool experience they had. These themes came out in an interview in 2015 with Hironori Yoshizawa, who succeeded his father, Hidenori, as Komatsudani's director in 2005; he described how they maintain such continuity as a *hoikuen*:

> One of the reasons would be our environment, here in Higashiyama, in Kyoto. It's a very stable neighborhood. If we were in another area of Kyoto, like somewhere that has experienced a lot of change, it would be a different story. The main thing is that children aren't different; the nature of children is the same. And we have had very little change of staff. We can stay the same because we are able to pass down our values. If we lost more than half of our staff, then Komatsudani might change a lot. Because we have mostly the same crew, when we do change something, it's always an evolution from something we've been doing. That gives us continuity even with change. For example, Nogami-sensei started here in 1981 as a student teacher. Now he's our head teacher. His philosophy is based on things that he was taught when he came here as a student intern.

Director Kamisakamoto went so far as to compare changing programs to changing husbands:

> We don't have a custom of moving, so most of the teachers work here for a long time. But we do have an exchange program with four other university-attached kindergartens. In my case, after many years at Ochanomizu, I went to Gakugei University–attached kindergarten for two years. It had a similar approach, but there were small differences, such as how to make lesson plans. It was difficult! I was so used to Ochanomizu that it was like I got divorced and remarried. Well, let's just say that the way of life was a bit different.

Comments by Morita, Nogami, and other experienced teachers as well as directors suggest that they view teaching expertise less as a set of skills they can carry from job to job and more as the ability to contribute to the collective enterprise and embody the ethos of their particular preschool. That being said, while teachers and directors at Senzan, Madoka, and Komatsudani emphasized the value of teachers' becoming enculturated into their particular approaches, to my eyes their approaches looked far more alike than different. By this I do not mean to suggest that Japanese teachers are easily interchangeable, but instead that there are aspects of expert Japanese teaching that are widely shared from school to school, one of which, ironically, is the belief that expert teaching is school specific.

I need to add some provisos. One is that poorer quality private preschools, with directors less idealistic and wise than the Yoshizawas, Kumagais, and Machiyamas and with head teachers less kind and insightful than Nogami, may have high turnover, odd curricular approaches, and a lack of communal spirit among the staff. As Director Miyasato explained:

> The private preschools that are strong have experienced teachers. In those preschools, teachers tend to not leave, which keeps the quality high. Those experienced teachers play a crucial role. If they are resistant to change, or if they are authoritarian, it becomes a scary atmosphere for the younger teachers. On the other hand, if they welcome new ideas, and if they have an attitude of being open to learn from young teachers, then the mood at the preschool becomes lively.

In good preschools, helping teachers to develop is seen as a collective responsibility. Professor Kawabe said of teachers who are struggling, "I would say this is not a problem of an individual teacher, but rather one of the preschool's weakness in management. It's not a question of individual responsibility. This struggling individual is working in a particular preschool. Therefore, if this teacher isn't making progress, it is this preschool's responsibility."

NONLINEAR GROWTH

Japanese participants described their growth as teachers as incremental but not linear. As in the case of Tanaka and Iwakura, the teachers at the Sapporo School for the Deaf, a long period of slow evolution was interrupted by a crisis in confidence in their approach, which led to a period of rapid and focused self-directed change. Director Miyasato described a similar arc in her professional development:

> What's the difference between young and experienced teachers? That's kind of difficult to answer because it's not like we follow a linear path. I guess my first answer would be "a wall." It's like at some point you're crashing into a wall, running up against barriers. But looking back, I can see that external challenges weren't the only reason I felt like I had hit a wall. It was also because something was lacking in me. The wall comes in various forms. First is when we get criticism from a boss, which is relatively straightforward to deal with. "Children in your classroom aren't developing." This we can resist! Second is when we realize that we aren't getting along very well with children. This makes us start wondering about our

teaching and to acknowledge that something we are doing is lacking. At these points, which probably come somewhere between the fifth and tenth years, there are teachers who quit. I did have a lot of moments where I might have quit. I was working while I was also raising my own kids. I was able to take three maternity leaves, which made it possible to take a break from work rather than quit. During these breaks from work, I had experiences outside of school that turned out to be beneficial for my teaching, like things I did in my community. Actually, being away from work had a bigger impact on me than becoming a parent. Another factor is that, here in Tokyo, teachers in the public preschool system can change schools. The experience of changing preschools gave me a chance to get vindication for things that didn't work in my previous school!

As Miyasato so vividly describes here, life happens. As teachers move through their careers, they not only gain professional knowledge and skills but also, at the same time, get older (and presumably wiser) and experience various predictable and unexpected events in their lives both inside and outside of school.

Having babies is one such event that impacts preschool teachers' careers. Teachers working in the public sector, like Director Miyasato, have the option of taking maternity leave and then returning to their jobs. This is more variable in the private sector, where employers are not required to rehire teachers following a leave of absence. Nevertheless, many preschool directors readily grant unpaid leaves in order to retain experienced staff. As Director Machiyama explained:

> HAYASHI: I've heard that many *yōchien* teachers will teach only five years or so and then leave the field when they get married and that this helps *yōchien* keep salary costs down. Is that true?
>
> MACHIYAMA: Well, it depends on the *yōchien*. There are *yōchien* that do as you say. But I have a different perspective on this. I think it's a frightening thought to have only young teachers. It is definitely true that experienced teachers can deal with a wider range of things. It's the best to have a mixture of young, intermediate, and experienced teachers.

This informal policy made it possible for Kaizuka, following the birth of her twins, to take nine years off from teaching at Madoka before returning to work. Kaizuka attributed much of her change as a teacher to the experience of parenting, which she said made her more patient with children. Several veteran teachers and early childhood experts who watched short video clips of Kaizuka teaching before and after her extended leave speculated on the impact on her teaching of marriage and parenting. For example, Setsuko Maki, a veteran teacher in Sapporo, said:

> I also took about six years off, like Kaizuka-sensei. Before having my own children, I thought that children listened to what adult say. But after six years of having my own children, I realized that no matter how many times we say something, there are things about children we have no control over.

Professor Kawabe suggested that not only parenting but also marriage and other life events impact teachers as they move through their careers:

KAWABE: It's amazing how much she changed. Did she get married?

HAYASHI: Yes. And she had twin boys.

KAWABE: Probably she now understands there are things that she can't do the way she wants. It's amazing how much she changed! Does she know that she's changed?

HAYASHI: I am going to ask her when I interview her again later today.

HAYASHI: Do you think becoming a parent changes teachers?

KAWABE: I think it's not a matter of having children or not. It is a matter of having experiences in life where we can't do things the way we want, and experiences that are very satisfying . These kinds of life experiences.

HAYASHI: The other teacher I focused on in this study, Morita-sensei, didn't have children, but she changed in a similar way to Kaizuka-sensei.

KAWABE: I don't think it's right to say that her changes are due to her having babies. I wouldn't like to think that teachers who haven't had their own babies don't become good teachers. I think, as a human being, when we live longer, we have a lot of different experiences and are faced with various responsibilities. These come out in our teaching. This is what is most valuable.

Tomoko Kumagai presented a similar perspective:

> Because it takes at least ten years to be a real veteran teacher, we want to create an atmosphere where teachers can keep working after marriage, as a mother or father. All those experiences are good for preschool teaching. Parents think a veteran teacher is anyone who is in her thirties. For us, as directors, we think veteran teachers are ones who have had many life ex-

periences, including having their own children. A veteran is a teacher who has had experiences that deepened their humanity. These veteran teachers understand many things quickly because they are fully human.

Director Yoshizawa, who has been watching over Morita since she started her career as a preschool teacher sixteen years prior, told us:

> To be honest, sure, she has changed. Well, I mean not only in her practice (*hoiku*). If we consider only her teaching, it's easy to see her in her classroom practices. But what I mean is that she has changed from the inside. If we talk about "experience," I think it is best to have experiences not only as a daycare center teacher but also as a person.

Coda: Morita and Kaizuka Then and Now

I was fortunate to have the opportunity in 2015 to make new videos in both Morita's and Kaizuka's classrooms. We shot these new videos, to the degree possible, with the same camera angles and framings used in the 2002 videos. I selected scenes from their 2002 and 2015 videos that were most alike in content (e.g., Morita leading art activities and Kaizuka dealing with disputes among children) and placed one-minute versions of these scenes side-by-side in a video, which I then used as cues for a new round of interviews with the two teachers, their supervisors and colleagues, and other Japanese early childhood education practitioners and experts. This turned out to be a particularly powerful new tool, one that stimulated new insights into the nature of how Japanese preschool teachers change with experience and how they conceptualize this change.

Morita and Kaizuka (figure 3), unsurprisingly, changed in their teaching in various ways between 2002 and 2015. In this section, I focus on changes in their embodied pedagogical practices. Based on microanalyses of videos of these two teachers at earlier and later stages of their careers, I argue that there is a directionality to the change in their uses of their bodies, a shift toward more self-restraint, composure, and tact in their use of gaze, facial expressions, posture, and gestures in interactions with children. I then end by suggesting that this trajectory of change in the embodied pedagogy of these two Japanese preschool teachers is consistent with the literature on nonembodied aspects of expertise in teaching in other countries, at other grade levels, and even in other professional domains.

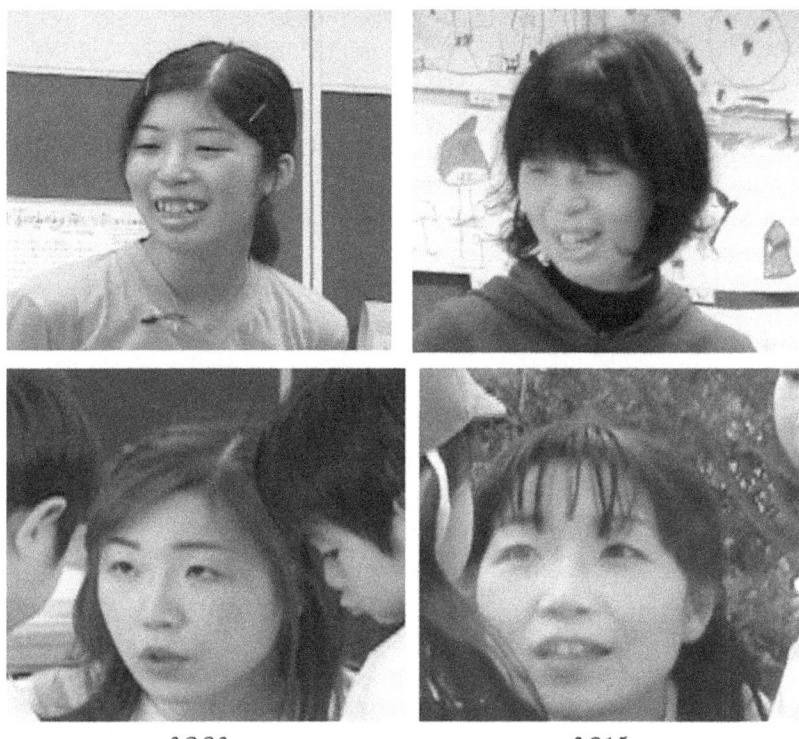

2002   2015

Figure 3. Morita and Kaizuka in 2002 and 2015

EMBODIED PEDAGOGY

There are aspects of teaching that are embodied in two senses (Hayashi and Tobin 2015). One is the way a teacher uses the body as a tool: using hands to gesture; using posture, gaze, and location to indicate varying levels of attention; and using voice to communicate empathy, frustration, or enthusiasm. The other is teaching practices that are tacit and lack premeditation. A challenge to studying the role of embodied practices in teaching is that these practices are nonverbal behaviors appearing in a field accustomed to describing things in words. Max van Manen describes such embodied pedagogical skill as "silent knowledge" that "is implicit in my world and in my actions rather than cognitively explicit or critically reflective. This silent knowledge cannot necessarily be translated back into propositional discourse" (1995, 10). The problem of studying expert practice is summarized by Michael Polanyi's dictum on the tacit knowledge of skilled practitioners: "There are things that we know but cannot tell" (1962, 601). This tacit knowledge is located in bodily practices, akin to the "muscle memory" of star athletes who in post-game interviews struggle to find words to explain how they knew in the moment precisely how hard, in what direction, and with what trajectory to hit or kick a ball. Conceiving of teaching as only or primarily a cognitive, conscious, pre-meditated activity leads to an underappreciation and scholarly inattention to embodied dimensions of pedagogy.

The recent theoretical turn in the social sciences and humanities toward a focus on spatiality, materiality, and embodiment has led to a rise in educational studies that use video to study spatial, material, and especially embodied aspects of teaching (Schreiber and Fishman 2016; Scopelitis 2013; Parks and Schmeichel 2014; Hayashi and Tobin 2015; Xiao and Tobin 2018). As Reed Stevens writes in a review of studies of embodied teaching, "Long banished from the main stage by an idealized, inside-the-head information-processing worldview, the body is steadily being rediscovered in the work of thinking and learning" (2012, 337). Even in a field as seemingly abstract as mathematics, researchers are using video to study how teachers use gestures to communicate concepts to their students (Alibali et al. 2014; de Frietas 2013). While these studies make the case for the value of gestures and other embodied techniques, they have not explored how a teacher's embodied pedagogy changes with experience.

The literature on the relationship of pedagogical expertise to experience suggests that through a process of trial and error, formal and informal mentoring, and thousands of hours of experience, teachers become better able to read a classroom (Berliner 1988), spontaneously make good pedagogical decisions (van Manen 1995), and be, in a word, more "withit" (Kounin 1970). Berliner describes experienced teachers as being able to transcend the self-conscious rational decision-making that characterizes younger teachers and becoming "arational":

> If the novice, advanced beginner, and competent performer are rational, and the proficient performer are intuitive, we might categorize experts as arational. They have an intuitive grasp of a situation and seem to sense in nonanalytic, nondeliberative ways the appropriate response to be make. (Berliner, 1988, 5)

With experience, alongside changes in knowledge, confidence, composure, "withitness," and pedagogical tact, teachers also come to use their bodies more effectively. In the sections that follow, I present the teachers' own observations alongside microanalyses of each teacher's one-minute side-by-side videos.

MORITA THEN AND NOW

In the 2002 video, we see Morita lead her students through a multistep origami activity, resulting in each child eventually making a paper fish. After distributing a piece of origami paper to each child, Morita folds her paper in half and holds it up as she says, "First we make a triangle. That's right. Our fish are now triangles. And then fold in both sides, right, like that, just like when you make a tulip. Then fold the two corners in, like this. And one more fold, like this. Got it? Good. No? Here, I'll help you." For about the next ten minutes or so, children sit in groups around tables, folding their brightly colored sheets of paper as Morita circulates from table to table and child to child, observing their progress and, when she sees a child struggling, reaching in to demonstrate or unfold and refold their mistakes. Throughout the activity, her intonation is upbeat as she continuously describes the steps, encourages the children, and praises their progress (figure 4).

In the video we made in her classroom in 2015, Morita introduces an art

Figure 4. Morita's 2002 origami lesson

activity by telling the children they will be making telephones out of paper cups and string and then showing them one she had made. After Morita passes out the materials, the children get to work at their tables. Morita circulates around the room, saying little, and offering help only when children appeal for her assistance.

The most striking change in bodily techniques revealed by watching the 2002 and 2015 videos side by side is in Morita's posture and the positioning of her arms. On the left (2002) side of the screen, we see Morita walking from table to table, not only talking more and more animatedly but also leaning slightly forward, with her arms held in front of her and her hands open, ready to reach out to offer assistance. In contrast, on the right (2015), her posture is consistently more upright and her arms are most often clasped behind her back. Her general demeanor, conveyed with her voice, facial expressions, movements, and posture, is generally less exuberant and more restrained in 2015 than in 2002 (figure 5).

I showed the side-by-side videos to Morita and her colleague Nogami and asked for their reactions:

MORITA: This [on the left] is an intense Morita. This [on the right] is a bit more relaxed Morita. On this [right] side, I'm waiting for the children's autonomy; on this [left], I'm not. On this [left] side, it seems like I was busy. On this [right] side, it seems like I move more slowly.

NOGAMI: Wow! I didn't expect to see such a huge, huge difference! I think with her body, she is unconsciously communicating to the children, "Try to do it on your own." It's not conscious and on purpose, but she is creating an atmosphere that "I trust you." Our hands come out in front of us when we are worrying, like, "Oh, be careful" or "Oh, you have to stop" or "I need to do something." You didn't have those feelings [pointing to the 2015 video] so you could hold your hands behind you, on your back. On the left [in the 2002 video], it just looks like she is moving around with a look on her face that suggests that she is trying to make the children do something. On the right, it looks like she is moving around showing an attitude of "Why don't you give it a try? What do you want to do?"

Morita went on to comment on how her movements and posture in 2002 and 2015 communicated different assumptions about what children can handle on their own:

At that time [pointing at the 2002 side of the video], I knew in my head what four-year-old children could do. However, I moved around more

2002   2015

Figure 5. Morita in 2002 and 2015

than I realized. I was continuously moving and looking around the room, with a feeling of like "What are you doing?" This year [pointing to the 2015 video], I had a special needs child in my class, but even with him my approach was "Well, to the best of your ability, go ahead."

Morita observed that in her 2002 video, her movements and demeanor made her too visibly present to the children, in contrast to her being less demanding of the children's attention in the 2015 video. She suggested that with experience, teachers learn to give children more latitude to act independently by minimizing their presence: "There are times that it's better that we position ourselves so children can't see us. It's like we try to erase our existence."

Morita was livelier at twenty-five than she was at thirty-eight, but from a Japanese pedagogical perspective, she was also less skillful, as her nervous energy dominated the origami activity, giving her students less room to explore and struggle than her students enjoyed with her much more restrained use of her body in the paper telephone activity she conducted thirteen years later. In the 2002 video, Morita communicated with her body that she was paying close attention to the children's progress and tribulations in their paper folding, which had the effect of decreasing their confidence and making them seek her help more. In contrast, in the 2015 video, Morita's more upright posture and arms held behind her back communicated that she was not worried about their ability to make the phones on their own and that, while she was available to offer assistance, she would do so only if necessary.

Many of the comments from other experienced teachers on Morita's teaching then and now used the term *zentai* (whole) as a way to describe her increased ability, with experience, to attend to the class as a whole and to have a wider perspective, both literally and metaphorically:

> IWAKURA: When she was young, she was moving around so much! In this new one, she has really slowed down. By not moving around so much she can take in the class as a whole (*zentai*).
>
> OTANI: We don't see any rush in her. She has become able to watch the whole group (*zentai*), while at the same time catching children's voices.
>
> WATANABE: If we focus only on where she stands. Earlier in her career, she was standing right next to the table, which means she was always showing her back to some of the children in the classroom, as compared with the later version, where she was standing near the same corner of the table, but in a location from where she was able to see everything (*zentai*). With experience, it seems like she has become able to interact with children with attention to the whole class. The overall mood is very calm, which we can feel by the way she moves and where she stands.
>
> SASAKI: We can see her change from her movement. In the 2002 video, she only focused on what was right in front of her. In the 2015 video, she responds with both her eyes and ears, picking up on children's whispers. In the first one, it's like in order to know how the children are doing, she has to move around from one to the next. In the second video, we can see that her perspective has become wider. Children can feel and respond to that.

In these experienced educators' comments, we see a parallel to Jacob Kounin's concept of "withitness" and van Manen's concept of pedagogical tact. Like these concepts, *zentai* emphasizes the experienced teacher's ability to have a pedagogical presence that allows them to deal in the moment with a classroom of students both as individuals and as a group.

In the 2002 Madoka Yōchien video, as the children are preparing to go home at the end of the day, we see Nobu, in tears, approach Kaizuka and complain that Yusuke pulled his hair. Kaizuka spends the next ten minutes mediating the dispute, squatting between the two boys, looking back and forth intently from one to the other as she presses each to explain his version of what happened and to take responsibility for his actions. Throughout this interaction, both Kaizuka's tone of voice and her facial expressions are anguished. Eventually, Yusuke, in tears, admits that he started the fight and then, with Kaizuka's encouragement, the boys apologize to each other (figure 6).

In Kaizuka's 2015 video, there is a similar scene. A girl in tears approaches Kaizuka and complains that another girl won't let her join in a game of hide-and-seek. As in the 2002 video, Kaizuka squats between the two children, turning her attention from one to the other, talking through what happened and how they can resolve the situation. Watching these scenes shot thirteen years apart, what is immediately striking is the similarity in Kaizuka's approach. In both scenes, she inserts herself in the middle of the dispute and

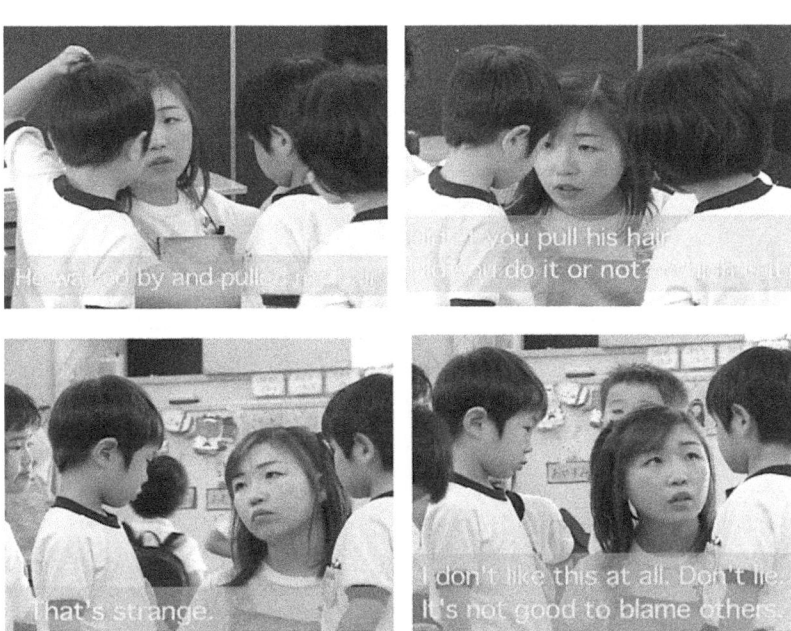

Figure 6. Kaizuka in 2002

urges the children to share their versions of what happened and to work toward a resolution. There is great similarity in her use of bodily techniques, including squatting down to be at eye level with the children, making intense eye contact, positioning the children with her hands to face each other, and holding their wrists for emphasis. However, alongside this continuity in her embodied pedagogy, we can identify a marked difference in her demeanor: her voice, body, and the set of her eyes and mouth are much more intense in 2002 and are more relaxed in 2015 (figure 7).

When I showed Kaizuka her side-by-side videos, she reflected critically on the way she talked to the two boys in 2002. She identified subtle aspects at these two stages of her career of her ways of interacting with the children:

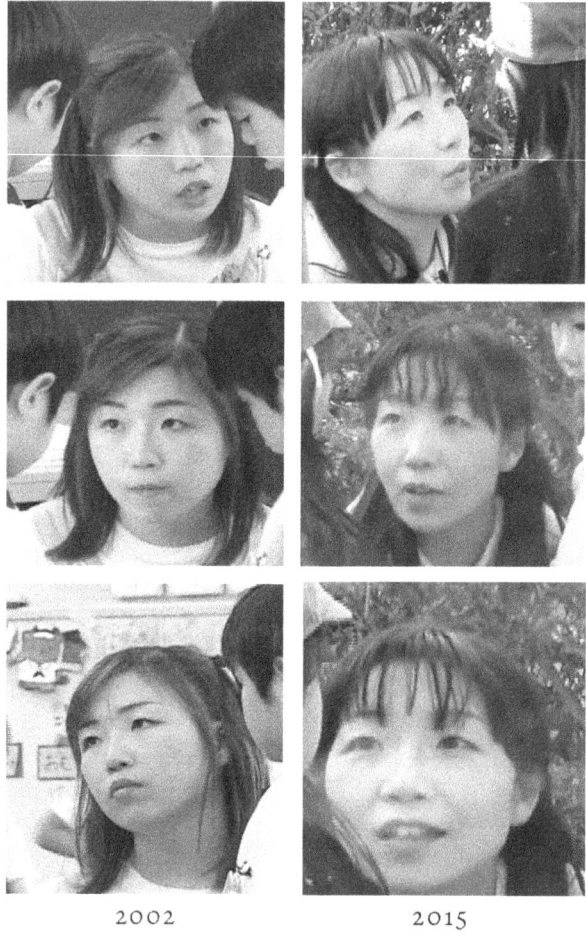

2002   2015

Figure 7. Kaizuka's facial expressions while dealing with disputes in 2002 and 2015

What a lack of patience (*yoyū*)! In this scene, I was in such a rush. I gave the children barely any room to talk. In contrast, on this [2015] side, I asked them: "What happened?" My intention was that I wanted *them* to talk. I wanted to create an environment that would encourage them to talk. I intervened only when they needed me. I waited for their words. I had *yoyū*. Here [pointing to the 2002 video], I was continuously trying to force them to say things in a certain way and, as a result, my facial expression revealed my anger and frustration. Of course, these two conflicts weren't exactly the same, but nevertheless viewing these two videos side by side really makes the point that having or not having *yoyū* is a big difference in my teaching, a difference you can really see in my facial expression. Here [pointing to the 2002 video], you can see from the hardness of my facial expression that I lacked *yoyū*. I must have scared the kids! Here [pointing to the 2015 video], because I have *yoyū*, I was able to hold myself one step back, watching the children's facial expressions.

These observations by Kaizuka were echoed in interviews we conducted with experienced Japanese early childhood educators to whom we showed Kaizuka's side-by-side videos. For example, an assistant director of a kindergarten commented, "Here [on the right] in the later version, she has become much softer. I can't hear what she is saying but we can tell that she is listening to each child, taking in what they say, and then responding." Veteran teachers in a deaf kindergarten program that emphasizes signing and embodied communication were adept at reading Kaizuka's embodied expressions:

TANAKA: The facial expressions are totally different!

IWAKURA: Yes, very different. She was scary in the first video! But here [in the 2015 video], her smile, her eyes indicate that she is ready to listen. In the earlier video, she is determined to reach her goal. She is the only one talking. The children look stunned, like they've been shot by a gun! It seems like she was thinking about herself. In the new video, as she talks to the children, we can tell that she's thinking about them, with empathy.

TANAKA: Notice the difference in her gaze. When she was young, she was looking straight at the children's faces. But here, she is looking in the direction the children are looking.

These comments suggest that a key difference between beginning and expert teachers is that the experts have become more coordinated and fluid in the use of their bodies. Because children attend not only to what their teachers say but also to what they communicate, intentionally or unintentionally, nonverbally (through facial expressions, gestures, posture, and location), teaching expertise is not only cognitive but also embodied (Hayashi and Tobin 2015).

"IT TAKES AT LEAST FIVE YEARS"

When Ritsuko Kumagai watched Kaizuka's 2002 video, she commented, "For a teacher to be able to really do *mimamoru* (to hold back from intervening too quickly), it takes at least five years." This invites the question: at least five years to become able to do what? The bodily techniques that Morita and Kaizuka acquired with experience (various ways of employing gaze, touch, posture, and facial expressions) are not in themselves hard to learn. What takes time to master is learning when to use which bodily technique. Director Kumagai went on to explain that while there are some things one can teach a young teacher, many key aspects of good practice cannot be directly taught or rushed. Consistent with Kumagai's observation, this study suggests that inexperienced teachers can have an intellectual understanding of what they should do and yet be unable to do so. Morita as a young teacher understood the concept of *mimamoru*—of the pedagogical value of holding back to encourage children to work things out on their own. Her body, however, conveyed the opposite message in the video we shot of her leading an origami activity in her third year of teaching. Her movement around the room during the origami activity, with her body leaning forward and her hands held out in front of her, conveyed not confidence in the children's abilities to cope with the task on their own but, instead, her determination to get the children to each produce a fish and, more generally, her need to feel helpful.

Similarly, once Kaizuka as a young teacher decided that she needed to extract confessions and apologies from the fighting boys, her eyes and mouth conveyed an urgency for them to comply that was too intense for a routine dispute between four-year-old children. Moreover, the intensity of her gaze focused on the boys narrowed her perspective, distracting her from her duty to supervise the whole class. At this early point in her career, although she understood intellectually that she should balance attention to individual children with attention to the class as a whole, Kaizuka lacked the embodied skill of being able to attend to the boys standing in front of her while at the same time distributing her attention around the classroom.

I suggest that such tendencies to struggle with distributing attention, to convey too much eagerness to help, and to push hard for an outcome (whether it be correctly folded origami fish or confessions and apologies) are more characteristic of teachers early in their careers than of teachers who have years of experience. Before they become skilled practitioners, beginning teachers have to develop not only pedagogical knowledge and tact but also bodily techniques that can convey their pedagogical intent. Such bodily techniques, because they are mostly tacit, are difficult to learn in a didactic way, and instead must be acquired, gradually, on the job. As Morita commented while watching her then-and-now video:

> In 2002, I am sure that Nogami-sensei often told me to relax, to take it easy. But the thing is, I couldn't tell when I was relaxed or not. I was young and I didn't have enough experience. The Morita of today can understand what Nogami-sensei tells her, but the 2002 version of Morita was like "What? I am overwhelmed."

TRAJECTORIES OF EMBODIED EXPERTISE

Morita and Kaizuka were dissimilar in their pedagogical approaches when they were young in 2002 and they were no more like each other in 2015. And yet, with experience, they evolved along similar trajectories. Morita as a young teacher had a relatively hands-off, low-intervention approach to dealing with children' disputes. Thirteen years later, in dealing with children's disputes, she was still hands-off, but even more so. Kaizuka as a young teacher was much more hands-on than Morita, as we see in her handling of the hair-pulling dispute in her 2002 video. In her handling of the hide-and-seek dispute in 2015, she was still hands-on, but a bit less so, with a softer touch and gentler facial expressions. While a comparison of the 2002 and 2015 videos gives an initial sense that each of these teachers has retained a personal style over the years, microanalyses show subtle shifts in both of their embodied practices, as they become less dramatically performative, talk less, and hold back more. Respondents to Morita's then-and-now videos noticed a change in her ability to hold back from intervening:

> TANAKA: I think when she was young, she was worried that children couldn't follow her instructions.
> IWAKURA: In 2015, she leaves things up to the children, encouraging them to do it on their own. Like Morita, I often did too much for children when I was young.

However, not everyone who viewed these videos was impressed with Morita's change over time, including these teachers at Makomanai Yōchien:

ENDO: Particularly with this comparison, sure, she has changed a lot over the years. But in my opinion, she is now too calm. I like the previous version of her better.

INAFUNE: On the one hand, she has changed in a positive way, such as now being able to catch children's voices. But on the other hand, she might look scary. It's like I want her to show a bit more attention, as she did when she was younger. I also like her younger version.

OKAUCHI: When I started teaching, my mentor told me that holding our hands behind our back gives children the impression that we are strict and demanding.

Professor Usui, who observed this focus group discussion at Makomanai, told me afterward that he disagreed with their assessment:

Superficially, Morita-sensei's movements looks very conservative. So, it looks like her style is not very engaged. But personally, although the Makomanai Yōchien teachers don't like it, I like Morita's style. She creates a very comfortable atmosphere. The children are not being forced to be either hushed or energetic. If we think about these two teachers (Morita and Kaizuka), we can say that with experience they have each developed their personal style. My impression is that their fundamental teaching styles have been maintained over time. Very interesting!

This suggests that, while my Japanese participants indicated that with experience preschool teachers generally change in similar ways, there are different styles of teaching well. Morita's expertise takes the form of being very calm, quiet, and steady; other veteran Japanese teachers are livelier, like Kaizuka. They each became a better version of themselves, but not alike. They each hold back more with experience, but in different ways. Both teachers evolved toward employing bodily techniques that show more patience and restraint and that communicate to children that they trust them to be able to work out their own solutions. Their embodied expressions become less controlling of and more receptive to their students. This observation of these two teachers leads me to hypothesize that with years of experience, teachers do not become like each other, but they move in a similar direction, along similar trajectories.

This is a case of two Japanese preschool teachers. However, there is nothing necessarily either Japanese or early childhood educational about the points I am making here. Research on teaching expertise across grade levels suggests a trajectory similar to the changes with experience I have reported. While these studies of pedagogical expertise do not focus on changes in embodied practice, they identify a movement toward more intuitive, present, and tactful teaching that is consistent with the changes I have documented in Morita and Kaizuka. For example, David Berliner, based on a comparison of novice and experienced teachers, found that as teachers gain experience, they become increasingly "arational"—they become less rule driven, less consciously deliberative, and more confident in following their intuition. Max van Manen, building on a concept first developed by Johann Herbart, introduced the term "pedagogical thoughtfulness and tact" to describe the way expert teachers employ "the improvisational pedagogical-didactical skill of instantly knowing, from moment to moment, how to deal with students in interactive teaching-learning situations" (1995, 8). Xiangming Chen writes in her study of expert Chinese teachers, "These teachers try to keep a balance between non-action and action. In fact, the term 'non-action' here does not mean that these teachers do not act at all but that they act in such a way that it does not interrupt the natural growth of their students" (2015, 198). These conceptions of expertise, while not directly addressing embodiment, are consistent with the changes with experience we see in the then-and-now videos of Morita and Kaizuka.

3 China

When the *Preschool in Three Cultures* research team made the videotape of a day at Sinan Road Kindergarten in Shanghai in 2002, Jian Wang and Jingxiu Cheng were the co-teachers of the school's four-year-old class. At the time, Wang was twenty-six years old and in her second year at Sinan Road, after having taught for several years in Xian following her graduation from high school. As Wang explained:

> When you made the video, I had just come to Sinan Road Kindergarten. It was my second year teaching there. When I got the job at Sinan Road, it was like I was a new teacher because at Xian—I don't know if you know the situation of education in Xian—the level of education was far behind Shanghai. Getting hired at Sinan Road was a great opportunity for me, a new beginning for me as a teacher. I was lucky to have experienced teachers like Cheng as mentors.

In 2002, Cheng was thirty-eight and in her eighteenth year of teaching at Sinan Road. She, like Wang, came to her first job straight from completing an early childhood education program at a vocational high school. Cheng began at Sinan Road as a teaching assistant, later became a lead teacher, and eventually came to be paired each year with younger teachers, such as Wang.

When we went to Shanghai in 2015 to interview these two teachers about how they had changed over the intervening thirteen years, Cheng was working as an administrator at another Shanghai public preschool and Wang was the director of a large private education company that runs over one hundred preschools. The divergent career paths of these two teachers, one working in the public sector and one in the private, reflect structural features of contemporary Chinese early childhood education.

Wang and Cheng overlapped at Sinan Road Kindergarten for eight years, but they only co-taught during the one year the research team videotaped them. Wang left Sinan Road in 2007 and Cheng left in 2010. In 2015, Joseph Tobin and Hsueh Yeh, who were co-principal investigators of the research

Figure 8. Wang and Cheng, 2015, watching their 2002 video

conducted at Sinan Road in the early 2000s for the *Preschool in Three Cultures Revisited* study, helped me arrange a reunion interview with Wang and Cheng (figure 8). It had been several years since the two teachers had seen each other. They were happy to have a chance to catch up, reminisce about the old days at Sinan Road, and reflect on the experience of being in the 2002 study. They described their old working relationship as co-teachers as close and harmonious. When I asked them directly, "Do you two consider yourselves to be expert teachers?" they laughed, and Wang replied, "After all these years, we should be!"

Wang: Carrying Progressive Ideas into a Challenging Private Sector

Chinese teachers fortunate enough to get jobs working for a city or provincial preschool rarely leave the public sector. A teacher may change from one public school to another, but they are unlikely to give up the security of being a public-sector employee, which gives them not only status, job security, and a good income but also a lifetime housing subsidy, health insurance, and a pension. Wang's decision to leave Sinan Road Kindergarten was therefore highly unusual. Wang had a baby in 2007, took three months of maternity leave, returned to her teaching at Sinan Road, and then quit several months later. She explained that she felt she needed to spend more time with her baby than was possible given the demands of her position as a teacher at Sinan Road: "After our students went home each day, we teachers were expected to work on lesson plans and other things until at least six each evening, which meant I didn't get home until well after seven, which was too late for my baby." Under the leadership of Director Zongli Guo, Sinan Road was engaged in a continuous process of program development and professional learning. Teachers worked collaboratively every afternoon into the early evenings in study teams, developing new lesson plans and reviewing and critiquing each other's teaching. This contributed to Sinan Road becoming known as one of the most respected preschools in Shanghai, a "model" or "window" kindergarten routinely visited by directors and teachers from all over China, and its innovative approaches to curriculum and pedagogy have been disseminated widely. Many of the school's teachers eventually become head teachers or directors for branches of Sinan Road and other public preschools eager to hire staff members who bring with them Sinan Road's expertise. Sinan Road's long hours and high expectations for its staff led Wang to make the radical decision to leave Sinan Road and become the assistant director at a private preschool nearer to her home. She reasoned that it would be less demanding to be the assistant director at a private kindergarten than a lead teacher at Sinan Road. This plan did not work out as Wang anticipated, as she explained:

> I left Sinan Road Kindergarten to be the assistant director of Gubeiyuan Kindergarten. But just a month or so after I got there, the director had some problems and she quit suddenly, and I was thrust into the role of director. Over the next few years, the company kept growing and I moved quickly from directing one kindergarten to overseeing many.

With the knowledge and skills she acquired at Sinan Road, Wang rapidly rose through the management ranks as her private preschool grew into a large company. When I interviewed her in 2015, Wang was the head of a network of preschools. Wang, who as a young teacher and new mother at Sinan Road was ambivalent about her job, said, with a sense of irony, that now she is the one who must try to convince young teachers to stay after school to do paperwork and participate in study groups—and to not quit when they run into professional and personal frustrations.

She said that her current job, in which she hires, mentors, and retains teachers, is challenging because private preschools, owing to having lower status and fewer benefits for teachers than public preschools, struggle to hire and retain teachers, and most of her teachers are young and inexperienced in dealing with children and their parents:

The young teachers who were born at the end of the eighties and the early nineties are all only children. It's hard to mentor this kind of teacher because when they run into a conflict with a child, a colleague, a supervisor, parents, or anyone, they can't cope with frustration and difficulty so they come to their director and say, "I'm going to quit." One of the main problems these teachers face is that their students' parents, like their children, are spoiled only children. These parents complain to the teachers, "You are treating my daughter harshly!" Whenever I get together with preschool directors, we all say that we have to coax our new teachers and comfort them. We have to persuade them to make some accommodations to parents, without going too far and making the teacher quit the job. Most of the generation of teachers from the nineties can't take responsibility. They are so spoiled that often one of their mothers will come to school to complain to me that we are being too hard on her daughter! I have to explain to these mothers that their daughters will face similar situations in any job.

Wang also emphasized that the job of preschool teaching and directing is more difficult now than in the past because of what she sees as a deterioration in parenting skills, and consequently a rise in the number of what she calls "maladapted" children:

These day, the most frustrating thing teachers encounter in their daily work comes from poor parenting, the maladaptation of children's emotional development, and a lack of parent trust in teachers. Often a preschool will discover that there is an online parents' forum where parents of children in the school complain. These young parents go online and get ideas from the West, which leads to a one-sided view that favors appreciating and praising children and making sure the children always feel happy and satisfied. This isn't desirable or realistic. Two teachers with thirty little children have to deal with so many problems. Some children will get upset about something at school and not tell their teachers and then tell their parents when they get home. Then the parents will contact the school and complain: "You criticized my child!" or "The methods you used are not suitable."

Wang explained that being a teacher or administrator in the private sector requires being especially responsive to the preferences of parents as customers:

It is difficult for parents to get their child into highly rated public kindergartens, which means that at a kindergarten like Sinan Road, they don't have to worry about enrollment. However, in the private kindergarten sector, enrollment requires continually attracting parents and then keeping them satisfied. I often joke that we are in the service industry. Service is a big part of a teacher's job here. And the pressure to satisfy parents is bigger in a private kindergarten. On the plus side, in a private preschool, we don't have to deal so much with politics, the Communist Party, the Communist Youth League, and so on as public kindergartens have to.

When Wang became the assistant director at the private preschool, she came to the realization that having become a parent had changed her perspective on preschool teaching:

> After I finished my maternity leave and returned to work, I discovered that I knew and understood more about parents' thinking than I had before. When I was teaching before I was a mother, my attention was primarily on what the children learned each day. After I became a mother, I could see things from the parents' perspectives, and I understand their concerns for their child being safe and happy at school. I've heard many teachers say, "When I became a mother, I came to understand children and my relationship with parents improved."

Cheng: A Career in the Public Sector

If Wang's professional trajectory reflects the rise of entrepreneurialism and privatization in Chinese early childhood education and, more generally, in Chinese society, Cheng's typifies a life in preschool teaching in the shrinking, but still important, public sector. Cheng has worked in the public sector her whole career. In 2011, after teaching at Sinan Road for twelve years, Cheng and two other veteran Sinan Road staff members were selected by Director Guo to open a new branch called "City Garden Preschool," which was intended to serve children from overseas families. When this plan didn't work out, the education department of the Luwan District of Shanghai made the site a new public preschool independent of Sinan Road, and Cheng became the new preschool's manager of human resources, the job she still holds. Cheng spends some time in classrooms, but her work is centered on hiring new teachers and other personnel-related duties.

When City Garden Kindergarten opened, Cheng and the other staff descended from a "first rank, first level" model (*shifan* 示范) kindergarten to one that was not yet ranked. Cheng explained that such a move, while not the most common of career paths, is not unusual or necessarily undesirable:

Many teachers want a position in a first rank, first level kindergarten, and if they have a chance to move to such a program, they will. But other teachers find the pressure of working in high-ranked preschools like Sinan Road to be too much and prefer a less stressful job.

Many of the responses Cheng gave to questions about how she had changed as a teacher over the course of her career combined reflections on her individual growth with a discussion of the impact on her and others of paradigm shifts in Chinese early childhood education. We can see this hybridity of discourses, for example, in Cheng's reflections on how her views on the teacher's role in children's art activities have changed over the years:

These days, we stress the importance of the teacher observing children. When I began teaching, I designed the curriculum from the teacher's perspective. My focus was on teaching children to grasp a concept or master a skill. Now, my focus is on noticing a problem a child is dealing with, and then thinking how I can help him. The kind of problems I mostly help children with aren't academic concepts or skills, but rather things like the courage to overcome difficulties and frustration or how to get along with others. In the old days, we required the children to draw a car that looks like a real car, but that's no longer our concern. Now we pay more attention to the feelings and experiences children put into their drawings.

The mixture of personal and collective change in this comment from Cheng is even harder to disentangle in the original Chinese version, which doesn't include the pronouns "I" or "we." Such mixtures of the individual and collective, and of personal growth and paradigm shifts, are typical of many of the responses Chinese participants provided to questions about the development of expertise. We were able to get Cheng to talk more explicitly about the relationship of personal expertise and experience when we asked her to reflect not on how she has changed over the years but rather on what, as an administrator, she sees as the main differences between younger and more experienced teachers. Cheng sees young teachers as having both shortcomings and advantages compared to their more experienced coworkers:

Our new teachers all graduate with bachelor's degrees from good universities. They know a lot of theories but lack the ability to work effectively with parents and children. Their professional skills are worse than ours, but they are more open to new ideas than we are. We experienced teachers tend to have a fixed style of working with children and we stick to our old routines. But we have a lot of experience, such as how to lead the class and how to deal with parents, things we can pass on to young teachers.

A core component of this expertise of experienced teachers, Cheng explained, involves the ability to not acquiesce to the appeals of young children to give them more help than they need or than is good for them, a mistake she suggested is commonly made these days by both parents and inexperienced teachers:

> For example, when the children in the youngest class arrive at school, they need to take off their coats and hang them on hangers. The teacher's role should be to support the development of such self-care abilities. But today's young parents, when they enter the classroom with their young child, if the child doesn't know how to hang up her coat, the parent will be worried and she will help her child do it. Young teachers think the problem here is just to get the children's coat on the hanger, so they help the children do it or say nothing while a parent helps her child. In contrast, the experienced teacher will encourage the child while at the same time explaining to the anxious parent, "You see, today he is doing great. He's trying so hard to put the coat on the hanger by himself. If he fails the first time, we should give him a chance to try again, okay?" By handling the situation this way, the teacher lets the parent know, "Oh, the teacher is caring for my child." Experienced teachers know how to speak simultaneously to parents and children.

When we asked Cheng what helps young teachers gain expertise, she responded:

> For example, a parent will complain to the director about something a teacher has done. Then the director will have a meeting with the team of teachers to discuss the situation. Each teacher, experienced as well as young, will explain her way of dealing with such a problem. Through this experience, the young teachers gain expertise, bit by bit. We have a saying: "The more trouble you encounter, the stronger you become." When you encounter more of these kinds of weird parents with weird complaints—well, I shouldn't say weird—but when we encounter problems like this, if we face each case head on, our experience gives us more strategies to use next time.

Chinese Directors' Judgments
of the Expertise of Wang and Cheng

In contrast to participants in Japan and the US, Wang and Cheng had much less to say about how they changed with experience. This may be in part because when the research team first interviewed them in 2002, they were already experienced teachers (especially Cheng), and in part because by 2015, they had left the classroom for administrative positions. As administrators, they had much more to say about differences between young teachers today and teachers a generation ago, the challenges they face supervising the current generation of young teachers, and dealing with parents than about how they have changed as teachers. Wang and Cheng answered many questions about teaching expertise by talking about curricular and structural changes in Chinese early childhood education since they entered the field. This was characteristic of my interviews with educators across China. I suggest that this is because the rate of educational reform and social change over the past two decades has been so rapid that it drowns out the quieter, subtler, incremental growth in expertise of individual teachers.

To get Chinese participants to answer questions about the relationship of teaching experience to expertise, we found that an effective strategy was to start the focus group sessions by showing the twenty-minute video the research team shot at Sinan Road in 2002 and asking the participants if the teachers in the video (Wang and Cheng) looked more like beginners or experts, and how they could they. The sections that follow present Chinese interviewees' thoughts about the development of preschool teaching expertise in sections organized around the themes of practical versus theoretical knowledge, the ability to control a class, the role of formal teacher evaluations and mentoring, and paradigm shifts and cohort effects.

The 2002 Sinan Road video includes several scenes of teachers dealing with children's disputes and mediating their learning and social interactions (figure 9). In one scene, we see Cheng mediate a fight between two boys over a basketball, and in another, she comes up with a solution to the problem of a boy who announces he does not want to eat any of the beans the class has grown in the school garden. In the longest sequence, which shows an extended dramatic play session where children play the roles of store clerks, doctors and nurses, hair dressers, and police officers, there is a fight between a boy and a girl over who gets to use the comb in the beauty shop, and two children playing police officers come over, guns drawn, to settle the disagreement. In another long scene, Wang leads the children in a spirited discussion

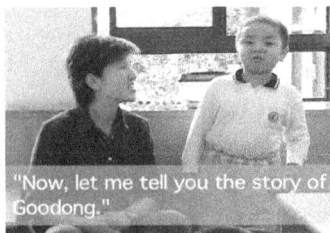

Figure 9. Cheng mediates a fight (left); Storytelling King (center); dramatic play session (right)

about whether a child has told a story to his classmates well enough to deserve the accolade "Storytelling King."

My former classmate and colleague Jie Zhang, who is now a faculty member at East China Normal University, arranged a focus group with staff from three experienced preschools and a "senior highest-level teacher" (*tejijiaoshi* 特级教师) who now provides in-service support for preschool teachers. As soon as the video ended, these experienced early childhood educators jumped right into the task of commenting on the expertise of the teachers in the video:

DIRECTOR GU: From watching the video, I can tell that Cheng-laoshi is an experienced teacher. For example, in the debriefing that followed the role-play game, she interacted well with the children, showing awareness of their level of social and cognitive development skills. Throughout the video she, demonstrated the ability to consider all aspects of children and to pay attention to many things happening at once. And she didn't impose her teacher's thinking on the children.

DIRECTOR WANG: I agree with Director Gu. The biggest difference between an experienced teacher and a young teacher is whether or not she puts the children in her heart. Cheng's performance demonstrates that she listens thoughtfully to what the children say and then responds in a way that shows an understanding of children. The other teacher, Wang, I would say that if we compare her with teachers in many kindergartens, she should also be considered an experienced/expert teacher. But if we compare her with Cheng, she is a little bit weak. Her weakness can be seen in the Story King activity, where she repeats children's words and sometimes she seems to miss the meanings of things the children say. And most of her questions to the children were closed-ended.

DIRECTOR FENG: I feel that both of them are experienced teachers, but they have different methods of working with children. I feel that Teacher

Cheng's methods are strict in contrast to Teacher Wang, whose approaches are more relaxed. Cheng, for example, with the boys fighting about the basketball, she said directly, "He hit you, right? He said he didn't hit you," and so on. And when she led a discussion with the class about the role-play game where the policemen threatened to arrest the child who wouldn't relinquish the comb, she only asked, "Can a policeman arrest someone for that?" That's all she said. Wang's teaching methods are looser. For example, when she led the discussion about the storytelling, she encouraged the children to state their opinions and asked, "Who agrees, who disagrees?" In my opinion, Wang gives the children more freedom. She let go more (*fangshou* 放手). In contrast, Cheng is stricter with the children. In their different ways, both of these two teachers are expert/experienced teachers. We can especially tell from how well they handled the whole-class activities that they both are skilled at organizing and leading children.

TEACHER YUAN: I see a bit of myself in both teachers. The way Wang related to the children is like she wanted to be more like a playmate, and she wanted each of the children to express themselves on equal footing, like with the voting activity. In comparison, Cheng, who has so much experience, is calmer (*congrong* 从容). I saw her play many roles: a caretaker, who wiped the children's backs, like a mother; a playmate who played ball with the children, even though she is old; a judge or referee, who decisively ended a dispute by telling a boy, "Do something else for a few minutes and you'll forget about it." These role transformations indicate she has extensive experience and command of many teaching methods. And she is skillful at handling problems, like when a boy says, "I don't like to eat broad beans," she tells the class, "If you like beans, you can eat two pieces; if you don't like them, you can eat one." And she supported the children's language development throughout the day in various ways, like the way she had children share during morning opening, and in the way she debriefed the dramatic play. I can see myself in both teachers.

This conversation captures many core Chinese emic understandings of expert preschool teaching. In the sections that follow, I use these comments and comments from other Chinese participants to discuss these emic concepts and to locate them in the context of the structures of Chinese preschool career ladders, paradigm shifts, and curricular reforms in Chinese early childhood education and larger social change.

Ranking Teachers' Expertise

These three directors and a teacher trainer, based on just one viewing of a twenty-minute video of teachers they had never seen before, were able to make astute comments about Wang's and Cheng's teaching experience and expertise. They not only correctly guessed each teacher's number of years of experience but also made insightful comments on how each teacher's actions, as seen in the videos, reveal the sophistication of her pedagogical skill. Moreover, they backed up their judgments with accurately recounted versions of the things children did and said in the video and how their teachers responded. After the session with these four expert participants ended, Yeh Hsueh, who had interpreted the session, explained that making such on-the-spot evaluations of teachers is a core component of the job of being a Chinese preschool director. Not all of the Chinese directors and teacher educators we interviewed made comments on the video as insightful as these four, but most found the task more familiar than did their counterparts in Japan and the US.

Each year, most preschools in China gets a ranking from 1 to 5 on two measures: one score for its facilities ("hardware"), and another for its curriculum and pedagogy ("software"). Different provinces and districts have different policies. In Shanghai, most bureaus of education choose to conduct evaluations on preschools every year. And each year, preschool teachers get rated in two ways: how diligently and how effectively one teaches . This evaluative process has consequences for a teacher's salary. But all the directors in the interviews told us that the purpose of the policy is not about the ranking itself and that it is instead intended to motivate preschools and preschool teachers.

Schools have some latitude in how they handle the annual evaluations of how well their teachers are doing their jobs. Many schools have their teachers do self-assessments, based on their own recordkeeping of their activities, and give themselves scores based on how well they handled various tasks. But most schools combine such self-reported data with evaluations by administrators. As Wang explained:

> We used to use a self-evaluation scoring form, but we found that this was not objective, so we dropped that approach. Now the leader of each of the groups, the youngest, middle, and oldest class levels, gives a score to each teacher in her group. Then the school's head teacher gives scores, and then the director, or the vice director, who is responsible for work evaluation. We combine the average scores of these three main scores to determine

their job performance rating. There are scores for attendance, ethics, lesson teaching, physical care, and so on, for various aspects of the job, and whether they attended any extra meetings beyond the regular school hours. All of this is recorded on this form. Points are added and subtracted for each item. Each teacher gets a score for the month, and at the end of the semester a score for the whole semester, and at the end of the year a score for the year. Based on her scores, she gets a monthly bonus. For example, one point represents a three-yuan bonus. We don't show the whole form to the teacher, but if she wants to look at her scores, she can go to the vice director's office to look at it, and when she look at the score, she can ask, "Why have I had points deducted in this category?" She also gets a bonus at the end of the year based on her score. These scores have some relation to expertise and to experience, but not a direct correlation. A younger teacher could get a higher score than a more senior one. And the scoring tends to measure how hard they work more than their level of expertise, which is measured in a different way, based on putting together a portfolio, taking a test, and being evaluated by the local education officials.

Cheng explained that evaluations and bonuses are handled a bit differently at her school:

We use portfolios and records that include judgments of the teacher's ethics and scores from satisfaction surveys of parents. But we use these measures not to determine bonuses but to determine job titles (*zhicheng* 职称). In China, everyone who works gets a job title, and every year or two you can apply for a higher job title. For public preschools, the titles are senior level, first level, second level, and third level. If you seek a promotion, the local educational authority will review your performance and determine the appropriate job title. This job title determines your salary, even post-retirement. For example, there are nine senior-level teachers in my kindergarten, and each year these nine teachers are ranked from first to ninth within this job category, so she knows where she stands. And the same thing is done for the teachers in each of the levels. If you rank for several years in a row in the upper half of the teachers in the school, you have the chance to apply for a higher job title. We handle the monthly bonuses much like Wang does at her private school. We have monthly scores that are a combination of peer evaluations and evaluations by the group leader and director. Your job title has no relation to the size of your bonus, but it is part of determining your starting salary for the next year, which is based on your job title and your previous year's performance evaluations.

Each educational authority, which has a limited number of slots for preschool teachers at each level of expertise, will let each preschool in its district know the number of high-senior, senior, first-level, second-level, and third-level teachers they can have. In theory, these numbers are based on the size of the preschool, but in reality, other factors come into play. For example, a preschool like Sinan Road Kindergarten, which is rated 1/1 (first level on both software and hardware), will have more teachers holding high-level job titles than a school with lower ratings. And teachers at private schools tend to have a much harder time being promoted than in public schools, as Wang told us:

> To get a higher job title, you need to apply to take the test in the district education department. But the proportion of higher-level jobs the education department gives to private schools like ours is very small: they don't give us any job titles at the level of senior teacher. Zero! Very, very difficult. In our kindergarten, I'm the only one with the ranking of senior teacher.

There is also a special category, "senior high level" or "expert teacher," a rank only a few experienced teachers can achieve. One director commented, "If you become one of these, you will be famous." One of our interviewees, Yuan Jingjing, is one of these famous preschool teachers who has achieved this highest teaching level. She explained the arduous process she endured to be promoted:

> You submit many administrative forms and lesson plans. And you should have a research agenda and publish some papers or a book, presenting the results of your research. And you need some honors. You need to have earned many certificates, such as a "First Prize for Excellent Teaching" at the city level. A district-level prize won't do.

While very few preschool teachers in China achieve this highest ranking, the existence of this highest level serves the interest of the whole system by providing paragons of the profession. As Lynn Paine, who studies professional development of teachers in China, explained:

> These ranking systems are based on the assumption that in teaching, as in other domains, it is possible and desirable to define both the ideal form of the practice and the steps or levels of expertise below this ideal that practitioners can ascend. It's like the way people study the violin. You may never become a highest-ranked teacher, which would be like becoming a concert violinist. But in teaching, as in music, the whole system benefits from

an explicit model for developing and evaluating expertise, a pedagogical model for everybody.

This process of being publicly evaluated and given a formal ranking is a cultural practice found in many domains of Chinese society. The Storytelling King activity in the Sinan Road video is an example of how early this process starts, and it helps to explain how being formally evaluated and assigned a title based on one's performance comes to be a familiar and accepted part of Chinese life.

Teachers in China, as in Japan and the US, have a subjective notion of their expertise and how it changes with time. But of the countries in this study, it is only in China that there is also an explicit and formal public ranking system of teachers. Chinese teachers may not always agree with the rankings they are given, but I did not hear the kind of discomfort with the idea of being formally evaluated in China that I heard from my participants in the US, where such practices are being introduced by policy makers and resisted by teachers, or in Japan, where such evaluations, for now at least, are unimaginable.

Implicit Definitions of Teaching Expertise

Alongside the formalized, explicit categories preschool directors use for determining bonuses and educational authorities use for ranking teachers' professional levels, there are implicit notions of expert teaching, notions that only partly overlap with the formal criteria. I divide these implicit cultural notions into categories of expert practice: care, practical knowledge (what is elsewhere sometimes called pedagogical tact, "withitness," or judgment), teaching without consciousness, and "dancing with shackles" (practices for coping with the demands and frustrations of everyday professional life).

CARE

Many Chinese interviewees contrasted the dexterity and ease with which veteran teachers deal with the bodily care of children to the awkwardness and inconsistency typical of less experienced, younger teachers. Director Liqun Gu, for example, said that one way she could tell that Cheng was experienced was the way she wiped each child's back as they came into the classroom, sweating from morning exercise. Even though most Chinese preschools classrooms have an assistant who is tasked with serving meals, cleaning up, and children's bodily care, veteran teachers still pride themselves on their ability to provide expert physical care to children. For example, a teacher in Kunming told me, "A young teacher may not realize that a child has a fever. But a veteran teacher, especially one who herself has the experience of being a parent, when she notices that a student in her class is out of spirits, would go over and feel his forehead and know if he has a fever." Chun Fu, a professor of early childhood education at Yunnan Normal University in Kunming, said, "Bodily socialization is very important. Teachers should touch, hug, and feel children's skin and not raise their voices. Their touch is more important than their voice."

The value placed on skill in the physical care of children is rooted in the history of Chinese early childhood education giving great importance to the safety and health of the children placed in their charge by parents. This emphasis, if anything, grew when China's one-child policy went into effect. As Tobin, Wu, and Davidson wrote in *Preschool in Three Cultures* (1989), "It's like a deal: you have one child and we will take care of him." This emphasis can still be seen in such practices as preschools having one or more nurses on duty who check children's health each morning as they enter the preschool gate; the great attention put into preparing, serving, and supervising meals; and the emphasis given to hand washing, wiping off sweat, and making sure children dress properly for the weather.

Wang emphasized the importance of care, lamenting that this is a shortcoming of her mostly young staff of teachers:

> The word for what we do, *baojiaoheyi* (保教合一), combines the characters for "care" and "teach." The term gives caring and teaching the same importance, but over time, especially after having my own baby, I came to understand that the caring part is much more important. Young teachers may be okay at the teaching part of the job, but most are weak at the caring part and at working with parents. I tell my young teachers, "When the children get home from school, their parents look to see if their kid is wearing his underwear inside out, or if he peed in his underpants. If you didn't help the kid change his wet underpants, the parents will be upset. Compared to whatever you taught their child that day, the parents' first priority is their child's life."

PRACTICAL KNOWLEDGE AND PEDAGOGICAL TACT

Several directors contrasted the facility of their young teachers with the latest educational concepts to their inability to deal with the everyday aspects of the job:

In universities, students learn so much theory these days, things older teachers have no idea about. But in their first few years here at our school, these smart young teachers don't have any idea how to deal with children's physical needs, or mediate their disputes, or how to talk with parents. They are strong on theory, but weak on practice.

In these and other comments, Chinese early childhood educators spoke of expertise in binary terms, contrasting practical with conceptual knowledge and being skilled at the physical care of children with the ability to teach in accordance with the latest educational principles. As Xiangming Chen writes about Chinese emic notions of teaching:

Experts and teachers have different mind-sets. Experts are more concerned about what to do, that is, theories and principles as to what to teach in the reform, while teachers are keen on how to teach in the classroom. The former can be too abstract and impractical for schoolteachers. (2015, 200–201)

Ping Xie, a director at Daguan Kindergarten in Kunming, said:

The young teachers who join us each year start from zero, because what they learned at university is different from the practical realities of kindergarten. There is a wide gap between them. It takes several years to turn what they learned in textbooks into pedagogical practice they can use to guide children's daily routines in preschool. It takes at least three years for a teacher to really start her career, because it takes that much time to connect ideas with practice. It takes time to translate the knowledge found in textbooks into practice.

Director Guo commented:

The knowledge students learn at university gives them a foundation for their professional practice. I tell our new teachers that they shouldn't throw away their textbooks. When we discuss a new curricular idea, I ask the teachers to go back to their university textbooks to learn more about the underlying core concepts. Then we discuss how to put these core concepts into practice in a real classroom situation. This is where they struggle. For example, new teachers don't know how to pay attention to all the children in a classroom; they tend to see only the children closest to them. And they have no idea how to deal with behavior issues. Even though the new teachers have read many books and articles about child psychology, the universities didn't teach them strategies for dealing with specific situations. The knowledge they learn in university is necessary, but not sufficient. They need to figure out how to practice what they learned (*xueyizhiyong* 学与致用).

Xueyizhiyong, the ability to put concepts into practice, is a Chinese version of what van Manen, after Herbart, calls *pedagogical tact*. Like the concept of pedagogical tact, *xueyizhiyong* is the art of expert teaching, the ability of expert teachers to be flexible rather than rigid in their pedagogy, to draw on a wide repertoire of strategies, and to make good decisions in the moment about how to respond to unanticipated events in the classroom. Jingjing Yuan, the famous preschool teacher in Shanghai, said:

> I have another example for why I think she is an experienced teacher. When I was a new teacher, when I saw a child crying, I would be very worried and unsure about how to deal with it. However, with experience I came to accept children's crying as normal, and I no longer see it as something I needed worried about or do something about. Many new teachers, when they see a child crying, they will run to the child. Experienced teachers deal with such situations calmly, which comes from their accumulation of experiences.

Professor Cao of Yunnan Normal University in Kunming explained:

> I think that the main difference is that an experienced teacher knows how to adjust her teaching based on her picking up on the changing moods and concerns of her students. She adjusts her strategies (*celue*) and is willing and able to drop one strategy if it's not working and switch quickly to another. Less experienced teachers tend to lack this ability to be flexible and to adjust their teaching in the moment.

Several Chinese interviewees said that experienced teachers differ from their young counterparts in being more able and efficient in how they read their students. For example, Xie commented, "Young teachers would talk too much, while an experienced one can get a sense of what is going on with a child from just a gesture or the expression in her eyes."

Professor Jie Zhang suggested that for their first several years, most young teachers need to follow lesson plans, as they lack the ability to teach in a more spontaneous, free-flowing way:

I am teaching preservice early childhood education classes. In my courses, I emphasize child-centered practice, as do the kindergartens where they get hired when they graduate. We teach them these approaches, but once they are faced with the reality of teaching, they find these ideas hard to execute. They seem to need guidelines. When these beginning teachers flounder, their more experienced colleagues give them a basic lesson plan to follow. The first few years, a teacher may follow her kindergarten's lesson plans, which has goals, steps, and activities. After four or five years, with experience, she should be able to teach without following someone else's lesson plan. You start at zero and gradually become an experienced teacher who can handle every situation you encounter.

Director Wong based her judgment of Cheng's teaching expertise in large part on how well she dealt with spontaneous events that arose in the course of the day, including disputes among children, like the policemen activity during the social play:

The trick here is knowing when to intervene strongly, and mediate an interaction, and when to pull back, and give the children room to work it out on their own. If the children in this class have just added the role of policemen to their social play, I would hold back, and watch, and encourage them to keep the play going and then perhaps at the end of the day's play, engage with them in a discussion, like Cheng did, asking them some questions about what policemen do and don't do. But if this policemen role-play has been going on for a while, I might decide that in this case it has gone too far (*guohuole* 过火了) and that these children who are playing the role of police aren't really doing this role sincerely, but instead are just finding fault on purpose, so they can feel important. In this kind of situation, the experienced teacher should put an end to the activity, without making a big deal of it. Just tell them to stop.

Director Feng followed up on this point:

Whether and how to intervene depends on many factors experienced teachers know how to take into account, including children's past interactions with each other, what has happened today and in recent days, the age of the children, their life experiences, the kind of community they live in. We can see this in how well we see Cheng handle the social play in the video, where a child calls the police to deal with a dispute in the beauty parlor. It takes real experience and wisdom for a teacher to know what to do in such a situation. Police officers are both familiar and distant figures to children. Children may see police officers every day on the street, but they know little about police work. An experienced teacher thinks about all of these and other factors and then decides in a given moment whether to push the children to go deeper in their discussion or not. It's not a question of one choice being wrong or right. It's a question of the mindfulness an experienced teacher brings to her decision-making.

Professor Yong Jiang of East China Normal University connected this sort of spontaneous, thoughtful decision-making with equivalent Western concepts:

> Experienced teachers have more *shijian* (实践), which means something like "practical wisdom." Or we can say they have more *jizhi*, which is the Chinese word for "wit," but which is also used to translate van Manen's concept of "tact." This is also related to the concept *zeyi de, shengcheng de*, which is how we usually translate Schwab's notion of flexible habits of mind, or emergent practice. An experienced teacher can react spontaneously to events in her classroom, choosing the approach she considers most appropriate, based on her experience. There is no doubt that experienced teachers have more of this kind of wisdom.

TIGHTNESS AND LOOSENESS

Commenting on the Sinan Road Kindergarten video, Director Feng described Cheng as tight, Wang as loose, and both as skilled educators. This judgment suggests that tightness and looseness are both valued characteristics in expert teachers. Inexperienced teachers can be too tight or too loose, or they can be tight and loose at the wrong times. Expert teachers come in both stricter and looser varieties, but both are able to find the right balance between being tight and being loose, and to employ the proper characteristic according to the demands of a situation.

An inexperienced teacher may err on the side of being too loose, which may then lead them to lose some control of their class, with the consequence that then, in an attempt to regain control of the children and get their lesson plan back on track, they swing too far in the other direction. As Yuan, the preschool teacher of the "highest rank," commented after watching the Sinan Road video:

> Wang had some innovative ideas, the kinds of ideas typical of many teachers who began their careers during the time of the second curriculum re-

form in the early 2000s. The way she related to the children is like she wanted to be more like a playmate and she wanted children to each express themselves on equal footing, like with the voting activity. Wang embodied the spirit of being free and open with her students. But when she had to deal with a problem among the children, perhaps because she didn't have enough experience, she would stop being open and return to controlling the children, like by ending the children's debate by stating that the boy had told a good story. I feel she was conflicted here. On the one hand, she wanted to give the children the freedom to express their feelings about the storyteller in their own words and in their own child-like way. But on the other hand, she wanted to keep control of the discussion, to bring it to a clear conclusion. Her effectiveness, in her mind, required that she get the children to reach a goal she had set up for them, which is indicative of a power/controlling type of teacher.

Yuan contrasted Wang's swinging back and forth from being loose to overly controlling with Cheng, whom she described as calmer and in control, reasoning that Cheng can be calm because she establishes control by "holding the class firmly":

Cheng in comparison, who has so much experience, is calm and unrushed. Because this is a Chinese setting and there are more than thirty children in one class, she must have the ability to keep control. But her way of controlling is calm, stable.

Yuan argues here that because class sizes are so large in China, being too loose will not work. I suggest there is also another, deeper line of implicit reasoning in her phrase "because this is a Chinese setting." Chinese teachers need to have control not just or primarily because their class sizes are large (in fact, the preschool student-teacher ratio is much higher in Japan than it is in China, and the ratio in China is similar to that in the US) but because looseness is not consistent with Chinese pedagogical, parental, and social practices. In contemporary China, curriculum reform efforts calling for teachers to be less controlling and more "child-centered" and to give children more latitude have produced hybrid pedagogical practices that balance looseness with control.

Across the interviews in China, participants described expert teaching using terms such as "authoritative," "tight," "strict," and "controlling"—terms that were rarely used positively in my interviews in Japan and the US. Yuan praised the way Cheng handled the situation in which the boys fought over a basketball with the word *ducai zhe* (独裁者), which in this context could mean "decider" or "authority," but which more literally means "autocrat" or even "dictator." Her point was not that teachers should always be dictatorial but rather that the strategic use of decisiveness should be part of an expert teacher's pedagogical repertoire.

Several Chinese participants described experienced teachers using the terms *na xia* (拿下), which literally means "to hold down" and also means "to capture, seize, or defeat," and *guan*, which literally means "to govern" or "to manage." For example, Haiping Gao, assistant director at Daguan Kindergarten, commented, "Young teachers know the new curriculum ideas, but old teachers know children and *na xia* (how to seize control of a class)." These terms are positive in the Chinese context because they imply a strong connection between the teacher and her students and the ability of the teacher to establish a positive mood for the class as a community of learners. In this sense, *na xia* and *guan* are related to Jacob Kounin's conceptualization of expert classroom management as "withitness," which is defined as a teacher not only knowing what students are doing but also communicating with students, through embodied presence, that they know what the students are doing and that they are in control.

Two professors of early childhood education contrasted beginning and experienced teachers in terms of their ability to have a firm grip on their class:

CAO: In China, what an experienced teacher has and an inexperienced teacher lacks is the ability to *na xia* a class. An experienced teacher can hold the whole class, manage the whole class, and build up close relationships with children.

HUA: Experienced teachers think younger ones are too idealistic. The truth is that sometimes children will not follow what you are teaching if you are too tolerant, but only will when you take control and train them to be obedient.

This is not to say that a teacher should always be strict or controlling. The art of expert Chinese preschool teaching is in establishing management of the class (*guanli*) by balancing *na xia* (a firm grip) with *fangshou* (letting go). Chen writes:

To use Laozi's metaphor, a bowl is comprised of a substantive wall outside and an empty space inside. The visible wall only provides a condition for the invisible space to function as a bowl. The empty space is more crucial than the wall for the bowl to be a bowl. Similarly, these teachers' non-action is like the empty space provided to their students, while their action is like the wall of a bowl. It is in their adequate interplay between non-action and action that brings their students' learning to a fuller play. (2015, 198)

In other words, expert teachers provide a strong, stable structure that, like the outside of a bowl, creates an empty space inside, which can be filled, in the case of preschool teaching, with children's creativity and interests. In what may sound paradoxical to some Western ears, by providing clear structure in the classroom, the teacher allows for children's creativity and freedom. Or we can flip it and say that without providing a clear boundaries and limits, there can be no creativity and freedom.

Chen describes expert Chinese teachers as artfully combining not just tightness and looseness, but also non-action and action:

These teachers . . . try to keep a balance between non-action and action. In fact, the term "non-action" here does not mean that these teachers do not act at all but that they act in such a way that it does not interrupt the natural growth of their students. Their typical class looks "loose outside and tight inside" with a seemingly dispersed appearance but having focused sub-stance. Having acquired enough confidence in both their own capacities and their students' potentials, they know what is going on even though they do not always act physically. . . . Their calm presence and timely guidance show that they have reached a certain acme of artistic connoisseurship in teaching (Eisner, 2002/2008). (2015, 198)

The Chinese term for *non-action* or *inaction* is *wuwei*. In one of the focus groups, participants discussed how expert teachers balance *na xia* with *wuwei* to create a classroom governed by the principle of *wuweierzhi* (无为而治), meaning "ruling by inaction":

YUAN: Laozi's concept of *wuweierzhi* has been used in various areas. In edu-cation, it requires teachers to respect children's nature and trust children's ability and potential. Let children try, learn, discover, even destroy. If they fail or make mistakes, it's okay, because they will learn from these failures and mistakes. All the teacher should do is create the necessary conditions for the children to thrive in her classroom. When an experienced teacher achieves a state of *wuwei*, she is able to make the choice to do nothing, or we can say, nothing other than to act naturally and just go with the flow of the children in her classroom.

DIRECTOR GU: But to have *wuweierzhi*, first the teacher needs to establish rules and routines. Once the teacher has established rules and routines in her classroom, she no longer needs to actively manage the children, or even talk. At that time, we can say she has reached *wuweierzhi*. The children now know the rules of each activity and have the capacity for self-discipline, so there is no need for the teacher to say anything. This is *wuweierzhi* in its purest form.

DIRECTOR WANG: It's like a Buddhist grandmaster, who over many years of encountering all kinds of situations and concentrated study, achieves a state of mastery, which then allows him to deal with new situations in a calm (*danran* 淡然) manner. When he encounters a problem, he no longer needs to think in a conscious way of how to act or what methods to use. It's a kind of state of emptiness, but an emptiness that is full.

Wuweierzhi—ruling by inaction—does not mean doing nothing, but rather not intervening too much. In other words, it is a philosophy of letting nature take its course, which gives rise to a creativity that allows for the achievement of self-realization.

THOUGHTFUL THOUGHTLESSNESS

Some Chinese participants who were impressed with Cheng's ability to employ a range of strategies and seamlessly switch from being "loose" to being "tight" according to the situation suggested that such fluency can only be achieved with experience and a letting go of conscious decision-making:

DIRECTOR WANG: In the flow of the day, with so many children in a class and so many rapidly changing situations, it is not possible to make these kinds of teaching decisions consciously. Therefore, I believe Cheng's decision-making must be subconscious (*qianyishi* 潜意识).

TEACHER YUAN: Yes. We can say that with experience, Cheng has reached the point where she can act automatically, without needing to think consciously (*ziranerran* 自然而然). It takes years of experience to teach so naturally and spontaneously.

Director Feng, on the other hand, praised Cheng for "the thoughtfulness she brings to her decision-making." From a Western point of view, it sounds contradictory to describe Cheng as being simultaneously thoughtful and subconscious in her teaching. However, a Chinese perspective sees no contradiction here, and in fact, as several of my participants told us, being too conscious in one's teaching can interfere with teaching thoughtfully, in the sense of being in tune with and responsive to students and situations.

Xiangming Chen (2015) lists "thoughtful thoughtlessness" (*wuwei* 无为) as one of the core characteristics of expertise. The participants in her study, who were high school teachers, told Chen that with experience, teachers can learn to empty their minds of conscious attention and intention and, as a result, be more effective.

In an interview, Professor Zhaocun Li explained expert teaching by citing a quote from novelist and philosopher Jin Yong: "Nothing is better than everything. There is no sword in the mind" (心中无剑). My colleague Lin Chen provided an interpretation of Jin Yong's words:

> In Buddhism and Taoism, there are metaphors that suggest that letting go is more effective than trying to hold something too tight. For example, you can carry more sand in your hand if you hold it loosely than you can if you make a fist. In teaching, trying to teach a lesson or control a class will go better if the approach is looser, more empty, more embodied, spontaneous and natural, and in harmony with the setting and the children. In Jin Yong's phrase "The mind has no sword," the sword is a metaphor that symbolizes tools, such as a weapon, or more abstractly, law, morality or ethics, or any man-made product that carries human will or desire. In a sense, "sword" here is "intentionality" or "agency." So, "no sword in the mind" means a good leader—or, by extension, we can say a good teacher—should let go of desire and control.

DANCING WITH SHACKLES

Another form of practical knowledge are the tactics teachers use to cope with top-down reform mandates and directives from superiors. A common saying in China is "There are policies (from above), and coping tactics (from below)." At all levels of Chinese society, people, including teachers, need to know how to be resourceful and flexible with directives from above, which Xiangming Chen discusses:

> One popular saying among the teachers in our study is "to dance with shackles" (*daizheliaokaotiaowu* 带着镣铐跳舞), which vividly portrays their efforts in trying to keep a balance among different tensions. As teachers, they have to "dance" (perform their duties and fulfill their responsibili-

ties), but with "shackles" on their body, their dance is heavy and restricted. Just as life is full of paradoxes, teaching is also full of paradoxes, especially in times of top-down reform. The "shackled dances" (strategies) of the teachers in our research mainly include self-reliance and reshaping the reform discourse with their own, among others. (2015, 200)

Chen refers to the teachers' use of "strategies." I would suggest a better term here would be "tactics," following Michel de Certeau's (1984) argument that those above use strategies and those below respond with tactics.

Experienced preschool teachers need tactics to deal with the reform mandates issued every few years by various levels of the government that call on them to change their practice. Teachers often find these reform directives to be abstract or even unrealistic, and the directives frequently arrive without clear ideas about how they might be implemented. Therefore, to survive professionally, teachers need to have tactics for avoiding implementation while not visibly resisting. As Chen writes:

"Self-reliance" refers to the strategy that many teachers have employed to ignore what has been advocated by "experts" in the reform, and go ahead with their own personal experience. . . . Experts and teachers have different mind-sets. Experts are more concerned about what to do, that is, theories and principles as to what to teach in the reform, while teachers are keen on how to teach in the classroom. The former can be too abstract and impractical for schoolteachers. (2015, 200–201)

Preschool teachers must acquire skills for coping with demands from above in the form of the ranking, evaluation, and promotion system; the expectations and rules of their directors; and directives from national, provincial, city, and local curriculum guidelines, which seem to be continually changing. The phrase "dancing with shackles" is used to describe not only how teachers deal with orders from directors but also for how directors deal with orders from the local government, and how local governments deal with national directives. These shackles, for the most part, are accepted as natural and inevitable in Chinese society. Instead of demanding to be released from the shackles or complaining about the constraints placed on them, the art of teaching lies in creatively working within these restraints. This is a skill that takes teachers years to develop.

Professor Li contrasted the earnest idealism of beginning teachers with the pragmatism of experienced teachers, a pragmatism that includes such practical considerations as how to look good when teaching in front of visitors:

When we visit kindergartens, we find that younger teachers teach based on logic and theories. They may not totally understand the theories they learned in school, but they nevertheless try to follow them faithfully. In contrast, experienced teachers are more practical. For example, when she knows an evaluator will be coming to watch her teach, a veteran teacher may rehearse her lesson several times with her students. A younger teacher might consider this to be a kind of cheating. But a veteran teacher knows the importance of protecting her school's reputation (*she hui xiao, she hui xing xiang*).

Professor Aihua Hua of East China Normal University added, "Li Zhaocun means that younger teachers tend to be idealists (*li xiang hua*) and veteran teachers realists. Veteran teachers know that there are times when it is necessary to be practical."

Contexts of Preschool Teaching Expertise in Contemporary China

While many aspects of expert teaching in China transcend context, enduring from generation to generation and holding true from region to region, many participants also emphasized what they saw as significant variations in teaching expertise by type of preschool, region, and cohort.

THE PRIVATE AND PUBLIC SECTORS

Wang and Cheng both began their careers in the public sector. However, once Wang made the radical decision to move from Sinan Road Kindergarten to a private preschool, she entered a different world of preschool status, educational backgrounds, career trajectories, and job stability. As Xiao-xia Feng writes:

> Most kindergarten teachers work in private kindergartens and are not formally recognized as "teachers," as they do not have *bianzhi*, a hallmark of a formal teacher, especially in rural areas (Hu & Robert, 2013). Therefore, these teachers do not receive the same wages, benefit, and privileges provided to teachers in publicly funded kindergartens. (2017, 67)

Because private preschools have a difficult time attracting and retaining teachers, compared to the public preschool sector, job tenure in the private preschool sector is, on average, much shorter and the level of professionalism is significantly lower. Even if they stay in their positions for many years, teachers in private preschools, as Wang explained to us, have a difficult time having their expertise recognized, as they have limited opportunities to rise in job ranks or achieve higher titles. Private preschool teachers also tend to have fewer opportunities for quality in-service professional development.

However, the stark disparity between the levels of expertise and career possibilities for teachers in the private and public sectors may be shrinking, as China is in the midst of a rapid privatization of early childhood education (ECE), as Hui Li and X. Christine Wang write:

> Since the 1990s, the central government started shifting responsibility for funding and managing ECE to the private sector. . . . Consequently, the number of private early childhood centers has drastically increased, from 25.2% in 2000, to 62.2% in 2008 (Zhou, Zeng, & Fan, 2010). At present, the existing public ECE centers owned by various levels of government are still supported by educational authorities, albeit with a gradually decreasing annual budget. In 2005, the budget for ECE was drastically cut to zero in the annual budget plan of the Central Government leaving local governments to sponsor several public early childhood centers, with no more than 1.3% of the entire educational budget (Li, 2006). . . . This so-called "market-oriented" but laissez-faire policy had unfortunately placed public kindergartens in a disadvantaged situation, and caused overall decline in quantity and quality of early childhood education in China (Li & Wong, 2008). (2017, 237)

It remains to be seen how this rapid withdrawal of government support and the shift from public to private provision will impact teaching expertise in the years to come. One implication is that as government support is reduced, public preschools will have more difficulty retaining experienced teachers and providing the kind of support that allows expertise to grow. As the private sector grows, it is very likely that private preschools that serve wealthy families will attract and retain top teachers and provide them with possibilities for career advancement and professional development, leading to levels of expertise comparable to the top public programs, such as Sinan Road Kindergarten, today. At the same time, private programs that serve less wealthy families, have lower status, and, as a result, have much smaller operating budgets will see a further decline in the overall levels of expertise among their staff.

A significant limitation of this study is the lack of interviews with educators in rural preschools. Research conducted in China shows the disparities between the working conditions in rural and urban preschools and emphasizes the need to disaggregate urban from rural teachers in conceptualizing teaching expertise in China. As Xiao-xia Feng writes:

> A survey in Anhui province found that in rural areas, about 76% of the kindergarten teachers had a strong wish to leave their job. Teachers who were younger, who had higher educational qualifications, and who received relatively lower wages reported that they were more likely to resign than other teachers (Feng, 2015). Hence, teacher wastage and attrition continue to be problems in the preschool sector. (2017, 67)

Because the university faculty members and teacher trainers who are most knowledgeable about the kindergarten curriculum reforms are based in Beijing, Shanghai, and a few other cities in the eastern part of the country, preschool teachers in western China, and especially in China's rural areas, lack access to the kind of training they would need to implement pedagogical approaches they have heard about but do not fully understand. There are no highly ranked preschools for teachers in rural areas to visit, and there are few opportunities to attend workshops or be visited by qualified scholars or educators.

In the *Preschool in Three Cultures Revisited*, Tobin, Hsueh, and Karasawa recorded a complaint about this situation from Guimin Su of Southwest University in Chongqing:

> The experts' presentations rarely help teachers. When I visit kindergartens in small towns and rural areas, a comment I often hear from teachers about the reform is "We understand what you are saying; but can you show us how to *do* it?" There is no coherent, adequate plan for teachers' professional development, leaving most preschools unable to bring their staff up to speed. The *Guidelines* are vague and they do not make enough allowance for local conditions. Also, teachers in most areas of China are faced with heavy pressures to survive in their local market economy; the *Guidelines* run up against parents' demands for didactic instruction, special interest classes, and early preparation for success in schools and on examinations. (2009, 86)

Professor Hua of East China Normal University explained:

> If a teacher in a rural preschool has seventy children in her class, how can you ask her to pay attention to each individual child and to respect their individual needs? It is understandable that practitioners in many parts of China cried out, "It's so difficult to implement the *Guidelines!*'"

Professor Hua emphasized that the reforms are being held back by a shortage of qualified trainers, especially in the countryside:

> The success of the reform depends on teachers' understandings of how and why to teach children in the ways the *Guidelines* suggest. But many of the supervisors whose job is to facilitate teachers' efforts to change are themselves muddle-headed about what the changes mean. The integrated curriculum requires skills and perspectives that teachers did not acquire in their professional training in school. Teachers are paralyzed, so to speak, and at a loss for what to do. Eventually they resist the reform.

It is also a question of motivation; rural teachers have little incentive to improve, as there is no career advancement ladder, and many quit each year or find themselves with no choice but to stay. On the other hand, being far away from Beijing and Shanghai has its advantages, as Professor Li explained:

> Teachers may feel rushed (*zhao ji*) when they begin their jobs at a kindergarten. But that depends on the circumstances at that kindergarten. If a teacher works at a kindergarten in the countryside, where there is no strict system and little pressure, she can gradually discover her own approach to teaching. On the other hand, in Shanghai, with its strict system and high expectations, teachers feel rushed and pressured and do not feel free to develop their own ideas. A schoolmate of mine who went to the countryside to teach after graduation from university felt no stress about her professional development. I asked her about the availability of in-service training opportunities and she said it wasn't a problem because there is little pressure. She can teach half the day and play with the children the other half. She is relaxed.

In her dissertation, Yi Che (2010) found that some rural teachers are quite skilled at practical wisdom and teacher-directed instruction; they are only behind if they are measured by Beijing and Shanghai standards.

Nevertheless, rural teachers have considerable disadvantages: while they have practical wisdom and skill at handling children, without adequate pre-service or in-service education about early childhood education and child development, there is the risk of preschool becoming mostly childcare and, consequently, preschools not being able to help rural families catch up with their urban counterparts.

COHORT EFFECTS

Daguan Kindergarten was a key research site for both of the *Preschool in Three Cultures* studies. In 2015, Tobin, Hsueh, and I showed veteran teachers and directors at Daguan a video the research team shot at their preschool in 1984 and asked for their reflections. Xiaojing Tang, who was a featured teacher in the 1984 video, spoke with a sense of nostalgia and sadness:

> Children at that time were very *guifan* (well behaved), and they followed their teachers. Children today are *zizhuxing* (autonomous) and *zizhu* (independent). Time brings great changes. Watching it, I got a kind of feeling of loss. For example, in the old video, we see children playing with blocks by trying to build a structure following a drawing we gave them. However, children now are good at exploring, so we let them go, and they make something that comes from an idea in their head or based on a building they have seen on television. They are very clever. They can *dongnaojin* (use their head) and can build without depending on a drawing we give them.

Tang's colleague Rui Zhang added:

> The children we see in the video were born in the 1980s. They look so *tinghua* (obedient). They followed what you told them to do. But children born in the 2000s are different. Since those days, there have been great changes in children, parents, and teachers. The young teachers at our school are very different than we were when we began. Although the young teachers get professional training at school, they lack practical experience, and they need to be guided by older teachers. These teachers are weak in helping children with daily routines, so they need help and guidance from the older ones. Younger teachers are better at pedagogical theory, but they are lacking in the skills for organizing kids' daily routines. But in terms of pedagogy, young teachers know more than older ones do. But even with pedagogy, they still need to learn practical teaching skills from the older ones.

Director Yonghong Shi of Daguan Kindergarten explained how she approached the implementation of the new curriculum ideas:

> We have actively explored the new ideas and introduced them to our teachers. Some teachers have started to try out these ideas. But this is not yet the case for the majority, in large part because we administrators have been hesitant to make any radical changes. We are afraid that only a few teachers would be able to thrive, but many others would be at a loss for what to do. For this reason, we do not want to plunge into a radical change. The *Guidelines* encourage us to follow children's interests and to tap their potentials. But if you let children take the lead, what then is the role of the teacher? We have been thinking about this issue for several years. Furthermore, our country is known for its emphasis on traditions such as patriotism and morality. If all we do is follow children's interests, I don't think we will be able to impart these traditional values; the guidance of teachers is necessary for such education to occur. Unless we figure out ways to solve these problems, we do not want to try out one approach today and then try out another tomorrow, running around searching for what works. Instead, we prefer to build on our established foundation and to follow traditional pedagogy.

Like teachers Tang and Zhang and Director Shi, many of my Chinese participants referred to older and younger teachers as members of different cohorts, with very different initial training, social experiences, worldviews, and strengths and weaknesses. Successive cohorts of preschool teachers over the course of their education and careers have been exposed to different paradigms, and as a result they have different levels of knowledge of and comfort with various educational approaches. When there is a paradigm shift, experienced teachers who developed their ease and skills in teaching in a particular way, such as in teacher-directed whole-group lessons, suddenly find themselves at a loss. Younger teachers find themselves pulled in two directions, between their attraction to the contemporary ideas they learned in their university coursework and workshops they attend and the advice they get from their more experienced colleagues. In a focus group interview conducted at East China Normal University with four faculty members in early childhood education, Professors Aihua Hua and Jie Zhang, who were themselves trained in different early childhood education paradigms, explained how these generational dynamics play out in contemporary Chinese preschools:

> HUA: Over the last hundred years, China has been through a series of "grand theories" that have governed early childhood theory and practice.

Different generations of teachers were trained in different early childhood traditions. Today's oldest generation of teachers and directors received their initial training, as I did, in an era of heavy influence from the Soviet Union. Then, after the progressive curriculum reforms of the 1990s, when these experienced teachers attended training in the new paradigms, they were confronted with a gap between their knowledge and the new ideas, which produced in them a painful sense of inadequacy. In contrast, a younger cohort of teachers attending the same training sessions found the ideas familiar and comfortable. For example, nowadays, we pay more attention to the differences in children's personalities and abilities, and our practices are more child-centered, while the tradition of teacher education in China had been to pay attention to the overall characteristics of children, according to their age and developmental stage. And today we focus more on play, while older teachers were taught how to teach different subject areas. As a result, these older teachers now wander at the edge of the classroom. They know they shouldn't do direct instruction, but they don't know what their role is in a classroom where children are playing independently. These older teachers trained in the old traditions often find themselves in conflict with the younger teachers, trained in the new approaches, and they feel it's hard to talk with them.

ZHANG: I see something else going on in the kindergartens I visit. Just as Professor Hua described, we are in the midst of a process of moving from traditional ways to new ways of teaching. So what happens in a kindergarten that has both older and younger teachers? What should a young teacher with little experience do if she finds herself working alongside an older teacher who has more traditional beliefs and practices? For example, in planning a painting activity, a new teacher's inclination would be to give children freedom to paint and create without instructions or limits. But her experienced colleague might tell her, "Your approach may be ideal, but it's not realistic. The reality is that parents want to see their children bring home from school certain kinds of paintings that meet their expectations for what children in their middle and older kindergarten grades should be able to produce." The same thing happens with expectations for classroom management. Younger ones believe in respecting children, so they are loose in their discipline. Older ones tell them that as a practical matter, there are times when it is necessary to be strict with children. These mixed messages, arising out of different theories of early childhood education favored in different eras, leave young teachers confused. Some young teachers will follow the lead of their older colleagues, while other young teachers will stick to the new ideas they have been taught. This is the reality of the lives of younger and older teachers in an era of curriculum reform.

Expertise and experience have a more complicated relationship in China than in Japan or the US because the pace of change—social, cultural, economic, and educational—in China means that knowledge and skills acquired earlier in one's career are a devalued currency. One impact of the dramatic paradigm shifts that have characterized early childhood education over the past generation is that older teachers are often perceived as having out-of-date beliefs and practices and difficulty adapting to new approaches. This can create an upside-down situation where a recent university graduate who has learned about new approaches in their university coursework is perceived as more competent in some ways than a veteran teacher. On the other hand, the young teacher who is up to date on new theories and practices soon discovers that she is by no means as competent as her older colleagues in the realities of running a preschool classroom, handling disputes among children, and dealing with parents.

Professional Development

The binaries of private and public schools, rural and urban settings, and older and young cohorts interact. A private, low-ranked, and poorly resourced preschool in a town in the west of China with an experienced staff without much formal education is at a great distance not just geographically but also economically and in terms of cultural capital from an elite, public preschool in a wealthy area of Shanghai, such as Sinan Road Kindergarten. The progressive curriculum reforms that Sinan Road's experienced, well-educated staff have been able to fully implement have had little impact on preschools that have fewer resources and lack access to high-quality professional development. Therefore, I cannot compare the levels of expertise of teachers in such disparate settings using the same criteria. Nevertheless, the interviews we conducted in varied settings across China suggest that there are shared characteristics among Chinese preschool teachers in how they acquire expertise.

APPRENTICESHIP LEARNING

Looking back on her years as a young teacher at Sinan Road Kindergarten, Wang emphasized how much she gained from being paired for a year with the more experienced Cheng:

We were a kind of ideal model of one experienced teacher and one young teacher working together. We were a real pair. There is a saying in China: "When a man and a woman work together, they will not feel tired." I guess this is also true for pairing a younger and older teacher!

Wang and other preschool directors we interviewed told us that, while many factors go into their decisions about which teachers to pair in each classroom, they assign new teachers to work with veterans whenever possible. Director Guo of Sinan Road Kindergarten was especially insightful in her explanation of the logic behind this apprenticeship model, as she drew on Chinese emic equivalents of what Jean Lave and Etienne Wenger (1991) conceptualized as "situated learning":

> In the past, we called our approach to educating teachers "master and apprentice." I was guided by my master (我被我的师傅带出来). When we hire a new teacher, we have her co-teach with an experienced teacher until her professional skills have reached the point where she can lead the children's activities by herself. But the first three years, we always use this *dai* (guide) style. The benefit of this method lies in its real situatedness at that moment (*qingjingxing* 情境性). The master can impart her pedagogical, cultural, and practical wisdom to her apprentice in any place, at any time. The master's experience gives her knowledge that is not abstract, but rather situated, as it is tied to how to handle particular situations (*lingsan* 零散). For example, the master may say to the younger teacher, "This time, in this situation, you should deal with this problem in this way; but next time, the best way to handle it might be different. It depends on many things." It can take a new teacher several years to acquire the kind of flexibility that allows her to transfer skills from one situation to another and to know which approach to use for which situation.

It is not only the apprentice who benefits from this system. While the younger teacher in this system has the benefit of the wisdom of a mentor to guide her through her first few years, the older teacher may also benefit by learning new approaches from her apprentice, As Wang reflected:

> Now that I have experience as a director, I have learned that every experienced teacher who has had a mentoring experience feels that the best model is to have an old one and a new one teach a class together. In this way, they help each other. The old teacher provides experience and wisdom. And the young one also contributes. For example, young teachers

are much stronger than older teachers with new media and they may have many new educational ideas, like new and fashionable ways for decorating the classroom and for conducting an activity. The ideal model is that they discuss things with each other and find solutions.

Rui Zhang, a thirty-year veteran of teaching at Daguan Kindergarten, made a similar point:

> Our overall philosophy of staff development is to train the younger ones and change the pedagogical ideas of the older ones. Older and younger teachers working together offer mutual support. Older ones can guide the younger ones while younger ones—for example, young teachers have a knack for using computers, which would be helpful to old teachers who are not so familiar with new technology. Old teachers convey their working attitudes and experience to the young ones, while at the same time the young ones convey new ideas to the old ones. The young teachers had great motivation to do their jobs, but they had no idea how to do it.

These comments by Wang and Zhang, while no doubt sincere, may idealize the relationships between veteran and younger teachers. Several directors told us that they have to give a good deal of attention to creating master-apprentice pairs, and while they sometimes keep pairs together, they also change them, which may imply that not all matches work well. Wang's expression of how extraordinarily well she and Cheng got along during their year together also implies that some of her other experiences with mentors were not as successful. I heard informal complaints from young teachers about the conservatism of older staff and from senior teachers complaining about the poor attitudes and work ethic of the younger teachers they work with. Nevertheless, such generational tensions did not lead any of my participants to question the value of the apprenticeship model or the value of a beginner learning to teach on the job, in real teaching situations, from a more experienced colleague.

STUDY GROUPS

Many Chinese preschools have regular study groups for their teachers. Some are organized around lesson planning, some around topics, some around implementing guidelines, and some based on issues teachers introduce from their daily practice. Yuan Jingjing described the various professional development activities at her preschool:

I am the leader of the research group at my school. We have many kinds of teaching and research activities. Sometimes we have lectures. The assistant director, the educational director, or I will identify a problem, give a short lecture, and then lead a discussion. We also do a lot of role-play activities. The activity begins with experienced teachers performing scenes of typical problems teachers encounter with children or with parents, such as a child crying over a toy, a child who won't eat, parents who have trouble leaving their child at school each morning, and so on. When the role-play ends, we ask the younger teachers to share their thoughts, and then experienced teachers present methods, prescriptions, and approaches that would be most effective. So part of our training approach is indoctrination (*guan shu* 灌输式的). Another approach we use is to take videos of children in different situations in classrooms and then use the videos as cues for discussion. We ask the teachers, What are the characteristics of this child? How can we describe his behaviors? What might be his motivations? Based on our answers to these questions, how should we deal with this situation? We also have a comparative method. We might, for example, compare videos that show how several of our teachers handle nap time. This gives a young teacher the opportunity to compare her approach with those of more experienced teachers.

Director Guo described the study groups at Sinan Road Kindergarten:

In our study groups, we encourage our young teachers to be practical and we focus on embodied practice. We often have the teachers role-play or improvise. One teacher acts as the teacher, the others act as students. The teacher asks a question, and if she has asked it awkwardly, the others, who are acting as students will say, "We cannot understand. We don't know what you mean." Then we discuss how a teacher should handle such a situation. We also put a lot of effort into what we call "topical training." We begin by taking a professional standard from the Guidelines for Kindergartens, and then we concretize it by discussing how this standard can be put into practice.

Further, Guo made a very perceptive and useful contrast between what younger teachers learn from apprenticeships versus study groups. In each, new teachers learn from older ones, but in different ways:

In the one-to-one master and apprentice (*shitudaijiao* 师徒带教) system, the new teacher learns from her master through contextualized, variable, specific experiences. She can work through specific classroom issues and problems in real situations and, when needed, ask for her master's timely help. In this system, the new teacher needs to respect her master and follow her master's words. In study groups we have—which are made up of all the teachers, young and old, who work with children of the same grade—the new teacher should take a lot of initiative. She works with the new teachers who have similar professional backgrounds and abilities. In the master-apprentice system, if the master does not point out a problem, the apprentice may not become aware of it, and if the master does not explain why she does what she does in the classroom, the apprentice won't understand the underlying reasoning. But it's a different story in the group-learning context. Here, the new teacher can ask questions about what she doesn't understand. The teachers, old and new, discuss specific cases that they all encounter, and they brainstorm strategies. In this way, master teachers get to know their apprentices in a different way, which helps them in their role as mentors.

As Guo points out here, both apprenticeship learning and group study are grounded in actual classroom events and focused on practical rather than abstract thinking. The apprenticeship learning context has the advantage of being more situated and immediate. The study groups, by encouraging give-and-take among younger and older teachers as they reflect on events that transpired in their classrooms, allow for a meta-level awareness. The master-apprentice relationship is a context in which talking at a more abstract level, while not forbidden, is not customary. Context here is key: the younger teachers have just as much respect for the wisdom of their elders in the study groups as they do in their apprenticeships. However, the social codes and implicit discourse rules are different: apprenticeships call for learning by doing and observing rather than by reflecting and for a stance toward the mentor of obedience rather than questioning. The group context, in contrast, gives more latitude to younger teachers to raise questions and even at times to disagree while maintaining an attitude of respect that is expected in a Confucian culture, even one that values critique and is comfortable with heated discussion. Similarly, an expert teacher will generally hesitate to give critical feedback to a young teacher in a one-on-one context, whereas such critique is an expected role for experienced teachers in study groups. As Yuan Jingjing explained:

> Out of concern for our interpersonal relationships, we cannot—for example, when a new teacher is teaching, as an educational leader, I cannot jump into her classroom and see her do something I think is wrong and tell

her so. We cannot do that because in Chinese culture, this would harm interpersonal relationships between us. However, in a study group, we senior teachers can be quite direct with young teachers.

LEARNING EXPERTISE FROM OUTSIDE ONE'S SCHOOL

Teaching expertise is acquired not just within preschools, through apprenticeship learning and study groups, but also through various avenues for ideas to reach teachers from outside their school. As Yong Jiang, Li-juan Pang, and Jin Sun write:

> Today, many normal colleges and universities have established ECE programs at different levels and with different modes, for example, evening schools, "television" universities, open universities, and other forms of distance education. This has provided multiple ways of professional development and in-service education, and become the main approach to promote early childhood teachers' qualification in China. (2017, 88)

While such distance learning approaches are a common form of ongoing professional development, they were not mentioned by any of my participants as having been a key influence in their development of expertise.

Many preschool teachers have the opportunity each year to attend workshops offered by experts. However, because attending these workshops and bringing in experts is costly, poorer schools, including most rural schools, often lack the funds to either bring in qualified trainers or send their teachers to outside workshops. Jiang, Pang, and Sun write:

> Resources for in-service professional training are limited and unevenly distributed. There is a great training need for teachers working in the private and rural kindergartens but they rarely get opportunities for professional development (Xia, 2008). As Liu (2008) points out, there are many problems related to the mode and contents of current in-service training system, including a disconnection between teachers' needs and training contents provided, a lack of match between training contents and teachers' diverse backgrounds, unreasonable training time, inefficient training organization and management, and limited evaluation of the quality of the training provided. (2017, 98)

Even in large cities, at schools that have ample resources for professional development such as Daguan and Sinan Road, teachers and directors rarely listed outside speakers or workshops as having played a major role in their acquisition of expertise, giving more credit to their apprenticeships and in-school study groups.

Nevertheless, opportunities for teachers and directors to get ideas from outside their schools play a significant role in Chinese professional development. One form such learning takes is a preschool sending members of their staff to visit highly ranked preschools and come back to share what they learned with their colleagues. As Xie explained:

> The leaders (administrators) of our school believe that teachers learn by expanding their viewpoints. In our kindergarten, we have a research group, which combines young and experienced teachers, and they learn by communicating with teachers in other schools. For example, we send teachers to workshops and to visit other preschools and bring new ideas back to us. During this process, teachers gradually change their educational ideas.

The highest-ranked preschools and teachers play a crucial role in the dissemination of expertise across sites. For example, after going through an arduous process of examinations, applications, and competitions and earning the rare distinction of being a "highest-ranked senior teacher," Yuan Jingjing was released from her classroom duties to allow her to organize professional development activities in her school and to visit other preschools in Shanghai to provide workshops and give guidance.

Daguan Kindergarten, as one of the two highest-ranked programs in Kunming, is regularly visited by staff from other preschools. Sinan Road, whose reputation is such that visitors come from across China, sees these visits not as an imposition but as part of its mission and responsibility as a "window school," as Director Guo explained:

> The government gave permission to Sinan Road Kindergarten to become the first preschool in Shanghai for educating kindergarten principals. In 2006, Sinan Road was already the first and only place in Shanghai that educated principals. Around 2008 or 2009, we became the first professional school for developing teachers in Shanghai. Now in Shanghai, we are sending new teachers who just graduated from university to these kinds of good condition, professional, experienced, and accredited kindergartens. We are the first of this kind of kindergarten. Of course, we educate many excellent teachers ourselves, and they eventually become principals. At the same time, we also educate teachers from many other kindergartens.

Through serving as "window schools," providing workshops for other schools, and members of their staff moving on to jobs at other schools, top-ranked kindergartens like Sinan Road play a key role in disseminating teaching expertise, which filters down from "key" or "model" schools to less advanced ones. Sometimes, Sinan Road and other model schools extend their influence by opening new branch campuses. Some staff members spend their entire careers at Sinan Road, while others, including Wang and Cheng, move on to positions as teachers or directors at other preschools, where they disseminate Sinan Road's pedagogical approaches. Wang took the expertise she gained at Sinan Road to her work at a private school, where she oversees the professional development of over nine hundred teachers.

The Challenge of Developing Expertise Across China

There are so many differences in China between urban and rural, private and public, and wealthy and poorer preschools and between teachers of different age cohorts that there cannot be a single notion of teaching expertise or a single approach to teachers' professional development. Teachers and preschools across China are rated each year, but these official rankings cannot do justice to the various types of programs and conditions. For these reasons, some Chinese early childhood education professors and policy experts suggest there should be different goals for teachers in these different settings, as well as different professional development strategies. Professor Jiang explained a new teacher ranking system that is being used to match teachers to their professional development needs:

> We sort teachers into L1, L2, L3, and L4. L1 are teachers who just started, L2 are experienced teachers, L3 are expert teachers, and L4 are teachers who are not merely experts but who can also teach others to teach. We are developing courses to cater to the needs of teachers at each level. This is a way of sorting by the level of competence, not merely by age or experience.

His colleague Professor Hua added:

> We haven't found a linear trend that shows that experienced teachers are necessarily more competent than younger ones on specific skills, such as observing and understanding children. It has to do not just with experience but also with the training they received or didn't receive early in their careers and the kinds of experiences they have had on the job.

Many Chinese policy experts see the core problem of professional development as the inadequacy of the in-service training available in rural areas, which leaves rural teachers unable to develop expertise in the new pedagogical paradigm. Professor Jiaxiong Zhu of East China Normal University suggested that the challenge China faces in early childhood education is not the availability and quality of the training provided to teachers but rather the content of the training and, more generally, what he sees as a mistaken attempt to train Chinese teachers in constructivist pedagogies imported from the West:

> In the last two decades, the government, influenced by scholars in universities, has focused too much on trying to get kindergarten teachers to embrace constructivist theory. We now need to step back and ask some tough questions: Is constructivism suitable for the Chinese culture? And is it realistic to expect Chinese teachers to become experts in teaching in a constructivist paradigm? If we take a hard look at what has been the impact of these constructivist methods and theories in the western part of China, especially in rural areas, it's not a positive story. First of all, what is most important to poor people in rural areas is for their children to be able to catch up in knowledge and skills with urban children. And secondly, constructivist ways of teaching are just too difficult to implement in all but a few Chinese settings. We need to match our notions of best practice and of teaching expertise to the realities of the settings. Even in developed countries, constructivist practices, like those from Reggio, are very hard for teachers to understand and successfully and faithfully implement. Just one month ago, a foreign professor visited us and gave an excellent presentation about constructivist pedagogy, about how to observe, document, create learning centers, all these things. After his talk he asked me, "Did the teachers understand my presentation?" I said, "No, most of the teachers cannot understand what you are talking about." It's the same thing with most presentations by Chinese scholars. They give a lot of advice, but with little consideration for the teachers' prior knowledge and practice. This is why we are in a deep hole. Instead of helping, too much of the energy we have been putting into professional development has made teachers confused. That's the real situation in China. Even many higher-level teachers can't really put constructivist principles into practice. If you ask teachers in big cities like Shanghai, "How have you changed over the past several years?" they would say, "We have changed a lot. Now we focus more on children's needs." But this is not real. I believe that only a small fraction of these teachers who claim to have mastered constructivist pedagogies really have.

If Professor Zhu's pessimistic analysis is correct, what are the implications? Where does China go next? The new paradigm shift is toward "Chinization" (*ben tu wua*), a recovery, in various forms, of traditional Chinese pedagogical ideas and practices. As professors at East China Normal University explained in a focus group discussion:

> JIANG: Until recently, we were following British-American ideas. This meant not just importing curricula from abroad, but also had to do with how we conceptualized teaching. We have been emphasizing the idea of *youxiao* (effective) teaching. Now, however, we are emphasizing being a *hao* (good) teacher. "Effective" is an educational psychology concept, whereas "good" is an ethical one. In Chinese traditional culture, we focus more on teachers being "good." Today the Department of Education has a new initiative, the Good Teacher Project, which emphasizes traditional Chinese concepts of good teaching.
>
> LI: *Youxiao laoshi* (an effective teacher) cares more about the *jishu* (skills), while a good teacher would be a good teacher morally, ethically, and culturally.
>
> HUA: It's a question of knowing our history and culture and not having wrong understandings of our traditional pedagogy. Some people are of the opinion that Chinese culture is autocratic (*zhuan zhi de*), and that it emphasizes obedience (*bei dong fu cong*). But this is not the true history of Chinese education and these are not the aspects of our culture we should be holding on to. We should preserve the parts of our heritage that we think are good. Many pedagogical ideas that people mistakenly think came to us from the West can actually be found in ancient Chinese culture. For example, the concepts of *yin cai shi jiao* (teaching students according to their aptitude) and *xun xu jian jin* (step by step) anticipated Vygotsky's notion of teaching in the zone of proximal development. We have a long tradition of good teaching methods that did not come from the West. We have traditions of caring about children, and of valuing their experiences and creative learning.

It remains to be seen where Chinese early childhood education is headed under the current Chinization paradigm reforms. While paradigm reforms are being announced by government leaders, debated by professors, and implemented by officials in local educational authorities, veteran teachers are continuing to teach in ways based on implicit cultural practices and continuing to pass these practices on to younger teachers through mentor-apprentice learning relationships and study groups. The strength of Chinese teaching lies not in whatever paradigm is currently in favor but instead in emic notions of expert teaching that transcend and survive paradigm shifts. The experienced directors and teachers we interviewed said relatively little about paradigms and philosophies and instead discussed expertise as being about the bodily care of children, the use of practical wisdom, the balance of looseness and tightness, and the art of teaching in a way that is thoughtfully thoughtless.

4 United States

For the *Preschool in Three Cultures Revisited* study, the 2002 research team videotaped Jannie Umeda in her classroom at St. Timothy's Child Center in Honolulu, Hawaii, and Fran Smith at Alhambra Preschool in Phoenix, Arizona. At that time, Jannie was in her second year and Fran was in her sixth year as full-time preschool teachers. When we interviewed them for the new study in 2015, neither was teaching in her old school. St. Timothy's closed in 2008 and Alhambra closed in 2011. In 2015, Jannie was in her fifteenth year of teaching and in her third position, a kindergarten teacher at Kamehameha Schools, a private school with a distinguished history of serving native Hawaiian children. Fran had recently retired after over twenty years of working as a preschool teacher at several publicly supported preschools in Phoenix.

Jannie's and Fran's career trajectories reflect aspects of the disjointedness and instability of US early childhood education and care services. As they moved from position to position, each retained a commitment to a model of working with young children that she was exposed to early in her career. Each managed to maintain some continuity of practice in the face of the obstacles of having to change jobs when her preschool closed, dealing with new colleagues, and changing mandates and directives.

While neither Fran nor Jannie was comfortable describing herself as an expert teacher, when they watched videos of themselves teaching thirteen years earlier, they each noted a clear sense of having progressed. Each described herself as having become more spontaneous and less scripted, better at reading children, and when faced with a situation where children are struggling in some way, less quick to intervene and more artful in doing so.

Jannie: Carrying on the Pedagogy of "the Mothers of St. Timothy's"

St. Timothy's Child Center was one of the three preschools videotaped in 1984 for the *Preschool in Three Cultures* study. When the research team returned to St. Timothy's in 2002 to make a video for the new study, Jannie Umeda was the featured teacher. At the time, she had just finished her two-year community college degree in early childhood education and had been at St. Timothy's for three years, the first year as a part-time teacher and the last two as a lead teacher. Jannie completed a BA in 2005 after taking evening classes and then left St. Timothy's for a job as a preschool teacher at a progressive private school. In 2011, she earned an MA in early childhood education.

We sat down with Jannie in 2015 to watch the video shot in her classroom thirteen years earlier. Near the beginning of the video, we see Jannie call on the children one by one during morning opening, asking them to choose which activity they want to go to during center time (figure 10). After watching this scene, Jannie stopped the video and commented:

> In the large-group time in my class these days, we still acknowledge the children who are at school that day by calling each child's name. But now instead of me leading it, I have incorporated a daily leader, a person who does this job, the person each day who points to all the kids and calls their names. In this way, the children learn everyone's names and they get the chance to be responsible. It makes them feel really good when they're the leader, you know, for their self-esteem. And in the video, we see me tell them that there can be only four children in each area. But now I don't tell them anymore how many friends can be in each area. They have to solve it by themselves. If there are only four chairs in the area but there are ten

Figure 10. Choosing centers

Figure 11. Writing down children's words

people, *they* have to figure it out. Because after teaching for many years, I saw where I don't need to put limits on them. I realized I could have kids confidently and socially problem solving things. Basically, I let them do that. I can just scaffold them, rather than me always controlling things. Now, I let a lot of things go.

In a subsequent scene in the 2002 video, we see children drawing pictures in the writing center and then dictating stories about their pictures to Jannie, who writes down their words (figure 11). Jannie's 2015 take on this scene was similar to her reflections on the morning opening scene:

I still do that. But now, I have the children sound out their own words and write in their own way. Their job is to sound it out and write it and draw exactly what they mean. I let them do their own thing. It's just creative writing and drawing. And we have them decorate wherever they want to put it. Over the years, you learn more and you let go more, you just having them doing more, and I do less. I am just there to help them, to give them language, to scaffold them, and to challenge them more. But I guess in the beginning years, I saw myself more where I had to take charge of everything. Now that I have been in this field for a long time, I got to the point where I understand that when you let them do more, you see more language development and more critical thinking process as well.

At the end of this video-cued interview, Jannie summarized how she had changed over the thirteen years:

> I let things go more than I used to do. Now I like to see what happens if I let it go. I see them growing even more, being more independent on their own, and then you see more confidence coming into them, and that helps them a lot. It took me a while to get to the point where I am. I see everything. I know I did this again. How can I change? Every year, I don't do the same curriculum, but I do similar things. But I change it up every year. Before it was like, "I have to do this. I have to do that." It's different now.

We conducted a second interview with Jannie with two of her former St. Timothy's colleagues, Linda Rios and Lori Onaga. St. Timothy's was abruptly closed in 2008 when the board of the church where the school had been located decided to use the space for other purposes and announced the closing too late in the spring for teachers to find new jobs and for parents to find new preschools for the coming fall. Following a series of emergency meetings, a St. Timothy's parent, Cheryl Cudiamat, opened Keiki Care Center of Hawaii and hired Linda, Lori, and several other veteran teachers and staff with the goal of carrying on the St. Timothy's tradition.

St. Timothy's was founded by a group of early childhood educators in 1977. Lori, who joined the staff a year later, explained the origins of the program:

> The people that opened the school, the four teachers, had master's degrees. They're all retired now. I call them "the Mothers of St. Timothy's." They're the ones that created the basic foundation for what they wanted the school to look like and what they thought was important for the kids to have, different centers, choices. They taught me a lot.

Jannie, Linda, and Lori expressed a deep commitment to the St. Timothy's tradition of child-centered pedagogy and a focus on language development that is informed by the National Association for the Education of Young Children's (NAEYC) principles of "Developmentally Appropriate Practice." They described how this tradition has been largely passed down through a process of mentoring. Lori credits the Four Mothers of St. Timothy's for mentoring her when she was a beginning teacher in 1978. Twenty years later, Lori became Jannie's mentor and passed on the traditions. Jannie credits many of the features of her classroom arrangement and pedagogy to Lori. For example, in the video, we see Jannie lead a lesson on absorption involving bowls of water, sponges, and paper towels. We stopped the video at this point to ask about the origins of this activity:

HAYASHI: Where did the idea for this come from?

JANNIE: Lori did one like that and I learned it from her. There's a lot of things I picked up from Lori. Like charting stuff, language stuff—she did a lot of language. And literacy things, too. So all those things and then, because we didn't have budgets to buy a lot of stuff, Lori created a bunch of work jobs for children. And then I started creating work jobs. The teachers at St. Tim's would get together and have workshops on what work jobs we can have in our classrooms and how to create work jobs. So, I learned it from other people, and especially from Lori.

LORI: When Jannie first started, it was like, ah, we kind of know who will really make it, who has potential lead teacher material, and I knew from the start that Jannie had it.

JANNIE: Lori—I just learned stuff from her.

LINDA: Jannie teaches so much like Lori, we call her "Little Lori."

Jannie apprenticed with Lori and other more experienced teachers and directors who had a clear vision of a particular version of child-centered pedagogy. She carries this style with her to new jobs, keeping the St. Timothy's vision alive.

We conducted a focus group discussion about the 2002 St. Timothy's video at a community college in Honolulu with a group of veteran early childhood education professors and lab school directors, some of whom had taught Jannie, some of whom had placed student teachers in Lori's classroom, and some of whom had at some point worked at St Timothy's:

EMI: That was a very St. Timothy's kind of interaction. I mean, for those of us who have been working in this community for a while, we can immediately recognize that there is a St. Timothy's way. And she was definitely doing things the St. Timothy's way.

EMMA: And I was going to say if you think about Jannie and her time working with Lori, the mannerisms . . .

OLIVIA: . . . are very much the same as her mentor teacher.

HAYASHI: That's interesting how you picked up even their body styles being alike.

OLIVIA: Very much Lori. You could hardly ever hear Lori, she speaks so softly.

EMMA: Yes, yes, yes. And the same with Jannie. But she has that same command of the classroom. I mean it wasn't chaos. It was always, I mean, Lori is the same way.

OLIVIA: Yeah, and she wasn't . . .

EMMA: . . . she never had to . . .

OLIVIA: . . . no, she just talked softly and the children—like how the children sat in the circle and listened and they knew exactly what to do.

These experienced early childhood educators pointed to several things Jannie did in the 2002 video that they saw as typical of an early-career teacher. For example, several of these focus group participants commented on a certain rigidity they saw in Jannie's way of handling children's misbehavior:

AVA: I feel like she had one strategy and she would use it across situations. Like when the boy threw the plastic bowling pin, Jannie rushed over and said something like, "Is that the way to use a bowling pin? Do you throw it? No, what should you do instead? You can throw a ball." I think in 2002, that was a strategy that was used a lot. Ten years or more ago. I feel like she had that one way to go and that's what she was using.

ISABELLA: I think as you go on and you teach for longer periods of time, you find out what's important and what's not, what to spend your energy on and what not to expend your energy on.

SOPHIA: It sounded a little bit scripted to me, like you would expect from a new teacher just out of school. Whereas I think somebody who had more experience may have read the situation a little bit differently.

AVA: Yeah, I don't think I would have said as much as she said. I would have told the children, "Tell me what you're thinking." But maybe in my second year, that's what I did.

CHARLOTTE: She's trying to perhaps employ things that she had learned in college.

EMI: You know what I didn't see? A lot of times, she would talk one-on-one with a child. Whereas, I think that if she would have said something more out loud, other children would have gotten the same message. And the boys hitting the other boys—that's so typical of four-year-old boy rough-housing.

ISABELLA: But you know, I thought she had great control of a large group.

SOPHIA: I mean, for a beginning teacher, that was remarkable.

In this conversation, these veteran educators identified several key differences between beginning and more experienced teachers: new teachers are more likely than experienced ones to follow scripts, rely on single strategies, intervene aggressively, talk too much, and give too much attention to situations where their attention is not warranted or helpful. I return to these differences in teaching expertise later in this chapter, where I look at interview data from across the US.

Fran: Quietly Sticking to her Beliefs

When the research team videotaped her classroom in 2002, Fran Smith had been working with young children for ten years, but only for the last six as a certified preschool teacher. She entered the field as a volunteer at her son's private preschool. As Fran and her long-time colleague Jenn Mills related:

> JENN: Fran and I have known each other for quite a while. We met when I was a teacher at Preschool West. Fran at that time was a parent in the program. I had her son in my classroom. And it was then and there that she decided to go for the CDA training.
>
> FRAN: Being in the preschool classroom as a parent made me want to be a preschool teacher more than an elementary teacher because I thought that giving them their first start was the most important.
>
> JENN: And then I left and went to Alhambra Preschool and Fran became a teacher at Preschool West. And a year after I was at Alhambra, Fran came to Alhambra.
>
> FRAN: It was actually a couple years later, when Preschool West closed. I started at Alhambra in '95 and stayed until it closed in 2011.

The career path described here is a typical one for US preschool teachers. Fran was introduced to the field as a parent of a preschooler and then as a volunteer, and she was encouraged to pursue a CDA (Child Development Associate) certificate. The CDA credential is an entry-level step toward a career in early childhood education. It requires 120 hours of training and 480 hours of work with young children. By the late 1990s, many preschools, like Alhambra, required that their lead teachers have at least a two-year college degree in early childhood education. Fran completed her AA degree by taking night courses at Glendale Community College while she taught at Alhambra. In 2011, Alhambra Preschool closed when Arizona ended support for the Early Childhood Block Grant preschool program,[1] which was replaced by a new program, First Things First.[2] After Alhambra closed, Fran taught for three more years in another preschool program and then retired in 2015.

During her time working with Jenn at Preschool West and her first few years at Alhambra, Fran developed a strong commitment to a child-centered pedagogy. This approach was supported by her college coursework. However, at Alhambra, Fran was pressured by the school's director, Bonnie Lund, to teach more phonics and to use *The Letter People*, the packaged prereading program that was being used by all the other Alhambra teachers; but Fran was determined to stay true to the child-centered, play-oriented beliefs and principles she was introduced to when she entered the field. As Fran explained in a 2005 interview reported in *Preschool in Three Cultures Revisited*:

> TOBIN: Is the preschool curriculum changing?
>
> FRAN: [laughing] Well, they're trying to change me.
>
> TOBIN: You feel that pressure from the Bush initiatives?
>
> FRAN: Yeah. And that's hard. How do you deal with that when you don't agree? I don't totally disagree, because I think academics is important, but kids need to play. They can't learn if they don't first get to feel comfortable in the classroom, to know how to be in school.
>
> TOBIN: Where does the pressure come from? Is it just kind of in the air or, like the stuff we hear at meetings and on TV about No Child Left Behind? Or do you feel it directly, from Bonnie? It's not like she's coming in to your room every day.
>
> FRAN: [laughing] Not yet! But, to be honest, it is coming. Like *The Letter People*. Aren't we just here to teach the children the main concepts and to make them comfortable socially and emotionally? Just because a company came up with a curriculum, doesn't mean we have to spend all this money and buy it. When it's all written down like that and set in stone, I think sometimes that it can really limit your thinking. If Bonnie came to me and told me I had to do *The Letter People*, I guess I would have to do it, but that's not me. (2009, 178)

In a subsequent interview, Fran updated this story:

> I did hold out for a little bit with *The Letter People*. But then I couldn't hold out any more. Bonnie said it had to be done. So I did it for, I think, the last two years I was there. But it wasn't relevant to a child, especially somebody learning English. And 99% of our children were English learners. And I just, you know, "H is for Happy Hair." I mean, who has happy hair?

When the research team videotaped her in 2002, Fran had already been teaching for six years. But when she watched this video in 2015, Fran saw her-

Figure 12. Fran and her classroom wall

self in the old video as still very much a work in progress. She described this 2002 version of herself as "still growing up." Fran pointed out several things in the 2002 video that she would have done differently later in her career. Her first criticism was of the way she had set up her classroom (figure 12):

> I still like it. But it looks so busy! I remember that when you showed me this video right after you made it, I felt like there was too much on the walls. And looking at this now, it seems to me now like I had even had more on the walls then than I remembered.

Fran was also critical of the way she scaffolded the children's use of language. One of Fran's signature activities is "Buddy Bear," a stuffed animal Fran sent home with a different child every day (figure 13). As Fran explained in the book *Preschool in Three Cultures Revisited*:

> I've been doing it for about three years. I noticed that we were having trouble with sharing time, everyone wanted to share about a toy every day and they were getting frustrated waiting for their turn. So I decided to re-place sharing time with Buddy Bear. The journal has always been part of it. Buddy Bear and the journal go home together. In the front of the book I have "My name is Buddy Bear. Share me with your family. And then write in the book. And then bring me back to school to share with my friends." The children can write anything, and they get to color. And sometimes the parents write in there. They'll write a story, what Buddy Bear ate, what he did. Pablo's mom speaks English. She wrote in English. But some of the

Figure 13. Buddy Bear activity

moms write in Spanish and then I have to pass it on to Eva or Cindy, to translate. (Tobin, Hsueh, and Karasawa 2009, 181–83)

In the 2002 video, we see Fran helping four-year-old Pablo report on Buddy Bear's visit to his home. While still proud of this activity, in 2015, Fran pointed out ways she could have handled her interactions with Pablo differently: "I could have used more wait time, maybe asking him more questions about what his mother wrote in the book. And before reading the story they wrote, I could have asked Pablo more about what he and his family did with Buddy Bear." Fran was similarly critical of how she handled the conclusion to the daily Buddy Bear activity. Here's the dialogue from that scene in the video (figure 14):

FRAN: Now who's taking Buddy home today? Mariana? Mariana, come up here. Do you have your backpack today?

MARIANA: [Mariana struggles to get Buddy Bear into her backpack] Ms. Fran., Buddy Bear doesn't fit . . .

FRAN: He doesn't fit in your backpack? Well, what do you think you can do?

MARIANA: My backpack's getting little.

FRAN: Your backpack is little?

MARIANA: No, it's . . .

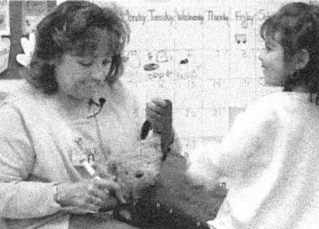

Figure 14. "Buddy Bear doesn't fit . . ."

FRAN: . . . it's getting little? Do you have too much stuff in there? I think . . .
MARIANA: No, I have . . .
FRAN: What?
MARIANA: . . . clothes.
FRAN: You have clothes in your backpack? Buddy has a handle on his bag so
you can carry it home like this.

Fran commented:

> Instead of saying "Your backpack is getting little," I could have said, "Why
> is your backpack getting little?" With experience, my questions got better
> for children, a lot better. I really got away from yes-and-no questions. I got
> better at "Use your words, I want to hear you." As I taught longer, what I
> learned is to give them more lead time. You know, wait for them to respond
> instead of giving them cues, unless they really need the help. And so I think
> looking at this video, I can see now that I was putting words in her mouth:
> "You have too much stuff in there?" I could say that I probably got better at
> waiting. Developing wait time is very important because in the beginning,
> you're afraid that if you don't keep things moving, you're going to lose kids.
> It takes years to get to that comfort zone of being able to take that time.

I asked Fran if we could interview her with some of her former colleagues,
and she invited us to have lunch at her house with Jenn Mills, Paula Harsh-
berger, and Christine Hogan. Fran taught with Jenn earlier in her career and
then, toward the end of her time at Alhambra, mentored Christine, who was
a new teacher. Fran met Paula through the Stepping Stone Foundation. In the
video, we see Fran leading the children in singing "He's Got the Whole World
in His Hands" and using hand movements she learned in hula classes as a
young girl growing up in Hawaii. At this point, we stopped the video:

HAYASHI: Do you think of that as Fran?

CHRISTINE: Oh, definitely.

JENN: I mean, it's Fran. It's her background. It's what's important to her.

FRAN: It gets the meaning across of what we're singing about. You know, the trees [doing her hula waving-trees gesture] and there's a movement with it. And I think it keeps them engaged.

When the video ended, her colleagues made comments emphasizing continuities in Fran's practice over the years:

JENN: I could walk into that room and know it was Fran's room.

CHRISTINE: Yeah, me too.

PAULA: Yes, it looks like the things I would see walking into your classroom.

JENN: That's Fran.

HAYASHI: What kind of things seem especially Fran?

CHRISTINE: The name chart.

JENN: Everything, children's names everywhere. All the language and pocket charts.

FRAN: I liked having that tree.

JENN: Your tree, yes. The tree has been there all the time I've known you.

CHRISTINE: She taught me how to make that tree.

The conversation then turned from continuities in Fran's practice to the ways in which she changed over her years of teaching. The group discussed what they saw as differences between teachers with less and more years of experience:

FRAN: Early on, it's like everything has to get done. You know, "I have to check this box. I have to check this box. This has to be done." And as the years go by it's like, "You know what? I'll get back to that later. I don't have to do it right now. Or maybe I don't need to do it all."

PAULA: But I think the more confidence you have in yourself and your ability to have control over the group, even though they're going all different ways, you know, learning to have eyes all over. Learning who you need to look at more.

HAYASHI: So the fear is, if I let go a little bit it'll . . .

FRAN: . . . cave in. Or explode.

HAYASHI: When teachers are beginning, what do you think makes it hard to wait?

JENN: We get anxious.

FRAN: Just wanting to help. We're helpers at our core. That's why we do this work. It's because we're caregivers.

The consensus of this group was that although they were less accomplished teachers when they began, it was easier to be a good preschool teacher in the past, when there was less top-down pressure, less paperwork, and more teacher freedom:

HAYASHI: Is the job getting less attractive?

CHRISTINE: It is. I mean, I still love it, but I mean, it's just . . .

FRAN: I mean it was better when you didn't have all this paperwork. And you could actually *do* things with the kids. I was seeing some things in the video that I used to do and I'm thinking, wow . . .

CHRISTINE: . . . you can't do that anymore.

FRAN: Earlier, I was telling Akiko that things just seemed so simple back then. I remember when Creative Curriculum[3] was the new thing. And we were in a training for it, where they told us about the anecdotes that you needed to be collecting and writing down. And all of us, our chins hit the floor when the trainer actually said, "During the day, you set aside fifteen minutes where you're just sitting and writing anecdotes. And if a child comes over to you and says, 'Will you read me this book?' you say 'No, right now my job is this.'" My head wanted to explode! I thought just, "No. I'm sorry. Not going to happen."

CHRISTINE: All the paperwork part of it and all that stuff that takes you away from the focus on the kids.

FRAN: After the preschool closed at Alhambra, I did one year in kindergarten. And everything was scripted. I mean, you didn't have any ability to teach anything in your own way. The reading was scripted. The math was scripted. The science program was scripted. That's when I retired.

US Early Childhood Educators' Reflections on Teaching Expertise

In addition to the individual and group interviews with Jannie Umeda, Fran Smith, and their colleagues, we conducted interviews with preschool teachers, directors, and early childhood education professors in Hawaii, Arizona, and Georgia. We used Jannie's video for the interviews in Hawaii and Georgia, and we used Fran's for the interviews in Arizona. After asking interviewees to comment on the classroom videos, we asked them how they changed between the early stages and later stages in their teaching careers and, more generally, what they saw as characteristic differences between beginning and more experienced teachers. Across these interviews, some clear themes emerged, as discussed in the sections that follow.

CONFIDENCE

US interviewees described the most significant change between beginning and more experienced teachers as a difference of confidence, with remarks such as "You get more confidence in yourself and your ability to have control over the group," and "It's all about self-confidence." As three experienced preschool teachers said:

> ALANA: I think the biggest thing is just becoming more comfortable in doing a job. Just having confidence. The kids are doing great. Maybe the success from the kids—they work both ways. I am confident, so they are going to be successful. You are successful, and that makes me confident, that's a circle.
>
> GRACE: I think getting more confident allows you to relax a little bit more, give them more time, get to know them a little bit more, give them even more than you thought—give them more than I thought I could give them.
>
> ZOEY: Yes. And with that comes the confidence. It's like a baby trying to learn how to walk. Right? It's like those first wobbling steps. I mean, it takes a while but you just keep giving them the opportunities to practice that and practice that and practice that. And then sooner or later, they're, like, so confident.

A professor of early childhood education, Bob Capuozzo, reflected:

> My first year in the classroom, I second-guessed everything I did. Like, I remember my director talking to one of the mothers of the kids in my classroom down the hall, and I was thinking that they were talking about me. And I was thinking that the mother wasn't happy having her son in my classroom. I was just sort of, "Oh my gosh, I'm doing something wrong." But it turned out that it wasn't that at all. And then six years or so into my career, I had a lot more confidence in my abilities in the classroom. And I stopped the second-guessing.

Behind the pride US early childhood educators take in their hard-won self-confidence, we can hear echoes of the insecurity they felt early in their years, an insecurity associated not just with their inexperience but also with the low status of preschool teaching as a profession in the US. Experienced preschool teachers feel not just more confident in their own abilities in the classroom but also more confident that they are professionals, and not just babysitters, whatever others may think. As Fran's colleague Jenn said:

> Self-confidence is hard at the beginning because, you know, you were always seen as just a *preschool* teacher and not a *real* teacher. It's like, my husband was in the fast-food industry, and when he was downsized, he wanted to move to a job in the full-service food industry. But employers told him, "Sorry, you don't have experience in full service." And it was kind of like the same thing for me: "Oh, but you're a *preschool* teacher." I had years of hearing that, so it was really hard on my confidence. I went back and got my early childhood certification and it still took years until my district began to recognize me as a real teacher.

US respondents used both the terms "confidence" and "self-confidence." What then, if any, is the difference between confidence and self-confidence? The "self" in "self-confidence" sounds redundant. But I suggest that experienced US early childhood educators feel that their (self) confidence, like other aspects of their expertise, is something that belongs to them, something that they need to cultivate even if others do not have confidence in them, and something that is a key component of their professional selves.

BECOMING MORE YOURSELF

In a focus group interview at the University of Hawai'i at Mānoa Children's Center (UHMCC), Gwen Dufault, a teacher in her sixth year, and Ana Hayward, a teacher in her fourth year, described their professional growth:

> GWEN: When you first start, you do what others are doing. You're usually partnered with a more senior teacher and you learn from that teacher and do what that teacher is doing just so you can survive and manage the group of kids. And then, as the years progress, you learn more, you pick up more things, and maybe you latch on to a passion you have and you develop that, and you bring that into your teaching. And so it gradually becomes more *you* and less someone else.
>
> ANA: I started out working at the Marine Corps base preschool and it was very structured and routine. Every day had a cookie-cutter element. Then I came here. And every year that I've been here, a little bit of that Marine

Corps experience has been chipped away. A little bit of that routine part goes away. And a little more flexibility comes in. And each year a little bit more of *me* comes out.

In these comments, both Gwen and Ana emphasize how, with experience, they have become increasingly themselves as teachers. Gwen describes this process as "becoming more you and less someone else." Ana is more figurative, as she uses metaphors to describe her early pedagogical practice as being like using a cookie cutter and the process of growing as a teacher as being like a statue's true form emerging through a process of extraneous elements being chipped away. This metaphor is reminiscent of a line attributed to Michelangelo's description of sculpting: "I break the spell to free the figure slumbering in the stone." Another preschool teacher also mentioned, "What you said is we were talking about being ourselves. When you're a new teacher, you're somebody else. You're a scripted teacher, right? You need to become conscious of the teacher you want to be, of being yourself, in order to become less conscious with experience."

However, this does not mean you would completely change. There are somethings that do not change, as Jannie mentioned:

> I am still meticulous about certain things, how I want things, each portfolio. It's always been like that from that time. It doesn't change. I have not let it go. It reflects me, basically. I don't like doing work halfway. I always make sure everything is in there and I can show parents because they aren't at school, so I can actually show this is what we are doing at school.

In other words, with experience you become not a different teacher but a better version of yourself. Jannie still makes portfolios or scrapbooks for each kid (now electronically) and Fran continued to do the Buddy Bear activity until her retirement. The underlying idea here is that each teacher has a true character inside that takes years to emerge through a process of experience chipping away the parts that are not true to who the teacher really is. I heard nothing like this from experienced teachers in China or Japan, a point I will return to in chapter 5.

VOICES, GHOSTS, AND SCRIPTS

Another way US respondents described this process of becoming both more confident and more themselves was as freeing themselves from the dominance of the voices of others they carried in their head from early on in their careers. As Sonya Gaches, a professor of early childhood education at the University of Otago in New Zealand, formerly working at University of Arizona, told me:

> When you are starting out and you get your own classroom, you're still kind of carrying those ghosts with you. Here you are, you're supposed to be your own teacher, and yet you've got those ghosts in your head. You've got your teaching team who's telling you, "Oh, you're a young teacher. And you have to do this and that." You just really don't know yet, so you listen to those voices. This creates this tension in young teachers because they are trying to find their own voice, their own way, but they've got the ghost voices talking to them. They've got the other people, competing voices talking to them. There are some things I do, and then I look back and go, "Whoa. What the crap was I thinking?" You know, "What was that? Where did that even come from?" That's what I mean by these ghosts we carry in our head.

The point is not that experienced teachers should or do break free of all the ghosts they carry with them from their teacher training programs and early years of teaching and being mentored. As Jannie reported, ten years after they first worked together, she was still carrying aspects of Lori's voice, demeanor, perspectives, and pedagogical strategies with her, and she sees this as a good thing. But with years of experience, teachers gradually internalize and integrate these influences so they become part of themselves and are no longer the voices of others in their heads. Even experienced teachers need voices in their head, scripts, and schema to fall back on. But it is only with experience that teachers feel that they can control access to these scripts rather than being under the control of them. As Sonya said:

> With experience, there are routines you fall back on. You still need that, to be able to call on a process of visualization, or to turn a script on in your head. Veteran teachers can resist those external scripts because they have their own internal ones. There is a danger with less experienced teachers that they run a script that shouldn't be run at that moment. Maybe that's what makes them brittle, because the script they're running doesn't fit, and they don't have a new one to put in there.

Other respondents referred not to scripts or schema but to "short cuts," "a repertoire of strategies," and "go-to moves" that teachers can rely on to skillfully navigate the day. Christine described this repertoire using a computer analogy: "With experience, you can access that full hard drive of information, of past learning and past experiences." The ability to draw on the wisdom of past experience allows teachers to be less fretful when encountering a potentially difficult situation because they have a sense of what is likely to happen. As a teacher in Georgia commented:

> A key difference is that experienced teachers are able to anticipate. The first time something happens in your classroom, it's like, "Oh my gosh. Oh my God. What am I going to do?" The second time it happens, it's a bit easier, like, "Oh, okay, I've seen this before." And then, over the years, you see variations of those incidents happen. So that by the time you've taught five, six years, things don't surprise you so much and you get better at anticipating what might happen.

Past experience not only gives teachers ways to predict potential situations but also gives them a way to be free from another type of ghost—rules. One experienced preschool teacher said:

> There's a more relaxed, responding-in-the-moment quality to a teacher who's more mature, who's able to say, "Yeah, there's this rule about how you do it. But maybe I'm not going to follow the rule this time."

LESS "IN HERE" AND MORE "OUT THERE"

Being more confident, less under the control of the ghosts of others, and having a larger repertoire of reliable pedagogical moves allows teachers to be more in the moment and more present to children, as described by a group of professors from the University of Georgia:

> VAIL: Like reading a story to kids. Beginning teachers are so focused on trying to read and be smooth and ask their questions that they're so *in here* [pointing to her head] and not [fanning her fingers out and away from her] *out there*. They are *in here* [touching her head], thinking about their own performance rather than [pointing] *out there*, paying attention to the effect of their performance on their kids.
>
> DRESDEN: I think that as they become more comfortable, they're able to really *see* the kids. When they have more experience, they start to move from this focus on themselves and this vision of teaching as a scripted performance to a vision of teaching as responsiveness to somebody else's needs.

VAIL: You're not worried about past or future, but you're *here*. You're not trying to fit the kids into a prescriptive "Here's what they should be doing next."

DRESDEN: It just kicks in.

These experienced teacher educators suggested that to be fully present in the classroom, teachers need to be able to relinquish the need to feel always in conscious, deliberative control, as their colleague Bridget Ratajczak explained:

By the fifth year of teaching, I'd get to school and it was like I finally knew, "Okay, this is how you teach. This is what you do." You reach a point where you just know these things. You know what to do without needing to overthink it. It just felt, ah, not automated in any way, but I somehow just knew what to do. So there was a lot less energy expended on all that stuff, and I was able to put more time into looking at my students' needs.

Fran and her colleagues described a similar shift:

JENN: Yeah, it just kicks in. It becomes more natural.

PAULA: In the beginning it has to be conscious.

JENN: And then later on it just kind of . . .

PAULA: . . . kicks in.

FRAN: You just *do*. You *do*. You don't even have to think. With beginners, it's like they have to think, "Oh, okay, I learned about this in college" or "I tried this before and it seemed to work." But with experience you just kind of skip all those steps and just *do*.

JENN: No more "What am I supposed to say? What am I supposed to do?"

FRAN: Like, let it go and just *do* as opposed to having to go through the process of all the steps.

EMBODIED EXPERTISE

As Tobin and I argued in the book *Teaching Embodied*, teaching is embodied in two senses:

One is a teacher's literal use of her body as a tool, how she uses her hands to gesture, comfort, and discipline; her posture, gaze, and location in the classroom to indicate varying levels of attention; her voice to communicate empathy, frustration, disapproval, and enthusiasm. A second, related meaning is teaching practices that lack premeditation and reflection and rely on "muscle memory" analogous to that of athletes and musicians. (2015, 7)

US respondents pointed to both of these senses of embodiment in their discussion of the differences between beginning and veteran teachers, both the way teaching with experience becomes more automatic and less consciously intentional, allowing for more fluidity and presence, and also how expertise is something teachers do with their bodies. US participants associated more expert teaching with both of these senses of embodiment. For example, in this focus group exchange, participants suggested that experienced teachers employ bodily techniques more fluently and intuitively than beginners do:

> VAIL: Well, I wonder if part of what makes things go more smoothly is you know where to put your body and how to move it.
> RATAJCZAK: It becomes almost instinctual.
> DRESDEN: But over time, I do think you get much better at it. Then I think a lot of it happens not completely consciously. Like, "Okay, those kids are getting rowdy." And you just walk over there without even thinking and it's a sort of a psychic energy thing. If you have to think sequentially, "Oh, they're getting rowdy. Oh, what should I do? I could do this, or I could do that, or I could do this. Oh, maybe I should walk over there," that takes too much time. Versus, with experience, you just walk over there.
> CAPUOZZO: Maybe coupled with that, I'm thinking in the video, the teacher in Hawaii seemed like she was talking a lot. If instead of telling the kids to stop their misbehavior, she could just walk over there and just use her body as a cue for them to behave. But it seemed like she was talking a lot, like a lot of young teachers do.

Many of my respondents commented on Jannie's and Fran's use of bodily techniques. Most of these comments were praise for their use of eye contact, positioning, and bodily demeanor, including "I think she positioned herself well. She was on the floor, actively playing with kids," "I liked her eye contact," And "You could see that Jannie was excited about the children learning about absorption. You could see it on her face. That's a key to teaching. We've got to show on our face and with our voice that we're excited about what we're trying to teach children." Gwen commented:

> With experience, I guess what exudes from you to those young children becomes different. It's like my control during group times is effortless now.

I don't mean that I'm like Attila the Hun,[4] you know, yelling at them, "You be quiet and sit!" It's not like that all. It's something very different. I don't know if it's the look on my face, the tone in my voice, or how I say it, but now I have control without needing to yell.

Interviewees also focused on the way skilled teachers have sophisticated use of their gaze:

EMILY: I love to watch seasoned teachers in action because I always learn a lot from them and pick up some new tricks, like the way they address a situation, even the way they give a look to a child.

ELLA: Speaking of looks, did you guys see a lot of side-eye from her?

CAMILLA: Yes, I did.

ELLA: What did you think about that?

CAMILLA: I think I could definitely give a look like that to any one of my preschoolers and they will know what it means.

GROUP: [laughing]

EMILY: They know from that look what I'm expecting from them. Well, not all of them all the time, but it usually works. Those looks don't always have to be from the side. It can just be a slight nod from across the room, and they get it, right?

Others mentioned the importance of positioning:

CHARLOTTE: You learn you can just walk over to them and stand there.

SOPHIA: I've learned that for some of them, me just moving two inches to the left does the trick. For others, I'm going to just come stand right behind them and then they're that much more focused or engaged.

Another embodied skill of experienced teachers is the ability to scan the classroom:

HAYASHI: How do you know someone might be heading toward trouble. It's very subtle what you are picking up, right?

JANNIE: Oh yes, you just have to know your kids. What you see and hear and pick up, and stop it before getting into trouble. I do even more searching of certain kids who I know tend to get in trouble. You are always scanning those kids. Once they start doing silly things, I'm on it: "Okay, make a different choice. Think about something else that you guys can do."

HAYASHI: You said, "scan"? What does that involve?

JANNIE: Just looking around and listening. Even though I am working with them, I am always watching and listening. I mean, even on the playground, we are always scanning all the time. You never know what can happen. Kids can get hurt.

HAYASHI: Do you think you did less scanning at the beginning?

JANNIE: In the beginning, you don't know what to look at. When you are scanning, it's really complicated. It's not like simply, "Just look." You might tell a new teacher, "Look around," but it's a process that takes time. Over the years, it's gotten a lot easier to scan the whole room.

Another experienced teacher pointed out how voice changes with experience:

AVA: I do know that there was this one time when I was trying to use my stern voice that a student assistant laughed. And I was like, "What?" She goes, "Is that you trying to be strict? Is that your stern voice?"

HAYASHI: Recently? Or when you were beginning?

ISABELLA: Yeah, beginning. And now, I don't need to do that fake stern voice anymore.

TRIAGE

To employ the right bodily technique for the right moment and to be able to teach in a less conscious way require the ability to scan a classroom, read children, and know which situations demand immediate attention and which can be left alone. Many US interviewees described this trait of experienced teachers, borrowing a term from the battlefield and the emergency room, as "triage." For example, Janna Dresden of the University of Georgia reflected:

Over time I became more efficient. I learned to triage. It's figuring out what's important to worry about and what's not important. As a beginning teacher, I worried about *absolutely everything* all the time. That got in the way of focusing on other things that mattered. I don't know if I could articulate what those things were, but with experience, I definitely became more attentive to some things and there were other things I just quit worrying about.

In their focus group, Fran and her colleagues made connections between scanning and prioritizing attention:

JENN: You learn to scan the classroom and then you can figure out there are things that don't need your attention.

FRAN: I think in the beginning, we just don't know that we don't have to do all of that. But as we gain experience, we prioritize. With experience we know that we don't have to do everything at once.

PAULA: I like that scanning notion. It's like a hospital. You can't give everybody the same attention. You have to invest where it will pay off.

Reflecting on her 2002 video, Jannie commented, "I am at the point where I can search more and scaffold more. I've got to the point where I can stand back more and be able to help those who need help more, in different ways." Other respondents made similar points:

ISABELLA: Hard to say if that's just her teaching style or something new. I think as you go on and you teach for longer periods of time, you find out what's important and what's not, what to spend your energy on and what not to expend your energy on.

GAYNEL: You learn to know which battles to pick and which kinds of battles to avoid.

The triage metaphor suggests that some situations in classrooms do not require a teacher's immediate attention but that others, as on the battlefield or in the emergency room, require immediate intervention. Many US respondents described expert teaching using terms such as "scanning" and "triage" that come from the battlefield and the emergency room. Other US participants used a different metaphor, one that suggested that preschool classrooms are unlike emergency rooms or battlefields because, in all but the rarest of cases, whatever a preschool teacher does or doesn't do in a given moment, "No one's gonna die," so there's no need to "sweat the small stuff, and it's all small stuff." The US interviewees can be divided into two camps: one that sees an essential skill of teachers as triage, or the ability to know which situations require their immediate attention, and another that believes that there are few such situations.

EMILY: I think there's a point where you learn to not sweat the small stuff. And you can actually be with the children. Whereas newer teachers . . .

ELLA: . . . you're sweating . . .

EMILY: . . . everything.

CAMILLA: I would get to the point where I would come home and take a shower right after work just because I sweated through my clothes, and I'm in tears because I felt like the day was such a disaster. It probably wasn't, but the seriousness that you put into thinking about how you taught that day . . .

EMILY: You make terrible mistakes. We all do. But hopefully we don't kill any children along the way!

ELLA: When you're a new teacher you think you *can't* make those terrible mistakes. But once you make those mistakes, and then you see that nobody died, and everything's okay, and the classroom's still intact, then you're like, you kind of ease back and you're able to become more flexible and have a calmer perspective.

LET IT GO

Some Chinese participants defined expert teaching by citing Laozi and some Japanese participants by citing Zen precepts. Many US participants, including Jannie and Fran, cited Disney:

JANNIE: I let things go more than I used to do. Now I like to see what happens if I let it go.[5] I don't even do these things anymore, like helping children make Mother's Day cards. Kids do all of it. They do everything. I told you, I let *everything* go now. It doesn't bother me anymore if things are nice or not.

FRAN: Like, let it go and just do, as opposed to having to go through the process of all the steps.

Given that previous studies have established the typicality of low intervention by Japanese preschool teachers in children's disputes (Lewis 1984; Tobin, Wu, and Davidson 1989; Tobin, Hsueh, and Karasawa 2009; Walsh 2002), it was not surprising to hear my Japanese respondents talk about the importance of teachers becoming more adept at employing the pedagogical strategy of *mimamoru* (teaching by watching and waiting). Given that research on US preschool practices has emphasized the importance of teachers mediating and scaffolding children's disputes and other interactions (Tobin, Wu, and Davidson 1989; 2009), it is surprising how many US interviewees referred to how, with experience, they had become less directive, slower to intervene and help children, more patient, calmer, less talkative, and more trusting of children. These characteristics form a constellation of a larger concept I call, based on the emic term used by many of the US participants, "letting go." I discuss aspects of this concept individually in the sections that follow.

Talk Less and Listen More

One way in which experienced teachers described themselves as having changed is that they have become better at letting go of the control of conversations with children. This involves talking less, being a more attentive listener, asking more open-ended rather than leading questions, and giving children more wait time. After watching their 2002 videos in 2015, both Jannie and Fran expressed regret over the way they took control of conversations. For example, Fran was critical of a scene in which she intervened in a disagreement among three children who were fighting over a toy:

> Instead of trying to help them so much and putting words in their mouths and saying things like "When you do that, it makes her feel bad," now I would have *them* voice how *they* are feeling. "How did that make you feel when she took it away from you? Can you tell her how that makes you feel?"

Fran's colleagues agreed with this assessment:

> JENN: Yeah, I don't think I would have said as much as she said. I would have let the children—"Tell me what you're thinking. And you tell me what you want to say. And you tell him and . . ."
>
> PAULA: As you go down your path of professional growth, you withdraw a little of your reacting, leaving more for them.

Jannie had a similar reaction to a scene in her 2002 video in which we see a couple of boys playfully spanking another boy. Jannie then comes over and intervenes quickly and assertively by telling the spankers, "Does it feel good to him when you hit him? How do you think he feels? It hurts his body." After watching this scene in 2015, Jannie commented:

> Well, now I would do it differently. It would've been way different if this happened in my class now. I would have them solve the problem situation. In the video, it's me telling them things. Instead of me speaking for him, I mean for the boy who was being spanked, I would have him speak to his friends.

A faculty member at Leeward Community College who had taught Jannie years before commented:

> She did talk a lot. She could've let the kids talk more. She had the answers to the questions before she asked them. I think it's much more exciting if you ask a question with no idea what the children are going to say, right? But I think that would be really hard for a new teacher, 'cause then they end up talking about things you don't want to talk about.

Some US interviewees suggested that in addition to learning to talk less, teachers need to listen to children more and with more insight. For example, a community college professor said, "I think I got better at reading kids the longer I taught, and at being able to understand what they were saying to me. I was understanding the words, but sometimes missing the meaning." An experienced teacher in Georgia explained:

> Little kids say so many things that when we are starting out, we tend to just dismiss the things they say that don't make immediate sense to us. But as I got more experienced, I learned to listen more patiently and to always try to find meaning in everything they say, because there is always some reason there.

A veteran teacher in Arizona similarly said:

> The longer I taught, the better I got at reading kids and being able to understand what they were saying to me. Earlier on, I was understanding the children's words, but sometimes not what they were really saying. But now from just one or two words, someone else listening totally could not understand what the kids are saying, but I get it. So it was just a process of getting to know kids better and what they could do the longer I taught.

Veteran teachers learn that children's conversations become richer when they ask more open-ended questions and leave more wait time. As Fran commented:

> With experience, my questions got better for children, a lot better. I really got away from yes-and-no questions. I got better at "Use your words, I want to hear you." As I taught longer, what I learned was to give them more lead time. You know, wait for them to respond instead of giving them cues unless they really need the help. And so, I think, looking at this video, I can

see now that I was putting words in her mouth. I could say that I probably got better at waiting. I think that I really grew in that area, probably more than anything else.

Faculty members in the University of Georgia focus group emphasized the importance of open-ended questions:

DRESDEN: And also the types of questions that they're asking. Like, are they using open-ended questions versus closed-ended? Jannie had a lot of closed-ended, yes-or-no questions.

VAIL: Right, like in the absorption lesson, instead of asking leading questions like "A sponge absorbs more than a piece of paper, right?" she could have asked questions like "What is the water doing when the sponge touches it? What's happening to it?"

RATAJCZAK: Hopefully, a more experienced teacher would have learned to do more open-ended questions with more discussion and conversation and getting deeper into the core ideas.

A Sense of Calm

Some young teachers enter the field, as one participant put it, "full of beans and raring to go" but unable to slow down and give themselves and the students they teach a chance to breathe, as Gwen and her colleagues at UHMCC reminisced:

GWEN: I've really slowed down. You should have seen me when I started out. I used to go, zing zing zoom.

LANI: Uh, you still go, zing zing zoom.

ANA: [laughing] No, you should have seen her before. She was scary!

WAYNE: It was exhausting!

ANA: We used to steal her Mountain Dew[6] because we couldn't have her go any faster.

A cost of such zinging and zooming is missing much of what children are thinking and saying:

GWEN: I eventually developed the patience to really listen to what children have to say.

ANA: Yeah, you need to have confidence to be more patient and to slow down, to listen more.

The opposite of such patience is the feeling young teachers have that they always need to be doing something:

> SONYA: Some veteran teachers reach the point where there's not always a sense of urgency about the way things have to be and the constant feeling that you have to be doing something. There is that sense that there is not always something you have to jump on. A sense of calmness.
>
> EMMA: Sometimes I have to tell people, like the Puritan work ethic, you know, the idea that you need to always be working, producing, moving, doing. That's really the wrong strategy. You really need to sit and wait and be quiet. And some teachers, they felt like they were not a good worker if they weren't always moving, watching, talking, doing.

This citation of the Puritan work ethic is insightful, as it suggests that many young teachers may confuse being calmer and more patient with appearing idle or lazy.

Several respondents contrasted Gwen's hyperactive early-career teaching style with what they perceived as Jannie's calmness, a characteristic they suggested is not often found in young teachers. Two colleagues we interviewed, Rich Johnson and Allison Henward, had trouble evaluating whether Jannie in the 2002 video was an experienced teacher who had mastered the art of being calm or a low-energy beginner:

> HAYASHI: What's your impression of her as a teacher?
>
> JOHNSON: I love her contact with the kids, being at their level physically, and how she made the children a real group, a team during circle time. She's very interactive even though she's very quiet. She's not yelling. I like that vibe.
>
> HENWARD: She's pretty connected to the kids and there's an easiness about her, where she's really not getting particularly excited about anything. She has this very level way about her. She doesn't overreact to anything. She's just responsive.
>
> HAYASHI: Is there any way you could, if you didn't know, could guess how long she'd been teaching when we videotaped her?
>
> JOHNSON: I would say a long time because, going back to my earlier point, to me she appears so comfortable. So at ease. Yeah, so I would say many years. A number.
>
> HAYASHI: So she doesn't look like a beginner?
>
> JOHNSON: Not to me.

HENWARD: My first impression when I first watched this video, I had the feeling that Jannie was, well, I would use the term "detached." She seemed very not overly enthusiastic or energetic. I thought that was just maybe her personality. But to put it more positively, there seems to be a comfort and a kind of automaticity about her. She is relatively calm. She's very even-keeled. She gives the feeling that, "This, too, shall pass," or like "The tide comes in, the tide goes out." She seemed to have the feeling that all of this is just the flow of life in the preschool classroom.

The metaphors used here to describe Jannie as having a calm vibe, being even-keeled, and rolling with the tide suggest that the preschool classroom is like a roiling sea best navigated by a teacher who has learned the wisdom of going with the flow and not fighting the waves and tides.

Jannie displaying some of the calmness of a veteran in only her third year of teaching alerts us to the complexity of charting expertise over time, as personal styles need to be taken into account, and teachers both earlier and later in their careers may not be equally expert in each task or domain of teaching. Jannie, by her own admission, had the characteristic flaws of a young teacher of talking too much and being too directive. And yet, like her mentor Lori, she also had a calm and low-key personal style that is more commonly found in more experienced teachers. This suggests that frenetic young teachers, like Gwen, tend to become calmer with experience and that precociously calm young teachers like Jannie tend to become even calmer.

Child-Driven

Fran summarized the ways she had changed with experience by saying, "I think I am now more child-based and child-driven." Many of the expert US participants made similar points, as in a discussion among experienced teachers at the Child Development Lab Preschool at the University of Georgia:

NORA: When I started teaching, it was like, "We are going to do it this way. Oh, I got a marvelous idea. Regardless of if you want to do it or not, you are going to do it." Not only that but, "This is what we are going to do today and you are going to like it." When I first started teaching, it was all precise learning activities. "We are going to connect the dots and make a letter." Now I am like, "Here is paper and here are some markers, and let's see what are you going to do with them."

LILY: When I was a younger teacher, someone gave me a big box and I told the kids, "This is going to be a fire truck." Last year, I got a big box and

I said to the children, "Oh, look, we got a box. What are we going to do with it?" All I did was provide materials and provide them a narrative that might help them along the way. I shifted from like a very teacher-directed to a very open approach.

ZOEY: I think the shift is from "self-monitoring" to more "child-oriented." Does that make sense? Through experiences, we become more "child-oriented" and tuned in to *their* thought process more than to our self-mind orientation. Like we start out saying: "This is what *I* want to do. This is what *I* want us to do. This is where we are going to go." With time, we become more child-oriented: "Hey, that's an interesting thing. Let's go with it." I think in the very beginning, you feel like you have to choreograph and direct everything. As you gain experience, you can take that step back. You get things done but in a different way. Instead of being directive, you just kind of get them going in the right direction without having to say, "You have to do this," or, "Why don't we do this?" That just comes with, with the aging process, with the experience process.

Few US interviewees reported having begun their careers believing in a teacher-directed, didactic pedagogy. Most said that their training exposed them right from the start to child-centered pedagogy, but this turned out to be very hard for them to enact in the classroom, and it took years for them to let go of control. They reported that over time they did not so much shift their philosophy from teacher-directed to child-centered as they became more able to teach in what they described as a more authentically child-centered manner. As Dresden described the process:

I think teachers become more comfortable with letting kids have more control. Early on, teachers feel like they need to be running the show so that they have control. Whereas later, they can learn and feel more comfortable with "If I let children do this, I'm still not going to lose the ship."

Letting Go Is Hard to Do

There are several reasons early-career teachers, despite subscribing to the virtues of child-centered pedagogy, find it so hard to let go of controlling their classroom. One reason, as hinted at by the teacher who referred to being influenced by the "Puritan work ethic," is that young teachers may feel that if they say less and hold back more, they will be perceived by supervisors, other teachers, parents, and maybe even their students as not being fully engaged. Another factor is that young teachers cannot let go because they have not developed sufficient trust in the ability of children to learn without being directly taught and to handle disputes and other classroom challenges without teacher mediation. This is related to a problem some of my participants described as an excess and misapplication of empathy:

> NORA: I was afraid of kids crying, so I felt like I had to run over and assure them that they were okay. I was afraid to be blamed by someone walking by and seeing children crying. Now I am comfortable. I don't like to hear children crying. I don't want them to be upset. But I know now how to proceed without trying to hush them, which I was really doing.
>
> DAVID: It's okay to let them cry. What looks like a failure turns out okay. You have to know your children.
>
> NORA: I tell young teachers, "Children are going to cry. It's okay to cry." It's a conduit for discussion. It's an opportunity for children to explore how they feel, how others are feeling, and how they might learn something from such situations as opposed to a teacher thinking, "I want you all to be happy all the time."
>
> AMY: We go into this field because we are nurturers. We need to learn to let kids struggle, to suffer, which is hard for us.

It takes years of experience to come to the realization, consciously or intuitively, that intervening too quickly when a child cries or is sad or angry is more about the teacher reducing her tension than about responding in a way helpful to children. Even after understanding that it is normal and even desirable for children to experience crying and strong emotions in preschool, it takes years to be able to control the impulse to intervene, as some preschool teachers expressed:

> ELLA: See, that's hard. My tendency would be to watch a little bit longer before intervening.
>
> CAMILLA: Have patience to really listen to what your children have to say. Just take that time.

Navigating a Career as a Preschool Teacher

Becoming a preschool teacher in the US is no guarantee that you will still be in the field ten years later. More than half of those that begin teaching preschool leave the field within three years (Bellm et al. 2002; Phillips, Austin, and Whitebook 2016; Whitebook and Bellm 1999; Whitebook 1999). Even among those who stay in the field, most will change preschools once or more in their first decade of teaching. Acquiring expertise in the US therefore requires the practitioner to manage their own career.

A focus group discussion we conducted with three experienced teachers at a child center in Athens, Georgia, brought out many of the key themes (which I have highlighted below in italics) teachers described as their processes and sources of professional growth.

> DAVID: I'm still trying to wrap my head around the question. What makes me change? What changes me as a teacher as I gain experience and grow?
>
> CATALINA: What I am thinking is experience. I was so young. I came right out of high school. Watching David and other experienced teachers, seeing where they were going, seeing where they were bettering themselves education-wise, bettering themselves from where they were at, getting themselves in a better situation to teach—that encouraged me to follow that track, too.
>
> DAVID: You and I started in the same place. My third year here was your first year. We both started working at another place and then I moved here and then you came a year later. One thing I learned when I first got into early childhood education was that *this school was the place to work if you were going to be serious about your job.* Anyway, when I think about you back then, you were such a *young girl.* And I remember we were at a banquet a couple of years ago and you were talking about all these things that you had to do to make sure food is safe, and I remember just going, "My gosh. *You're an adult!*" I was thinking *you've become an expert on this because you have education and experience* and confidence. The confidence comes from knowing what to do.
>
> ALANA: It's not really confidence. You always are saying, "I've got that bag of . . ."
>
> CATALINA: . . . know-how.
>
> DAVID: ". . . *bag of tricks.*" I know what to pull out and when to pull it out. And I know if it doesn't work, then you need to change it. You become more adaptable in the way you teach. You just realize, *through a process of elimination,* what's going to work, what might not work. Something that didn't work last year might work this year.
>
> ALANA: I think we change from seeing what each other is doing and, if it's working, trying it ourselves to see if we can adjust it to our way of working.
>
> DAVID: Every profession has its own vernacular. And when you first start, you are not really sure what it is and you are not sure how to use it. Then

you start understanding it and you start using it then you become more *entrenched* in that profession. That's how I see Catalina now. When I hear her talk about strategies she uses. I admire it. It's smart. *So I steal it.* Because if it works for her, it'll probably work for me.

CATALINA: The first three years of your teaching, you worry about lesson plans, you worry about getting your classroom ready, you worry about being perfect, perfect, perfect. Then, you look back after three years, and it's like, "I need to get to setting goals, like being more involved in working on getting to know parents, being closer to parents and families." I think once you get all of that hardcore stuff done, then you start looking at smaller goals for your teaching career. You start learning to get things done outside of the center, like learning more about parenting and families.

DAVID: Having opportunities to *interact with peers* is very important. During the summer, our attendance was very low, and so Alana and I had a lot of opportunities just to talk about teaching, which is a very rare gift to have. "Hey, why are you doing this? How do you do that?" Sometimes practical questions, sometimes big picture questions, like "Is this curriculum working for you?" It's just really very nice to have those conversations. And we had some *workshops* with Mariana Souta-Manning and we discussed issues about teaching, and issues about classrooms. It was just a great way to connect with each other, but also to kind of *vet* some things that you couldn't stop. You have to live through it. It's really nice to have that support. When I was—I was going to say a kid, but I was already in my early thirties—but I felt like I spent so much time *treading water*, trying to figure out if I was doing the right thing, if what I was doing was *appropriate for the children as well as for myself*. It's just a lot of figuring things out, like walking through a maze without a flash light, in the dark. While cold. [laughs]

BETTERING YOURSELF

Catalina reported learning in her first few years of teaching from her slightly more experienced colleague David the need for teachers to "better themselves education-wise." This comment succinctly captures the idea that for US preschool teachers, the responsibility for professional growth is primarily on the teacher. Some teachers are complacent and willing to move forward in their careers without pushing themselves to become more skilled. But those US practitioners who do become more expert do so through a determination to make themselves better. During the first stages of their careers, Jannie and Fran, like Catalina and most of my participants, reported looking to experienced colleagues for direction. But by their third year or so, most of these teachers took control of their professional growth, seeking out professional development opportunities and changing jobs, whether by choice or by necessity. With experience, they not only became more themselves as teachers, they also became more in charge of their professional growth.

BETTER SITUATIONS

Catalina suggested that teachers can "better themselves" by getting themselves in a "better situation." David echoes this point by saying that in the third year of his career, he came to the realization that "if you're going to be serious about your job," he would need to move to the best place to teach in his area. David identified a child center in Athens, Georgia, fitting that description, and he moved there. Catalina followed him a year later.

Several US interviewees, like David and Catalina, reported having changed jobs in search of the best match between their beliefs and their new preschool's approach. For example, Ana described the relief she felt when she moved from the Marine Corps base preschool and its "cookie-cutter" approach to teaching at the much freer UHMCC, which was much looser, more child-centered, and where she was able to "become more myself." Lani Au described a process of moving from school to school until she found a program that was just right for her:

> This is the fifth school I've worked at. And for me, the changes came as I went from structured to less structured to here, right? It was the change of place. Being at a place where the children were first, and the relationships with the families. When I first started preschool teaching, every preschool classroom looked the same. Everyone had the same yellow, blue, red color scheme and the same square lesson plans. It was interchangeable. Anyone could have been teaching. And as I've gotten older and spent more time in different schools, I realized I needed to be in a place where only I could be doing this. It matters that I'm here. I really value that.

Lani articulates the dream of finding a professional home where one doesn't just fit in, but where one can make a unique contribution. At her fifth stop on her professional journey, at UHMCC, Lani finally found her home, her right place where she can be herself and help other staff members to be successful and happy.

US teachers change jobs more often than do their counterparts in China and Japan; but it is not easy for them to move because they need the right match, what one of my interviewees called "a cozy situation," one where they can not only be comfortable but contribute. There is a romantic notion here that for every teacher, there is "the perfect match" somewhere. This contrasts with the Japanese approach, in which one gets 'one's first job at a preschool and then commits oneself to becoming the best teacher one can be for that school.

Experienced US teachers change jobs not just for better matches but also for better pay and benefits. Unlike in Japan, where salaries and benefits for preschool teachers in both the private and public sectors are much the same from program to program, there are wide variations in the US (Whitebook and Bellm 1999; Bellm et al. 2002). This is the case even within the growing public preschool sector, in which some preschool teachers are paid as much as their peers who teach elementary school, while many are paid much less. These disparities in compensation contribute to teachers' job changes. Many excellent private and non-private preschools pay relatively low salaries and provide limited benefits. This means that a teacher like Jannie, who felt at home at St. Timothy's and valued the program's approach, nevertheless left for a job that paid much better. A teacher like Fran, who completed her BA during her tenure in her first position, was able to use her new degree to trade up for a higher-paying job.

HIGHER EDUCATION VERSUS ON-THE-JOB LEARNING

David reflected on a moment at a banquet when he was suddenly struck by the expertise of Catalina, his colleague of many years. He attributed this expertise to a mixture of education and experience. A common discourse among US educators is praising what they learn on the job and denigrating what they are taught in university settings. As Janna, who teaches preservice and in-service early childhood education courses, told us:

> There's a culture of "What you learn in school is not that helpful. It's what you learn on the job that's most helpful. And a lot of what you learn at the university doesn't even relate to reality." And it's this, you know, on-the-job culture of this school and teachers you're working with and that's the reality.

Such sentiments can be explained in part by a strain of anti-intellectualism and a high valuation of practical knowledge in American society. When asked what contributed most to their professional growth, most of my participants did give most of the credit to their on-the-job experience. But many also gave credit to formal professional development activities and mentioned the value of workshops and university courses.

This is not to say that they value workshops and courses in general but rather that under certain conditions, these professional development activities can be helpful. Jannie, Fran, and most of the other US early childhood educators said that the majority of workshops they had attended had little impact on their professional growth. They mentioned occasionally picking up some tips at workshops and receiving necessary information, for example, about changes to guidelines for dealing with blood or reporting domestic abuse. But few cited workshops as having played a major role in them becoming more expert as teachers. This is consistent with the literature on professional development, which suggests that workshops alone rarely produce significant professional growth (Ko, Wallhead, and Ward 2006). Problems of workshops for in-service teachers include a lack of intrinsic motivation when the topics are chosen by others, resentment about giving up planning time to attend workshops or even attending workshops outside of their regular work hours, a lack of follow-up, and presentations not suited to their contexts and needs. A workshop presented to a group of practitioners at different stages of their careers, as if most often the case, is likely to be too basic for some and too advanced for others.

A few experienced participants described a workshop they attended as having catalyzed change in their practice. The key factor for this impact seems to be timing and motivation: the workshop presented them with an idea when they were at a point in their professional growth that made them ready for it and open to change. For example, one veteran teacher in Hawaii said:

EMILY: I was in my sixth or seventh year of teaching and then I went to a NAEYC conference where I attended a workshop on working with families. Two things I took away from it that I do to this day were one, to greet the parents every time they come into the class, and two, to let the parent know how much you like their child. That's what matters to them most.

The advice offered in this workshop should have been useful even to beginning teachers. But I suggest that for a message in a workshop to effect a profound change in a practitioner, it needs to reach them at a point in their career when they are ready for it. Few preschool teachers are ready to work effectively with parents in the first stage of their career, and therefore a workshop on working with parents, no matter how well delivered, may not be well received by a preschool teacher at an early point in their career concerned with other teaching priorities (Mahmood 2013). The literature on workshops suggests that a workshop is most effective when the participants choose the topic and they attend as a group (Wagner and French 2010). David praised a workshop he attended by citing not the content the presenter shared but the opportunity for discussion and connection with colleagues.

The story was similar for in-service university coursework, which many teachers took during their first few years on the job either as a requirement for keeping their jobs or because it would raise their pay. Problems of coursework include a sense of a divide between the realities of practitioners and the academic knowledge of professors and resentment about the costs of taking evening courses, in both money and time. Many US teachers work on bachelor's and master's degrees after beginning their first jobs. Some programs require teachers to complete a degree while working to keep their jobs. Degrees and continuing education credits make teachers more marketable. Unlike their counterparts in Japan, where preschool teachers rarely move and rarely pursue advanced degrees, and in China, where professional development is mostly offered by schools and districts for their programs' entire staffs, preschool teachers in the US are largely independent agents who acquire experience and degrees they can use to move from job to job.

Few interviewees credited their preservice or in-service university coursework as being the key factor in their professional growth, but as with workshops, several participants talked about the impact coursework at particular junctures in their early careers. For example, after several years of preschool teaching, Fran reached a point where she was ready for a shift in perspective and approach:

> When I started out, I did a lot for the kids and directed a lot. It was almost like, "Okay, we are going to do this now. Come on. Now we are going to that." It was like daycare rather than preschool. Then I started going back to taking early childhood classes in the evenings. I really enjoyed those. The teachers' ideas were very different from what I had heard before, like in working with young children, what counts is the process, not the product, and the importance of listening to children. It wasn't until I started going back to school that I kind of opened the door a little bit more.

Wayne Watkins, former director of the UH Mānoa Children's Center, said he went back to school at a point in his career when he became frustrated with his current teaching:

At some point it started being apparent to me that, "Okay, your guesses about what you do with this kid or what you do in this situation are not as on-target as they used to be or they no longer feel as on-target. What is going on?" I went and took a graduate class. I mean, I swore I would never do that again because the university, I thought, had screwed me up. But taking the graduate class did allow me an opportunity to get in a frame of mind where I was reflecting on things like, "Okay, the things I say directly affect the children's reaction." And so I started analyzing all that and I realized like, "Oh, duh." So I started deliberately saying things to children in certain ways. And you know, breaking old habits.

Fran and Wayne benefited from coursework at junctures in their careers when they had for some reason become dissatisfied with their current practices and felt a need to shift their perspectives.

ACQUIRING A "BAG OF TRICKS"

Alana, Catalina, and David, as well as some other US interviewees, described the acquisition of expertise as a process of gathering and mastering a "bag of tricks." This metaphor captures several aspects of how experienced US practitioners think about their expertise as early childhood educators. The first part of the metaphor, the bag, implies that expertise here is pictured as a collection of practices a teacher picks up as they move through their teaching career. The metaphor suggests that, as with a shopping bag, a practitioner has control over what they put into their bag of tricks. No two teachers will have the same tricks in their bags. In other words, the metaphor here is consistent with my larger finding that US practitioners see themselves as managing their own professional growth. A "bag of tricks" also suggests that preschool teachers see themselves as what the French call "bricoleurs" and Americans call "a jack (or jill) of all trades." In *The Practice of Everyday Life*, Michel de Certeau (1984) argues that those in positions of power can employ strategies, while those with less power must resort to tactics. Strategies are tools for those who can dictate the terms of their life and work. Tactics are tools for those who must be practical and clever in how they "make do" with the resources and latitude available to them. Preschool teachers in the US, like other bricoleurs, are necessarily pragmatists who—unlike, for example, professors—do not have the luxury of following a path of philosophical or ideological consistency. Most US participants were in general agreement with the NAEYC's principles of "Developmentally Appropriate Practice," but said they employed these principles in their own way, without feeling the necessity to do so with fidelity (a complaint policy makers often make about teachers). As pragmatists, experienced US preschool practitioners use the tricks in their bags that work and discard others. A "bag of tricks" is similar to another metaphor used by a few of my interviewees: they referred to their expertise as "tools" they have in their "tool kit," a metaphor that suggests a connection between preschool teaching and other skilled trades, like carpentry, rather than with professions like university teaching.

Where do these tricks of the trade come from? As David said in reference to a practice he observed his colleague Catalina using, "I admire it. It's smart. So I steal it. Because if it works for her, it'll probably work for me." David described this process with the word "stealing" rather than, say, "copied" or "learned from." The references to a repertoire of professional practices as "tricks" and to the mode of acquiring them as "stealing" carry a hint of the playfulness and even naughtiness that de Certeau suggests is characteristic of resilient skilled practitioners who find clever ways to "make do" within structures not of their own making.

The tricks and tools are acquired not en masse but one by one, through a process of observing, copying, experimenting, adapting, and discarding. Catalina said she thought teachers changed from seeing what other teachers do "if it's working." David said, "You become more adaptable in the way you teach. You just realize, through a process of elimination, what's going to work, what might not work. Something that didn't work last year might work this year." In a focus group in Honolulu, an experienced teacher said:

> You look and see what other teachers did because you can learn shortcuts and stuff like that. So I think that's really helpful. Workshops, no. Being around other teachers, being in that setting, yes. You know, being able to see what others are doing. This not only shows you new ideas but also shows you things you don't want to get in the rut of doing and stuff like that.

Teachers can pick up tricks from anyone they work with, but they focus their borrowing on the practices of senior colleagues. As a teacher said in a Honolulu focus group, "I learn so much from watching veteran teachers teach who I feel hold the same teaching values that I do, that have got a good fit. I learned a lot from these teachers who I would consider my mentors." Many US teachers reported having begun their careers in the position of assistant teacher, a role that facilitated learning from lead teachers. These statements suggest that teachers pick up teaching practices from coworkers, especially from senior colleagues whom they admire. However, this learning from coworkers does not fit usual definitions of mentorship. While lead-assistant teacher relationships are common during the induction stage of a career, they are not the principal way US teachers who stay in the field acquire professional expertise.

Jannie acknowledged that Lori was a model for her and that she picked up from Lori a lot of practices she still uses. But neither Lori nor Jannie referred to their relationship as mentor and apprentice. There are two versions—or two meanings—of the mentor-apprentice relationship. One is more formal, in which both mentor and apprentice take their roles seriously, with the apprentice faithfully internalizing all the mentor has to offer and the mentor not only providing examples but also giving tasks matched to the apprentice's abilities and feedback when needed. The other version is one in which a younger teacher, like Jannie, identifies a senior colleague, like Lori, she admires and with whom she shares "values," and learns from her without either acknowledging they have a mentor-apprentice relationship. The agency, the responsibility for acquiring expertise, is all on the one learning and not on the mentor. The younger one may describe what they do as "copying" or "adding something from her to my bag of tricks" but does not attempt to become a disciple. They will learn not just from this one senior coworker but also from others they get to observe. This second version is less mentoring than it is learning from one's seniors.

PARENTING

US teachers reported that one of the things they found most difficult early in their careers was dealing with parents. They cited several reasons for this, including not having had much preparation for dealing with parents in their university coursework and being younger than the parents and not having children of their own, therefore lacking both experience and credibility:

GRACE: I think a lot of beginning teachers . . .
ZOEY: . . . run away from parents.
GRACE: Particularly if they don't have children themselves.
ZOEY: Becoming a parent does change a teacher.
GRACE: Or feeling like your parents have confidence in you as a teacher makes you . . .
NORA: There's a certain type of parent at our university lab school that's similar to me that I can connect with more easily. I was a struggling college student with two kids once, so I can totally get that parent. But then we have children of professors, and then I have a harder time making that

connection. I feel a little nervous, but I have to push myself. They're human beings too, and they're trusting me with their child. So I respect and appreciate that. And I just have to work a little harder with those parents.

Some interviewees said that early in their careers, they viewed interacting with parents as a distraction from the love of children that drew them to the field:

LILY: We came to work with the children and then we discovered, "Oh, these adults come with them!"
NORA: I still say that all the time. I say, "I'm really good with kids and dogs. Kids and dogs. Don't give me adults."
LILY: There are some good teachers that are actually excellent with kids but not as great with adults.

Jannie also talked about becoming a parent as a turning point for seeing things differently:

Parenting does change you. It gave me a different perspective. Not having a child versus having one, you look at things differently. I have two boys, and with them, I eventually reached the point where I told them to solve their problems. You bring it back to school too. Before I was a parent, I was always having them do things. After having children, I got more relaxed and I let the children solve their problems.

A group of experienced educators in Hawaii, while not arguing that becoming a parent changes you as a teacher, suggested that experience in teaching, as in parenting, leads to a more relaxed approach:

EMMA: There's a parallel between teaching and parenting. The first child comes along and the bottle has to be given when the pediatrician said, and the temperature has to be just right, and on and on. And then the third child comes along and you say to yourself, "He's not crying. He's dry so, you know, he's okay." There's a more relaxed, responding-in-the-moment quality to a teacher who's more mature, who's able to say, "Yeah, there's this rule about how you do it. But maybe I'm not going to follow the rule this time."
OLIVIA: Yeah, they are really, really cautious about a lot of things. And looking to see if they're doing everything right. But by the time they have the second one . . .

AVA: The second one, yeah . . .
SOPHIA: . . . eating dirt, no big deal.

While some early childhood practitioners may never become comfortable dealing with parents, many interviewees reported that a combination of age, experience, and having children of their own not only helped them connect better with parents but also helped them become better at dealing with children. For example, some US teachers emphasized the impact of their own aging on how they were perceived by parents:

EMILY: When I started teaching, I was younger than many of the parents, so they didn't take me seriously. Then, like say, ten years ago, we were kind of like the same age and so they kind of saw me as a peer. But now, ten years later, they know that I'm old enough to be their parent. So there's a different kind of trust and a sense of respect. The role that I play for them now is also a little more mothering. Or I'm even more like the grand-mother. That happens with time, yeah. Natural aging.

Interviewees suggested that becoming parents gave them not just more status and credibility but also more perspective, wisdom, and patience. To make this shift, it is not necessary to become a parent—some expert early childhood educators never have a child—but most of the US teachers and directors credited having children of their own as having a major impact on their teaching. However, the impact of becoming a parent on teaching was not linear or necessarily entirely positive. In a focus group discussion, staff at a lab preschool in Honolulu brought up the complexity of this relationship between parenting and preschool teaching:

HAYASHI: So how does having kids change you as a teacher?
ANA: You learn how to manage your time better and you . . . it actually bal-ances you.
GWEN: You're less focused on work.
ANA: Your work and personal life.
HAYASHI: And that's a good thing?
ANA: Yeah, yeah. You have more on your plate and you just learn how to balance. It's like learning a new way to live.
LANI: When I teach preservice teachers, one of the things I always say to them is that parents think less of you if you don't have kids. They think you don't have enough knowledge, you don't have enough background, you're not a good teacher. But actually, it's totally the other way. Because I

was such a better teacher before I had my kids, because I care more about my kids than your kids, now. Right? Once I had my kids, I wanted to get home to them as fast as I could, so I left school as soon as I could and did my prep work at home. So they got more out of me before I had kids!

WAYNE: You're putting more energy into your own children so you have less available for the kids here.

LANI: Well, this job can eat you up, right?

ANA: What you want to do is you want to build up the relationship these children have with their own parents. You don't want to replace their parents. And if you think you should, this is really the wrong place.

HAYASHI: Are you saying that it's not good to care too much about your students?

WAYNE: With age, some teachers start recognizing the limits of their sphere of influence. It's not all the way through this child's life. It is during these hours. Period. Done.

LANI: These children belong to their parents. And I think one of the worst kinds of teachers are the ones that you interview and they say, "I want this job 'cause I love kids." And I say, "Go find a man and have a baby then!" 'Cause these kids aren't available, right? They're not. They're spoken for.

Lani makes a profound point here about how becoming a parent shifts a teacher's priorities and attention. On the one hand, the years when a teacher has young children of their own at home can have a negative effect on their teaching by reducing the time and energy they have for their students. Lani suggests, bravely and honestly, that becoming a parent can make a teacher care less about their students. But she goes on to suggest that this is not necessarily a bad thing. An implication of her reflection is that loving one's students as one would one's own children is not beneficial, as it may lead one to do too much for them, to make one competitive with children's parents for their love, to be too needy for children's love, and to be unable to step back and have perspective on children's needs. As Lani says, children have parents. What they need from a teacher is another kind of relationship with an adult.

AGES AND STAGES: FROM TREADING WATER TO SWIMMING

Several interviewees suggested that there are stages in a preschool teacher's professional growth, with the focus of the first few years being on determining that they are in the right field and acquiring basic skills to survive the rigors of daily life in a classroom with three- and four-year-olds. This is followed by a second stage, in which the focus shifts to the acquisition of higher-order reflection and practice. The stress of the first stage can be seen in comments made in separate focus groups by Cindy Vail, David Jones, and Jannie Umeda:

> CINDY: The main thing for me was how to survive a day without kids killing each other or killing me. So it was almost like going in with your battle gear on.
>
> DAVID: I felt like I spent so much time treading water, trying to figure out if I was doing the right thing, if what I was doing was appropriate for the children as well as for myself. It's just a lot of figuring things out, like walking through a maze, without a flashlight, in the dark.
>
> JANNIE: When you're younger, you just really, you're struggling just to stay afloat. You have to figure out how to deal with the kids, the parents, the curriculum, everything. And then, after you have the experience of several years, it just starts to come, and it just kind of settles you in more, and you kind of begin to realize, "Okay, what can I do better? What kind of things do I need more help with?"

The metaphors used here for the first stage of preschool teaching are striking: descriptions of the first stage of teaching as being like needing to put on battle gear, being in the dark, walking through a maze, and treading water poetically communicate a sense of struggling to just survive rather than to grow and thrive. This is akin to Maslow's hierarchy of needs: young teachers, in need of a feeling of security and self-esteem, are not yet able to put energy into higher-order concerns and instead focus on basic skills for getting through the day. After five years or so of working the field, in Jannie's words, "it just starts to come" and "settles you in." The passive voice of her construction reflects the feelings of a young teacher that one cannot will oneself into this second stage any more than a teenager can will herself into adulthood. The comments of experienced teachers suggest they have an implicit stage theory: if in the first stage of your career, you can master basic skills of teaching and get through the days and weeks and years without quitting, then you can eventually arrive at a point where you can teach more effectively and enjoy your job more. Fran points out that the best part of preschool teaching is the pleasure one gets from being with young children, but that this is hard to experience early in one's career because one is distracted by insecurity and the feeling of being overwhelmed:

> Everything is so new. You want to make sure everything is right. "Oh no, an observation is coming!" There is a lot of pressure. You just have to get

through it, believing that eventually it's going to be okay. You need to get to the point where you can just try to relax and enjoy it. Because kids are fun! If we can just get to that point at the beginning of our career, maybe we would stay longer.

Catalina, an experienced preschool teacher, described the change between the beginning and more mature stage as one of shifting from mastering "the hardcore stuff" to being able to focus on what she calls "smaller goals":

The first three years of your teaching, you worry about lesson plans, you worry about getting your classroom ready, you worry about being perfect, perfect, perfect. Then, you look back after three years, and it's like, "I need to get to setting goals, like being more involved in working on getting to know parents, being closer to parents and families." I think once you get all of that hardcore stuff done, then you start looking at smaller goals for your teaching career. You start learning to get things done outside of the center, like learning more about parenting and families.

Referring to higher-order practice as a "smaller goal" sounds paradoxical. But it makes sense if we interpret the distinction Catalina is making here as akin to a harried young parent struggling just to get food on the table versus a more mature parent being able to make a meal that is nutritious and delicious. Catalina's example of a "smaller goal" is getting better at working with parents and understanding the complexity of children's lives outside of school. This goal is smaller in the sense of being less basic, more sophisticated, and more focused. It is smaller in the way the more abstract goals at the top of Maslow's pyramid are smaller than the pyramid's large base.

For most teachers, the transition between stages is gradual and unmarked. But one US teacher, Emily, was able to cite an exact moment when she knew she had become a competent early childhood educator:

I remember not being able to handle or know what to do when a child threw a really bad tantrum. And I would always ask my co-teacher, "Can you please help this one particular child?" And he would. Until one day he just said, "No, you got it." And I'm like, "I do. I got this." I got it. And once I went through it with the child and he came out of it and we were fine, it was like, "Okay, I can handle anything. If I could handle that, I could handle anything." When he said "You got it," I was like, "Okay, you're right. I can. Thank you for that gift of telling me I could handle it and having that trust in me."

Not all of the reflections offered by US interviewees on how teachers change over time were positive. Some saw the movement of teachers through their careers as one with the potential not only for growth but also for stagnation and even decline. In describing the transition from the beginning to more mature stage of preschool teaching, David said, "You start understanding it and you start using it, then you become more *entrenched* in that profession." The explicit meaning here is that, with experience, teachers become truly and securely professional. But the use of *entrenched* rather than, say, *established* is a slip that carries a hint of a less positive trend—namely, the possibility of teachers becoming complacent and inflexible over time. This theme was stated more explicitly by several teachers and directors. For example, Emily said of young teachers, "They're new, and so they're very malleable." Her use of "malleable" here suggests a binary in which young teachers are flexible and older ones are rigid.

This point was made most explicitly by participants in our focus group discussion with early childhood education professors:

HAYASHI: If you picture someone in, say, their third versus, say, fifteenth year . . .

VAIL: I'm actually picturing one in my head right now. She's very comfortable in her role as a teacher and she's good with the kids. But a lot of what I see her do is not really thoughtful about some of the activities and materials that she chooses for kids. And I'm thinking, she's been doing this for so many years that in a sense it's a bit surprising she doesn't choose better activities and materials.

HAYASHI: Do you think she might have been better in her third year?

VAIL: I don't know. It could be that she just thinks, "This is what you do. And this is how I do it." And not really thinking a lot about . . . I don't know how to put it. You . . .

DRESDEN: It becomes automatic instead of . . .

RATAJCZAK: . . . get in a rut.

VAIL: This one I'm picturing, I think it's a rut. She goes to work and this is just what she does. I really don't imagine that there's a lot of forethought. It's almost like, "Okay, these are my kids. This is the kind of the stuff that they could work with." And it's not bad stuff. But it's not really engaging.

HAYASHI: So, confidence and having a bag of tricks can be negative for some people?

VAIL: And I think there's a certain amount of energy and enthusiasm that comes from doing something that's a little bit new, right? That same lesson might once have been great for kids, but when you've done something ten times, then maybe it's just not as fun anymore.

DRESDEN: We think as teachers, you know, "Improve, improve, improve." But then you start to burn out or get tired. So maybe the beginning careers of teachers are more similar, as everyone is getting better those first couple of years. But then after that, there's more individual variation in the direction they go.

HAYASHI: Are you suggesting that there's two kinds of trajectories? Some teachers grow with time, others get comfortable and master of a bunch of tricks and stop adjusting . . .

DRESDEN: Yes, some are like, "What worksheet am I going to pull out and do this time?" or, "What did we do last year?" or, "We're going to do just what we did at this time last year." The flip side of that would be—I'm thinking of a student I taught ten years or so ago and she's loving so much being in the classroom, and she just says, "I'm in my stride. I am now just really getting it after all these years." She's been probably about ten years in the classroom. And she, when you go in her classroom, it is, "Wow." She's using technology in innovative ways, engaging her students, being very thoughtful about her planning and her lessons. She's one of those superior teachers who is not just going through the motions. You do see both types.

Professionalism and De-professionalization

The US system of early childhood education is a patchwork of private and public, national and local, and accredited and non-accredited programs that have different requirements for teacher education, different levels of pay and benefits, and varying turnover rates, which makes it difficult to generalize about the career trajectories of US preschool teachers. There has been a consistent push to professionalize the field (Boyd 2013; Foundation for Child Development 2018; Goffin 2013; National Research Council 2015). In the 1990s, the federally funded Head Start program began to require that teachers have a two-year degree in early childhood education; by the 2000s, Head Start required lead teachers to have a four-year university degree. In state-funded programs and private preschools seeking NAEYC accreditation, there have been similar shifts toward requiring more formal education for teachers.

An irony pointed out by many US interviewees is that as the field has aspired to become more professionalized, the job of being a preschool teacher has been de-professionalized in many ways. Now at points in their careers when they feel most competent, experienced teachers complain that increasingly specific and demanding requirements for documentation, testing, accreditation, learning standards, and scripted curricula give them less latitude to put their expertise into use in their classrooms. These tensions came out in an interview with one of these very experienced teachers, Nancy Siket. I quote her reflection at length because her story reflects much of what I heard from other experienced US teachers about how their jobs are changing in ways that undermine their hard-won expertise. Nancy has thirty-some years of experience teaching in public and university-attached preschool programs in the Phoenix area. When I spoke with her, the child-centered preschool where Nancy had worked for fifteen years had recently been closed, and Nancy and a few other staff members were reassigned to another preschool under the leadership of a director with different priorities:

> When I started out, it was at a preschool that was pretty directive about what the kids had to do, yeah. "We do this, this, and this." It was a very structured curriculum, based on High Scope. And I was new and I bought it. Then I came to the Farmer Preschool and the director, Cheri, always understood and supported the play-based thing. And—I'm giving myself credit here—but I probably tightened things up a little bit, you know, by bringing in the idea that children should plan. I incorporated High Scope ideas. I brought it over with me because I felt comfortable with that, and it made sense to me. And Cheri was really open to a lot of different things. Cheri trusted the people she hired. And then we went through two accreditations with NAEYC. And you know, the last one, they had ramped it up big time. They have really ramped it up. And there was so much paperwork. I mean, doing documentation and paperwork isn't new for me, but these days, it is different. I was used to documenting from my years with High Scope, which has you document tons of stuff. And I always took a lot of pictures. So I was pretty solid on that stuff. But I mean, it's still a lot of work. And for parent-teacher conferences, I had to write up a narrative, three pages for each kid. It's like writing twenty term papers! It took me forever to do those. But I understood why they wanted all that stuff. I understood it.
>
> And then last year, when I moved up here. It's not just the way they expect us to control the kids. It's also the curriculum. Let me tell you. In the United States these days, people are *really* into early academics. And they think that this is the key to success. And in our program now they are having us do these assessments every few weeks. We go through the

whole alphabet with each child, see if they can identify the sounds, the vocabulary, and stuff like that. I said "I'm not doing this with three-year-olds. This is ridiculous." Is it important that you know the whole alphabet at three? I don't think so. Why would you want to know everything before you get to elementary school? Why would you even bother to go if you know everything? Should you really spend your whole life getting ready for the next thing? What about right now? The administration here tried to pressure me on this because they are really into early academics. But I told the director that, you know, "I'm a constructionist. I really am!" At this point in my career, with all my experience, I should be able to speak up and tell the director and the other teachers these things. But the curriculum here is different, and the structure, so they don't really want to listen to me. So I may need to move on.

When the school year ended, Nancy did move on to a church-run preschool. Nancy's concerns are about the impacts various education reforms and policies are having on both children and teachers. The changes she has seen mean that children's lives in preschools are more structured with academics, have more testing, are more controlled, and have less freedom to explore and to create and engage in meaningful learning. She said, in her colorful language, that she had seen lively children enrolled in programs dominated by these new approaches turned catatonic and into robots. She and other teachers are also victims in this dystopian tale, as they must spend much of their day on documentation, paperwork, and testing children, and their teaching is increasingly forced to follow curriculum standards and even to be scripted. Rebecca Buchanan describes the sort of phenomena that Nancy described in a 2015 paper:

> When there was a disconnect, or a lack of fit, between teachers and their school or district, one way that they solved for this tension was by pushing back. Pushing back is a form of teacher resistance (Gitlin and Margonis 1995; Pease-Alvarez and Thompson 2011) where teachers reject, negotiate, or reconfigure particular school and district policies with which they do not agree. (710)

And she continues:

> It also seems that a significantly tighter coupling of policy and classroom practice has occurred. Policies developed outside of the school can change teacher practices and shape their identities. The trade-off in a system of

tight coupling may be that teacher professionalism is sacrificed, because many teachers experience tighter coupling as a loss of professional autonomy. (715)

Interviewees in other focus groups made parallel points about the deteriorating conditions of preschool teaching. Some teachers echoed Nancy's story:

JANNIE: It takes a toll on you, because there are lot more expectations for teachers. You have to do all these things that are expected. Now you have no time to do other things. It's burnout, too.

ELLA: A lot has changed. I remember when play was really important. The amount of documenting that we need to do now is crazy.

FRAN: Those damn *Letter People*!

CHRISTINE: For me, 'cause we have a SFA (Success for All) curriculum and we have TSGs (Teaching Strategies Gold) and we have many other observations, it's hard to let go. We have to be on top of it. One right after another. It's stressful.

US expert interviewees emphasized the negative impacts of policy changes:

EMILY: I think the efforts to professionalize the field, in some kind of perverse ways, have taken teachers away from children.

LIEBERMAN-BETZ: A lot of the policy is moving people in the wrong direction.

DRESDEN: The hopeful trajectory of teachers as they gain experience going from focusing on themselves to focusing on their students gets interrupted and moved in the wrong direction by a lot of policies that are put on teachers now.

VAIL: Teachers have a desire to do their jos well. But I think what's happening is, when it's pushed down from above and they're forced to do it, and you have to implement that new policy right away, and then the training comes afterwards. Part of where that whole idea of resistance to change comes from is that it's shoved down their throats as opposed to "Hey, this is something I would have really liked to learn more about and really liked to work on as a professional to improve my practice."

LIEBERMAN-BETZ: We've laid new demands on top of other teaching tasks without really considering what our first and most important values were. Some of those ideas might appeal to teachers, but the level of tension in the room because of the political context overshadows any of the content.

RATAJCZAK: And they feel like, "What's coming next?"

LIEBERMAN-BETZ: Yeah. They feel like, "I just learned this, but now I'm going to learn something that's going to contradict it, so why bother even listening?"

RATAJCZAK: If we take teachers' agency away, then their desire to grow, to change, to learn—we've just smooshed their initiative.

Passion and Commitment

As Nancy related, the job of preschool teaching can be frustrating. The frustration leads some teachers to burn out. However, I saw no hints of loss of passion or commitment in the comments from any of the experienced teachers we interviewed. Frustration, yes; burnout, no. Some tactical accommodations, yes; but no giving up or giving in. The experienced early childhood educators quoted most in this chapter, Jannie and Fran, as well as David, Catalina, and Nancy, are strong, enthusiastic, committed, and passionate early childhood educators. They are battle-scarred, but also battle-toughened after years on the front lines of US early childhood education. I acknowledge a selection bias at work here: we interviewed no experienced educators who found the job so frustrating that they quit the profession; moreover, each of the programs where we interviewed teachers are accredited and of relatively high quality. If these programs were not so, my interviewees would no longer be working at them. Although my participants are not typical of the US early childhood education labor force in these senses, I argue they are representative of a sector within this labor force: certified teachers who have worked for many years in accredited programs.

The contemporary political context of early childhood education in the US, as I have shown above, sometimes has the effect of undermining the expertise of experienced teachers. On the other hand, the central takeaway from this chapter is that experienced US preschools teachers carry their expertise in them and with them. As a teacher moves through her career, she gets help from and learns from others along the way, but her expertise is something she has and owns. Curriculum and policy changes come and go, as do administrators. But a teacher's expertise survives. Part of this expertise is the effective ways of being with children they acquire. Part is knowing how to manage their own professional growth and development. And part is knowing how to navigate the system and how to deal with pressures from parents, administrators, and policy makers. In de Certeau's terms, teachers become skillful tacticians in the practice of everyday preschool life. Compared to policy makers, these teachers are politically weak, but with their years of experience dealing not only with young children but also with reforms, supervisors, and requirements, they have developed expertise not only for teaching children but also for resisting pressures from above that they feel impoverish the lives of the young children in their care.

When they were younger and less experienced, they did not yet have the confidence to resist. As Nancy said about her first job in a preschool with a highly directive High Scope curriculum, "I was young, so I bought it." Describing her acquiescence as a young teacher to a directive curriculum as having "bought it" implies a kind of gullibility and vulnerability to manipulation in her early career, as well as its opposite: the savviness and backbone she acquired over the years that enabled her to respond aggressively to directives she received in her recent job that she felt were bad for children. As their confidence and knowledge grows, experienced teachers develop a strong belief in their understanding of what's best for children, the utility of their own practices, and their reading of the politics and power of their situation, which allows them to choose their battles, giving in on less crucial things while holding the line on others. Because their expertise is inside them and transferrable to wherever they work, if necessary, preschool teachers can change jobs when they reach the conclusion, as Nancy did, that their current situation no longer gives them the latitude they need to teach in the way they believe best. Experienced teachers are very rarely fired for insubordination. If things get bad enough, while some do leave the field, many move on to new jobs in settings they feel will be less restrictive. The commitment and passion of these experienced teachers is impressive. Those US teachers who make it through the first stage of teaching emerge with confidence and determination. If they had stopped caring, they would not be so passionate about what they see as wrong-headed policy and curriculum changes. If they were burned out, they wouldn't care so deeply. Their words show their continuing passion, commitment, and wisdom.

5 Looking across Three Countries

In this concluding chapter, I step back and look across the interviews with experienced Chinese, Japanese, and US early childhood educators and identify differences and similarities in definitions of expertise, trajectories of change with experience, and the structural and cultural factors that they report support and, in some cases, impede professional growth. I conclude by suggesting that my findings may also apply to teachers in other countries, to levels of education beyond preschool, and to other fields of practice.

Pedagogical Expertise across the Three Countries

One challenge when conducting comparative research across countries is determining whether interviewees intended the same notion in using different language and vocabulary. This is a complex issue. For example, are "letting go" and "holding back" the same? Or, what exactly should be considered the equivalent of "let it go" outside of the US? The US participants' versions of "letting go" are a combination of two different but related things: one is letting go of the need to control children and the other is being more present in the moment. In the words of US teachers, "let it go" sometimes means "let go of the need to control/mediate children," and sometimes it means "be less hectic, less anxious, less in one's own head." The first is akin to what Japanese participants called *mimamoru*; the second is similar to *jibun de ippai*. In all three countries, participants described both of these two dimensions of expertise (having a lighter touch with children, being more relaxed and less anxious, and being more in the present and less in one's head).

In terms of vocabulary, there is some question as to whether the terms that emerged from the interviews for this study—Disney citations or Taoist and Zen terminology—will retain the same meanings with the passage of time.. There are terms used by the participants that were particularly related to the current context, such as "let it go." The interviews were conducted around the time the Disney movie *Frozen* was popular with children, and the US preschool teachers often used this line from the movie's most popular song in describing aspects of how they loosened up with experience. But the US participants also talked about this loosening up using other phrases and metaphors, including "be more relaxed," "hold back," "trust the kids," "no one's bleeding" (meaning there is no need to intervene), and "give the kids more room." The vocabulary might change with time, but I suggest that the core concepts are likely to transcend eras.

I still pay attention to the nuances and contexts of each language and set of vocabulary when I make comparisons, but the core argument here is not about the actual terminology; it is about the notions that the terminology embodies. In all three countries, participants used a range of words, metaphors, and tropes to describe what I am suggesting are dimensions of the same larger directionality of teaching expertise with experience.

The six Japanese, Chinese, and US teachers featured in this study were pedagogically dissimilar when the research team filmed them in 2002 during the early stages of their careers. The interviews with them conducted in 2015 show that they were still unalike. And yet, after watching videos of themselves teaching thirteen years earlier, these six teachers described having moved along similar trajectories. Looking across the interviews with the 112 educators in Japan, China, and the US suggests that they are describing much the same constellation of skills, perspectives, and habits of mind. In the sections that follow, I organize their reflections under five core concepts, with examples of the form each takes in each country.

A SENSE OF COMPOSURE

After watching the opening scenes of the video the research team shot in her classroom in Kyoto thirteen years earlier, Chisato Morita exclaimed in a tone that mixed surprise and chagrin, "Yoyū ga nakatta!" (I was in a rush!). As explained in the Japan chapter, the phrase Morita used here, can mean both not having adequate time to deal with the tasks at hand and experiencing the subjective sense of rushing more than is necessary. In this second sense, the phrase is similar to comments US participants made about feeling frantic as young teachers and comments from Chinese teachers about have felt overwhelmed in their first few years on the job by their duties and responsibilities. Veteran teachers in all three countries described themselves, as young teachers, both failing to keep up with their tasks and feeling *as if* they were failing to keep up and, therefore, needing to rush.

For example, David Jones, a veteran US teacher of over twenty years, described the younger version of himself as moving around the classroom "like a chicken with his head chopped off." Gwen Dufault described her earlier teaching as "zing zing zooming" and her colleagues concurred, joking that they "had to steal her Mountain Dew to slow her down." Sonya Gaches described the opposite of such franticness as the calmness that comes to veteran teachers with the awareness that they can be effective without needing to always be *doing* something. Veteran teachers were described by Chinese interviewees as *congrong*, which can be translated into English as "calm." These comments suggest that with experience, teachers reach a point at which they are no longer overwhelmed by a sense of "so little time and so much to do," and that they come to realize that they can be more effective by slowing down. As discussed in the sections that follow, this sense of slowing down and having adequate time for tasks is related to the ability to read classrooms more quickly and know what is important and what can be let go.

BEING IN THE MOMENT

Defining the essential quality of the practice of psychoanalysis, Winfred Bion wrote:

> Psychoanalytic observation is concerned neither with what has happened nor with what is going to happen, but with what is happening. . . . The psychoanalyst should aim at achieving a state of mind so that at every session he feels he has not seen the patient before. (1967, 243–44)

Substituting "preschool practitioner" for "psychoanalyst," this observation fits nicely with the reflections of Japanese, Chinese, and US early childhood practitioners on how they change with experience:

> *Educational* observation is concerned neither with what has happened nor with what is going to happen, but with what is happening. . . . The *preschool practitioner* should aim at achieving a state of mind so that at every day she feels like she has not seen the children before (substitute words in italic by the author).

In other words, as they acquire experience, preschool teachers become more *present*. Experienced educators from all three countries described this sense of presence using similar concepts and metaphors. Fran Smith suggested that with experience, she became more "In the moment." Cindy Vail of the University of Georgia used gestures to dramatize what it means to be present: "[Beginning teachers] are *in here* (touching her head), thinking about their own performance rather than (fanning her fingers out and away from her) *out there*, paying attention to the effect of their performance on their kids. You're not worried about past or future. You're *here*."

Several interviewees described the mental state of experienced teachers using the metaphor of throwing away scripts or rule books that prevented them from being fully present and in the moment as young teachers. For example, Director Hironori Yoshizawa said to Morita, "It seems like twelve years ago, you tried to do everything in the proper way. It's like you were following all the rules, according to the way you were taught at the university." Sonya Gaches suggested a more dramatic metaphor for the voices young teachers cannot get out of their heads:

> When you are starting out and you get your own classroom, you're still kind of carrying those ghosts with you. Here you are, you're supposed to be your own teacher, and yet you've got those ghosts in your head. [. . .] This creates tension in young teachers because they are trying to find their own voice, their own way, but they've got the ghost voices talking to them.

Many Japanese interviewees characterized beginning teachers by using the phrase *jibun de ippai*, which literally means "full of myself," but which I translate as "preoccupied by my own thoughts" or "too much in my head." Morita, faulting her earlier teaching for being too teacher-centered and rigid, attributed these shortcomings to her self-absorption and constant need to fill her classroom's time and space:

> I talked too much. I was frenetic. I felt compelled to keep filling the space with my talking. It's like I was following a script. There was no time or space for the children's reactions. I was too preoccupied with my own thoughts (*jibun de ippai*).

Director Eri Kamisakamoto of Ochanomizu University Kindergarten commented:

> It's crucial to face the aspect of ourselves that faces children. When we are young, we tend to be full of ourselves (*jibun de ippai*). Ears that don't catch children's whispers. Eye that don't see children. [. . .] It's like, "My focus isn't on the children, but me."

Her colleague Akemi Miyasato added, "It seems like we are thinking about children, when actually we're thinking about ourselves."

Several Chinese educators drew on Taoist principles to describe the state of experienced teachers' thinking. For example, Teacher Yuan praised Cheng for her spontaneity, which she ascribed to Cheng having transcended the self-consciousness characteristic of younger teachers:

> We can say that with experience, Cheng has reached the point where she can act automatically, without needing to think consciously (*ziranerran* 自然而然). It takes years of experience to teach so naturally and spontaneously.

These comments are consistent with the findings of Xiangming Chen (2015), who writes of Chinese pedagogy that teachers can become "thoughtfully thoughtless" with experience. They can learn to empty their minds of conscious attention and intention and, as a result, be more effective. It takes years of experience to teach so naturally and spontaneously. A US preschool director, Amelia Wright, made a similar point: "When you're a new teacher, you're somebody else. You're a scripted teacher, right? You need to become conscious of the teacher you want to be, of being yourself, in order to become less conscious."

FLEXIBILITY

The tendency of younger teachers to be bound by rules and scripts leads to a rigidity, a lack of ability to adjust one's pedagogy to different children and situations and to respond to the unexpected. As a preschool director said of Jannie Umeda upon seeing her 2002 video, "She's still a little rigid and rule-bound." The word "still" here implies that such rigidity is characteristic of teachers earlier in their careers. A US professor of early childhood education commented, "There's a more relaxed, responding-in-the-moment quality to a teacher who's more mature, who's able to say, 'Yeah, there's this rule about how you do it. But maybe I'm not going to follow the rule this time.'" Mariko Kaizuka said in reaction to seeing herself as a younger teacher, "You don't have only one way to deal with children." Professor Hiroshi Usui commented, "Beginning teachers tend to treat all children the same way. With experience, teachers gradually get better at noticing differences among children, and then they can begin to treat different children differently." Professor Takako Kawabe detailed the variety of roles teachers need to play and suggested a timetable for the development of this ability:

Teachers must take up various positions. Sometimes we have to be face to face with a child; the next time side by side, to give us and the child the same line of sight, so we can see and feel the same things. Sometimes we have to go ahead and be a model. And sometimes we have to be behind the children, to *mimamoru* (hold back). It takes time to recognize these four positions, and then another seven or eight years to be able to adjust positions unconsciously, depending on the situation.

Chinese early childhood educators made similar points:

Younger teachers will put something they learned at university into practice, but they don't have the ability to change very quickly (*sui ji ying bian*). The difference between them is that an experienced teacher would notice children's moods, the challenges that children are facing, and help children solve problems. She would change her strategies when the first one isn't working.

Several Chinese interviewees suggested that such flexibility is a key component of what they called the "practical wisdom" (*shijian*) that can only be learned with experience. Professor Yong Jiang of East China Normal University connected such flexible, practical wisdom to the concept of pedagogical tact:

The Canadian educational phenomenologist, Max van Manen, wrote a book we translated and published here. It is about the tact of teaching. It also could be called *jizhi*, which is usually translated into English as "wit," but which we also use as a Chinese translation of "tact." In English, it is what Schwab called "flexible habits of mind." There is no doubt that experienced teachers would have more of this kind of wisdom.

HOLDING BACK

Many of the Chinese, Japanese, and US interviewees cited the ability to hold back as the practice that most distinguishes veteran from beginning teachers. I am suggesting not that experienced Japanese, Chinese and American teachers hold back in the same ways or to the same extent, but rather that experienced educators in all three countries intervene less quickly and aggressively than they did when they were younger. Previous studies (Lewis 1989; Tobin, Hsueh, and Karasawa 2009; Hayashi and Tobin 2015) have shown that *mimamoru* (watching and waiting) is a pedagogical strategy widely endorsed by

Japanese early childhood educators. Interviews for this study add a temporal dimension to our understanding of *mimamoru*, as many Japanese interviewees argued that while younger teachers generally appreciate *mimamoru* as a concept, it takes many years before they can employ this strategy effectively. As Director Ritsuko Kumagai put it, "For a teacher to be able to really do *mimamoru*, it takes at least five years."

Reflecting on the video of herself teaching thirteen years earlier, Morita was critical of how, as a young teacher, she offered more help than was needed when her students struggled with their art projects. Kaizuka was disturbed by the heaviness the younger version of herself brought to mediating the aftermath of a hair-pulling fight. Watching scenes from their 2002 and 2015 videos side by side, both teachers were struck by how much better they had become at resisting the impulse to offer assistance more quickly and aggressively than what they had come to view as necessary or beneficial.

The *Preschool in Three Cultures* studies (Tobin, Wu, and Davidson 1989; Tobin, Hsueh, and Karasawa 2009) presented examples of Chinese and US practitioners making critical comments about scenes in Japanese classroom videos where, in their opinion, teachers failed to mediate children's disputes. Thus, I was surprised to find Chinese and US interviewees in this study praising the value of teachers holding back. Having previously conceived of *mimamoru* as an emic Japanese pedagogical concept, I now see it as a Japanese variation of a practice that is characteristic of experienced teachers. I am not suggesting that with experience, Chinese and US teachers come to hold back as much as their Japanese counterparts do, but rather I suggest that in all three countries, teachers move along similar trajectories, toward intervening less often and less aggressively when children struggle than they did when they were starting out in their careers. With experience, Chinese and US teachers report intervening less soon and less aggressively than they did when they were younger, but still sooner and more aggressively than their Japanese counterparts.

Watching her old video, Fran was critical of the habit she had as a young teacher of "rescuing" her students when they struggled. Experienced early childhood educators in the US who commented on Jannie's teaching in her 2002 video were critical of her overly zealous interventions with children, suggesting that she should have given her students more latitude to solve their problems. Many of the US educators, perhaps citing a lyric from *Frozen*, described their pedagogy of holding back using the phrase "let it go." For example, a veteran teacher of over twenty years described himself as "a big letter-go-er." Jannie often used the phrase "let go" in describing her evolution as a teacher: "Over the years, you learn to let go more, having them doing more, and I do less," "Helping them at the beginning and letting it go. Then I'm just watching and observing," and "Now I like to see what happens if I let it go. I just provide some scaffolding."

Watching a scene from her 2002 video in which she leads the children in a debrief of an altercation that had occurred during dramatic play, Jian Wang commented that with experience, she came to question the value of such interventions. A Chinese preschool director described a pedagogical skill of expert teachers as *fangshou* (放手). This term, which combines the characters for "release" and "hand," is usually translated into English as "let go." Several Chinese educators used the concept of *wuwei* (inaction) to describe a kind of artful holding back:

> All the teacher should do is create the necessary conditions for the children to thrive in her classroom. When an experienced teacher achieves a state of *wuwei*, she is able to make the choice to do nothing, or we can say, nothing other than to act naturally and just go with the flow of the children in her classroom.

My colleague Bing Xiao explained, "*Wuweierzhi* (ruling by inaction) does not mean to do nothing; it means to intervene as little as possible. It requires the teacher to know and respect children's ability and potential. Let the children discover, even destroy. Even when they fail, they learn from their failures." I suggest that *mimamoru, fangshou, wuweierzhi,* and "letting go" refer to much the same pedagogical concept: an ability that comes with experience to offer the minimum assistance necessary when children are struggling and, in this way, to give children the maximum opportunity to learn and grow.

Why does it take so many years to be able to let go? Interviewees pointed to many factors. One is the difficulty young teachers have in judging the seriousness of situations that arise in their classrooms, resulting in more frequent interventions than is necessary. Younger teachers are often anxious to both be and appear to be helpful to children, a belief related to the idea that good teaching requires constant activity. As teachers gain an understanding of children's resourcefulness and resilience, they feel less of a need to intervene when children struggle. Younger teachers less secure of themselves and their position may fear being accused of being negligent by supervisors or parents. Finally, less experienced teachers may fear that if they do not intervene quickly and aggressively, their classroom may spin out of control.

Experienced early childhood educators described teachers as not only gradually becoming more competent and confident but also getting better at communicating their competence to children, thereby putting the children they teach at ease. As Jacob Kounin (1970) suggested with his concept of "withitness," effective teachers are not only aware of what their students are up to but are also adept at letting their students know that they are aware. This combination of simultaneously being and appearing aware was cited in various ways by interviewees in all three countries as a meta-level characteristic of experienced teachers, one that combines the traits I have discussed above: composure, flexibility, being in the moment, holding back, and letting go.

Preschool teachers and their students are continuously reading and reacting to each other's moods, desires, and intentions, which they intuit not only from words but also from embodied actions. Responding to video cues, interviewees in all three countries pointed to the impacts a teacher's gestures, facial expressions, and postures have on students. For example, Professor Kawabe commented on Kaizuka's then-and-now video:

KAWABE: Her facial expressions are so different! This [pointing to the 2002 video] is such a scary, scary face. The frowning eyes and mouth. This is a face that makes children feel they can't say what they want to say. In contrast, here [pointing to the 2015 video] her face makes the children feel comfortable to draw close to her.

HAYASHI: The differences are subtle.

KAWABE: Yes, but children read these small differences.

As Tobin and I wrote in *Teaching Embodied*:

Teachers can modulate the degree to which they are present to children by adjusting their location in the classroom and the attitude of their body, with a posture that communicates attention, concern, casualness, or distraction. A skilled teacher strategically performs various levels of paying attention. If children seem too aware of her and dependent on her, the teacher adjusts her gaze and posture to appear to be too busy with a task to pay careful attention to them. In contrast, when a teacher senses children are about to spin out of control, she adjusts her appearance to seem to be paying more attention. Teachers also use posture, head tilting, touching, and other body adjustments, in addition to eye contact, to signal levels of attention/ inattention. (Hayashi and Tobin 2015, 24)

A group of early childhood educators in Honolulu commented on the way skilled teachers use their gaze and position:

EMILY: I love to watch seasoned teachers in action because I always learn a lot from them and pick up some new tricks, like the way they address a situation, even the way they give a look to a child.
CHARLOTTE: You learn you can just walk over to them and stand there.
SOPHIA: I've learned that for some of them, me just moving two inches to the left does the trick. For others, I'm going to just come stand right behind them and then they're that much more focused or engaged.

Morita and Kaizuka similarly noticed differences in their uses of posture and facial expressions earlier and later in their careers, differences that were subtle and yet, they suggested, crucial to how their students reacted to them.

In addition to using the performance of different levels of attentiveness to cue students, teachers also need to learn to direct their attention, a skill that can feel overwhelming to a young teacher faced with monitoring fifteen or more children who may be scattered across a classroom or playground. For example, a Chinese kindergarten director commented, "An important difference between new and experienced teachers is their field of vision (*shiye* 视野). Where a new teacher may see a single point, an experienced teacher can see a space." Another director said, "From watching the video, I can tell that Teacher Cheng must be a very experienced teacher. She can pay attention to all aspects of children. When she is taking care of the children, she has this kind of awareness. She pays attention to many things at once." Jannie emphasized the importance of learning to scan the classroom:

In the beginning, you don't know what to look at. When you are scanning, it's really complicated. It's not like simply, "Just look." You might tell a new teacher, "Look around," but it's a process that takes time. Over the years, it's gotten a lot easier to scan the whole room.

Commenting on Morita's teaching of an origami lesson in 2002, her supervisor, Takaya Nogami, pointed out that her preoccupation as a young teacher with getting children to pay attention to her instructions prevented her from being able to really see her students: "It seems that at that time, you were so focused on what you had to do that you hadn't reached the point where you could *see* each child. Your focus was only on getting the attention of the group." Reflecting on her handling of a hair-pulling argument, Kaizuka and her supervisor, Taro Machiyama, observed that like many young teachers, she had trouble distributing her attention between the two boys who were fighting and the rest of the class, a skill they agreed comes only after years of experience.

The combination of becoming skillful at both performing and paying attention produces the ability to manage a classroom with a light touch. Many interviewees in all three countries reported having struggled as young teachers with managing a whole class. Chinese educators emphasized the importance of a teacher learning to balance *fangshou* (letting go) with *na xia* (literally, to hold down or to capture). As my colleague Lin Chen explained:

> In Buddhism and Taoism, there are metaphors that suggest that letting go is more effective than trying to hold something too tight. [. . .] In teaching, trying to teach a lesson or control a class will go better if the approach is looser, more empty, more embodied, spontaneous and natural, and in harmony with the setting and the children.

US educators made similar points using different metaphors, arguing that younger teachers are so afraid of losing control of their classrooms that they err on either the side of being too lax or too strict. For example, a veteran teacher educator commented:

> I think teachers become more comfortable with letting kids have more control. Early on, teachers feel like they need to be running the show so that they have control. Whereas later, they can learn and feel more comfortable with "If I let children do this, I'm still not going to lose the ship."

Gwen reflected on how she changed after her first several years of teaching:

> With experience, I guess what exudes from you to those young children becomes different. It's like my control during group times is effortless now. I don't mean that I'm like Attila the Hun, you know, yelling at them, "You be quiet and sit!" It's not like that all. It's something very different. I don't know if it's the look on my face, the tone in my voice, or how I say it, but now I have control without needing to yell.

Putting these different dimensions of "withitness" together and looking across the three countries, we can say that with experience, teachers become better at finding just the right balance between holding tight and letting go. As argued above, a general trajectory of teachers in all three countries is toward intervening less often and less aggressively. We can now add more nuance to this argument by suggesting that experienced teachers in all three countries hold tight to their classrooms while appearing to hold back. A teacher who, earlier in her career, needed to raise her voice to settle her class down or to interrupt the flow of an activity to reprimand an individual child after years of experience can settle down her class or cue a misbehaving child with just an artful glance or a change of posture. As Xiangming Chen writes:

> To use Laozi's metaphor, a bowl is comprised of a substantive wall outside and an empty space inside. The visible wall only provides a condition for the invisible space to function as a bowl. The empty space is more crucial than the wall for the bowl to be a bowl. Similarly, these teachers' non-action is like the empty space provided to their students, while their action is like the wall of a bowl. It is in their adequate interplay between non-action and action that brings their students' learning to a fuller play. (2015, 198)

In other words, accomplished teachers, each in their own way, create a not-always-immediately-visible scaffolding that supports their students' learning and development and that allows them to intervene rarely and with a light touch.

The right balance between holding tight and letting go varies country by country, teacher by teacher, and activity by activity. In her comparison of bodily practices in Chinese and US preschools, Chang Liu (2017) found that Chinese teachers who keep a loose grip on their class during free play are strict during daily group exercise (*guangbo ticau*). Japanese preschools also have a version of group exercise (*rajio taisō*), but unlike their Chinese counterparts, Japanese teachers rarely correct children's movements during group exercise. In contrast, Japanese teachers tend to give more structure to morning greeting and afternoon departure rituals than do teachers in China and the US.

Tightness-and-looseness is a relative concept. What may seem like a tight hold on a classroom to a Japanese or US observer may seem loose by Chinese standards. The degree to which an experienced Japanese teacher holds back from intervening in children's disputes may seem extreme to Chinese or US observers. And the percentage of time an American teacher spends on one-to-one attention to her students may seem to Chinese and Japanese observers to be insufficiently attentive to her class as a community. Visits to classrooms of experienced teachers in Japan, China, and the US would not give one the impression that their pedagogical approaches are the same. And yet beneath the visible differences, there is a core of shared characteristics of pedagogical expertise, including an ability rarely found in beginning teachers to convey a sense of composure, flexibility, being in the moment, holding back, and being aware and conveying awareness.

Contextual Factors in Teachers' Professional Growth

I argued in the section above that Japanese, Chinese, and US teachers follow similar trajectories of professional growth. However, this study shows that the sources of support for their growth and the shapes of their career paths are quite different, reflecting differences in political, bureaucratic, social, and cultural factors. One major factor is the pace of educational reform. In times and places where rapid social change is accompanied by dramatic redefinitions of values and knowledge, the expertise that comes with age and experience loses value (Mead 1978). This has been the case over the past several decades in China, where waves of curricular reforms and educational paradigm shifts can turn notions about the relationship of experience to expertise on its head, with newly minted teachers trained in the latest government-mandated paradigm seen as sources of guidance for more experienced colleagues who were trained in approaches now considered out of date. On the other hand, the trendy knowledge of younger practitioners is a currency that rapidly loses its value when the next wave of educational reform hits. Meanwhile, what Chinese interviewees described as the "practical wisdom" of veteran teachers survives reforms and paradigm changes. While the pace of social and educational change in the US is markedly slower than it is in China, some veteran US teachers similarly described to me how top-down policy directives have worked to undermine their hard-won professional expertise, requiring them to employ packaged and even scripted curricula and to conduct forms of student evaluations and documentation that impede their ability to take full advantage of the expertise that has come with experience. In Japan, where early childhood education has experienced relatively little reform to curriculum or shifts in pedagogy over the past several decades, no interviewees reported more recently trained teachers being valued over veterans or policy directives constraining experienced teachers from employing their expertise.

Differences across the three countries in the status of preschool teachers impact definitions of expertise. In China, there is a system for evaluating and even quantifying teaching expertise tied to merit pay increases. Each year, every teacher is given a score on their pedagogy. While individual teachers may privately complain about having been judged unfairly by a particular evaluator, the system is generally accepted to be fair and beneficial. For example, in a discussion in Shanghai with experienced early childhood educators, the participant who had earned the designation of "first prize for excellent teaching" was treated with respect and deference by her fellow focus group members. In Japan, where rating and ranking teachers is unheard of, professional expertise is generally assumed to be closely tied to years of experience. In the US, increased demands for teacher accountability have had, in some situations, the effect of de-professionalizing teaching. As Rebecca Buchanan (2015) writes:

> Current policies that require value-added accountability measures aimed at evaluating teachers tend to isolate and quantify the value that individual teachers add to their students in order to rank and compare their effectiveness (Collins, 2012; Cuban, 2013; Harris, 2011). Contemporary education reform foregrounds instrumentalist notions of the teachers' role, which de-professionalizes the work of teachers (Mockler, 2011). (2015, 702)

Another major structural difference impacting teaching expertise is job stability. Most of my US interviewees reported having changed employers several times over the course of their careers and many even had to cope with the closing of their programs. In the US, where teacher turnover in early childhood education is very high and job changes are frequent (Bellm et al. 2002; Phillips, Austin, and Whitebook 2016; Whitebook and Bellm 1999), preschool teachers tend to see themselves as the agents of their own professional development and career advancement. In this context, expertise becomes something, like a resume, that belongs to the individual teacher that they can build on from one position to the next. Japanese preschool teachers move from one school to another much less often. After working for many years in the same programs where they began their careers, Japanese teachers come to think of their teaching ability as highly contextual and to define expertise not so much an individual quality as the ability to function effectively as a member of a team (Rappleye and Komatsu 2017). As Morita commented, "I don't know if I would be a good teacher at another *hoikuen*. I just know that I have learned how to teach well here at Komatsudani." In China, while teachers in public-sector preschools have the security of lifetime employment, rapid expansion of the early childhood sector, coupled with the rise of the private, for-profit sector, has created opportunities for changing jobs, often with the incentive of a higher-paid administrative role in a new school. A positive side of this dynamic is the spread of teaching expertise from the highly respected programs from which the accomplished teachers are recruited to less highly ranked programs hoping to improve.

What Supports Professional Growth

Preschool teachers in all three countries reported that they attended workshops, learned from colleagues and directors, and improved gradually from experience. However, across the three countries, these sources of support for professional development take different forms. We can conceptualize these differences along three continua: from high touch to low touch influences from authorities and mentors; from professional development as an individual pursuit to a collective pursuit; and from professional development as motivated more by extrinsic factors to more intrinsic factors. Using these conceptual categories, the Chinese approach can be characterized as high touch, extrinsic, and moderately collective; the Japanese approach as low touch, intrinsic, and highly collective; and the US approach as highly individualistic, with a mix of intrinsic and extrinsic motivations and high touch and low touch direction from others.

Lynn Paine, who has conducted research in all three countries on professional development in mathematics instruction, suggested conceptualizing the Chinese approach to providing critical feedback to young teachers as "high touch" rather than as "hierarchical" or "aggressive." This perspective suggests that Chinese supervisors are not less supportive than their counterparts in Japan and the US, but rather that they have different ways of being supportive. Providing critical feedback is seen in Chinese professional development, as in Chinese early childhood education (Tobin, Hsueh, and Karasawa 2009) and other domains, as a central component of good pedagogy and a way of showing one's concern (*guan*). Some Chinese teachers reported having been at times stung by criticisms from their director or other experts, but none suggested that such criticisms were inappropriate or unhelpful. The logic that criticism plays a vital role in the improvement of practice is a deeply ingrained, implicit pedagogical belief in Chinese culture.

High touch in the professional development of preschool teachers in China takes several forms: Directors do not hesitate to criticize mistakes of teachers. Teachers are observed and evaluated each year by outside experts as well as by their directors and given scores on a range of teaching measures; teachers also receive verbal and written narrative feedback and notes for improvement. Mentoring is high touch in the sense that it is specific, frequent, and critical.

There are many explicitly extrinsic incentives built into the fabric of Chinese professional development. Scores from the annual assessments of teachers are used in merit pay determinations. Excelling in teacher ratings can be a route to professional advancement, including, eventually, for a few, achieving the rank of "expert teacher," which brings not just higher pay but also acclaim and influence. Schools as well as individual teachers get scored each year, which gives directors a great incentive to provide critical feedback and advice to teachers they anticipate may contribute to their program falling short of receiving a high rating. In turn, the rating has implications for how much tuition a school can charge and how many children it will be able to enroll.

Schools as well as individual teachers receive annual ratings, which reflects the balance in Chinese professional development between a focus on the growth of individual teachers and on the school staff as a collective. This stands in contrast to the case in Japan, where professional growth is closely tied to being a member of a team of teachers, and the case in the US, where professional development is much more an individual than a collective pursuit.

Professional development in Japan is low touch. The implicit pedagogical assumption that leads Japanese directors to give minimal feedback to teachers is the same logic that leads Japanese teachers to be less aggressive than their counterparts in China and the US in intervening in disputes among children. This philosophy and practice of *mimamoru* (holding back) was most succinctly expressed by the lead teacher at Komatsudani, Nogami, who told us that when he sees a young teacher struggling in a classroom he tells the teachers "as little as possible."

However, this Japanese low touch approach to scaffolding teachers' professional development does not mean that there is an absence of critical reflection. Japanese teachers, both individually and in groups, engage in *hansei*, which literally means "self-reflection" but in practice here means "self-critique." We can say that one reason Japanese supervisors and mentors give so little criticism to younger teachers is that they are leaving space for teachers to engage in self-critique. Just as Japanese teachers hold back from intervening when children struggle to communicate, because it is the children's responsibility to work out their own problems, Japanese supervisors hold back from giving critique because they want teachers to know that it is the teachers, as individuals and as a group, who bear the primary responsibility for identifying and addressing shortcomings.

Hansei among teachers in Japan is both formal and informal. Most *yōchien* employ a preschool version of lesson study, in which a group of teachers working with the same age children meet to plan, critique, and improve their curriculum and pedagogy. They usually call this activity *ennai kenshū* (inhouse study groups) rather than *jugyō kenkyū* (lesson study) because they conceive of their curriculum as being composed more of activities than of lessons. An implicit logic here is that criticism is more useful and welcomed when it comes from oneself and one's peers than from above.

Most workshops for teachers in Japan are in-house, with a school's whole staff learning together. These workshops are consistent with the collectivity and incrementalism of Japanese preschool teachers' professional development, in which the focus is on the staff as a whole striving to ever more sincerely and effectively embrace their program's approach. There is no punishment or reward structure in Japanese early childhood education that would provide extrinsic motivations for teachers to pursue professional development—there is no merit pay and no custom of building one's own resume in order to move to a higher paying, more prestigious, or more influential position. What most drives the professional development of a preschool teacher in Japan is a sense of having a responsibility to one's school and to one's fellow teachers to do one's share as well as one can.

Professional development in the US features a variety of extrinsic motivators, including compulsory workshops, formal evaluations by both directors and outside program accreditors, and increases in salary tied to completing university coursework and earning further degrees. While US early childhood education increasingly features such extrinsic reward structures, teachers attempt to control the amount of time and effort they put into responding to these extrinsic factors. US interviewees made it clear that they view themselves as the ones most in charge of their own professional development.

Many US interviewees reported having learned from a mentor they informally selected, usually a more experienced colleague they would go to for pedagogical and career advice, encouragement, and commiseration. Some reported receiving useful advice from their director, but many more spoke of times when they resented getting unsolicited feedback or directives from someone who held authority over them. Mentoring was seen as most effective when it was unassociated with unequal power relationships and extrinsic consequences. For these reasons, we can describe the preferred form of mentoring in the US as low touch, mixed with some undesired high touch from directors.

Most US interviewees said they found workshops much less helpful when they were compelled to attend than when they went of their own volition. Some reported appreciating opportunities to engage in professional development activities with their fellow staff members, while others complained about having to extend their work time to attend compulsory workshops. Several interviewees described attending a workshop or taking a course as a turning point in their professional development. They speculated that this had as much to do with their being at a stage in their career when they were ready to change as it did with the strength of the workshop or course. Fran, for example, related that after several years of teaching in a relatively traditional way, she found herself dissatisfied with her approach and was therefore open to trying something new, which led her to enroll in a course at her local college that introduced her to a new paradigm that profoundly shaped her professional growth in subsequent years.

What is most striking about the professional development strategies of preschool teachers in the US compared to China and Japan is the degree to which they describe it as an individual pursuit. Many experienced US teachers reported having enrolled in university degree programs on their own, attending evening classes after full days of work. With a new degree in hand, many moved on to higher-paid positions at other schools. In this sense, US preschool teachers view their professional development as an investment in themselves, an undertaking that makes them a more effective practitioner while also adding new lines to their resume, which will open up new professional possibilities. Their career ladders are based on extrinsic motivators, but within this structure, teachers' professional development is also fueled by their intrinsic motivations, including the individual importance they place on becoming more accomplished professionals.

Life Happens

Between their third and sixteenth years of teaching, many preschool teachers have children (as did three of the six teachers featured in this study). During this interval, they also grow older and gain experience in the classroom. It is therefore difficult to separate the effects on teaching expertise of professional development from the effects of parenting and other life events, including aging. Nevertheless, several interviewees drew direct connections between their having become a parent and their growth as a teacher. They reported how the experience of parenting gave them a more rounded understanding of children and a more sympathetic view of their students' parents, while at the same time giving them greater credibility in parents' eyes. In one particularly lively discussion in Honolulu, a group of experienced early childhood educators reflected on the impact of having a child on their teaching. After several teachers commented on how becoming a parent gave them a richer understanding of children, another, Lani Au, wondered if this was true in her case:

> I was a better teacher before I had my kids because now I care more about my own kids than other people's kids. Once I had my kids I wanted to get home to them as fast as I could, so I left school as soon as I could. So they got more out of me before I had kids!

This comment led the participants in this focus group to discuss how having a child of one's own can work to free one from needing one's students' love and approval, which in turn can have a liberating effect on one's teaching. In other words, parenting, like other life events, has a complicated relationship with the development of professional expertise. The teachers in this study who became parents tend to credit parenting with contributing to their expertise; teachers who did not have children attribute their growth to other factors.

Complicating the Relationship of Experience to Expertise

Each of the six teachers featured in this study reported having become a much better teacher between their third and sixteenth years. Their colleagues agreed. Indeed, all of the experienced Japanese, Chinese, and US early childhood educators described how they changed with experience, and in each case, they described these changes as growth. However, this does not mean that the relationship of experience to expertise is linear or even always positive. Asking experienced teachers to reflect on how they are different now from their early years in the classroom does not allow for pinpointing when change occurs. We have consistent evidence of the direction of change but not of the rate, nor do we know whether the growth is more steady or sporadic.

I have identified a directionality to change and characteristics of change with experience that are strikingly consistent across my participants in all three countries. But this is not to say that this trajectory always follows a smooth path. Looking across the interviews from the three countries suggests a picture of professional growth that is difficult to break into a series of orderly stages. Instead, teachers' reports suggest a variety of trajectories. One of these trajectories is consistent with stage theories, as in the case of a teacher like Fran who reported having spent several years getting accustomed to life in the preschool classroom, settling into a comfortable pattern, and then reaching what Piagetians would call a period of disequilibrium, when a previously adequate way of operating no longer feels adequate. In Fran's case, her period of disequilibrium led her to a decision to take additional classes, which helped her make the jump to what she described as a higher level of expertise. Mizuho Tanaka and Sachiko Iwakura, teachers at the Sapporo School for the Deaf, related a more dramatic version of reaching a point of disequilibrium, when they came to the conclusion that, after ten years or more of systematically working to get better at teaching deaf children using oral methods, their whole approach was wrong-headed, leading them to start their professional growth anew, working to learn and master a new paradigm of deaf education.

These teachers did not so much move up to the next step on the staircase they were on as they jumped to a different staircase.

Several veteran Chinese teachers reported having gradually become expert within a teaching approach and then, following top-down educational reform, having to function within a new curricular and pedagogical model, which temporarily positioned them as less competent in the new strategies than their younger colleagues. Exploring the changes in "Western societies after World War II" and the "New Relationships between the Generations" that arose from these changes, Margaret Mead (1978) introduced the concept of a cultural shift from what she called postfigurative to prefigurative ways of teaching and learning. While in postfigurative cultures, which are more or less static, adults' knowledge and experience can be "passed down" from the older generation, providing the younger generation with adequate equipment for mastering their lives, this is no longer the case in modern societies under conditions of change. This could explain the discourse of how the pace of change in China makes experienced teachers' knowledge less valuable than in a postfigurative culture like Japan. While they suddenly found themselves in need of remediation in their understanding of the new curriculum, Chinese teachers remained accomplished in what they called "practical skills" for dealing with children and parents. This suggests that professional growth is both non- and multidimensional and that one can become an expert in some aspects of teaching while lagging in others. Other interviewees suggested that trajectories of expertise for some teachers take the shape of an upside-down U, as they improve at their craft for many years and then hit a period of "burnout," caused by exhaustion, personal crisis, or, in the cases of some veteran teachers in China and the US, becoming so disillusioned by top-down policy directives that they lose enthusiasm for teaching and even leave the field.

Preschool administrators in all three countries said that there are some teachers who never get very good at their craft and who plateau at a relatively low level of ability. The director of a preschool in Honolulu said, "I've worked with a lot of teachers who have been teaching for ten, fifteen years. They get to a maintenance level, and that's where it stays." A director at a private *yōchien* in Tokyo commented, "A few of our teachers are not strong when they begin and they never get much stronger, no matter how long they work for us. In these cases, we just support them as best as we can and try to put them where they'll do the least harm!" These reports are consistent with the literature on teacher development in the US. As David Berliner writes, "Evidence exists that some teachers remain fixed at a less than competent level of performance" (2004, 207).

Conceptualizing Expertise beyond Preschool Teaching

This study is a contribution to the understanding of the link between experience and expertise. Although the findings are based on the study of preschool teachers, the findings may be applicable to other levels of education and even to other fields and domains. Studies of fields of practice other than preschool have shown similar characteristics of the kind of expertise that comes with years of experience. For example, Xiangming Chen (2015) writes in her study of expert Chinese secondary teachers, "These teachers . . . try to keep a balance between non-action and action. In fact, the term 'non-action' here does not mean that these teachers do not act at all but that they act in such a way that it does not interrupt the natural growth of their students" (198). Max van Manen, building on a concept first developed by Johann Herbart, introduced the term "pedagogical thoughtfulness and tact" to describe the way expert teachers employ "the improvisational pedagogical-didactical skill of instantly knowing, from moment to moment, how to deal with students in interactive teaching-learning situations" (1995, 8). Experienced teachers achieve a kind of fluency and spontaneity that is seen in what Berliner describes as *arational*, Polanyi describes as *gestalt*, Gladwells's (actually Erickson's) violinists with ten thousand hours under their belts, Spiro's ability to function in ill-structured domains, Bloch's non-linguistic knowledge, Kounin's "withitness," and Csikszentmihalyi's flow, lack of self-consciousness, and awkwardness. These conceptions of expertise are consistent with the changes with experience described by the Japanese, Chinese, and US early childhood educators we interviewed.

The preschool teachers in this study report becoming, with years of experience, less anxious, more relaxed, and more present—characteristics that have been found in other domains as well. As David Berliner (2004) wrote while reflecting on decades of studying teaching expertise:

> Experts in teaching share characteristics of experts in more prestigious fields such as chess, medical diagnosis, and physics problem solving. Thus, there is no basis to believe that there are differences in the sophistication of the cognitive processes used by teachers and experts in other fields. (26)

The concept of tacit knowledge suggests that across domains of professional practice, practitioners become less consciously intentional and more intuitive and physically adept (Polanyi 1962). The ability to retain composure under pressure and to take time to slow down, allowing for nuanced decision-making under tense conditions that demand action (or holding back), has been attributed to skilled, experienced pilots (Hutchins and Klausen 1996; Bellenkes, Wickens, and Kramer 1997); surgeons (Polanyi 1966; Hindmarsh and Pilnick 2007; Ericsson 2004), computer scientists (Dreyfus and Dreyfus 1986), musicians (Ericsson, Krampe, and Tesch-Römer 1993), and athletes (Jackson and Marsh 1996). To perform at a high level in each of these fields requires a similar ability to slow things down in order to make good on-the-spot decisions, an expertise that takes years of experience to master.

Acknowledgments

I would like to thank the Spencer Foundation and the Japan Society for the Promotion of Science (JSPS KAKENHI Grant Number JP17K14021) for their support in funding this research project. I offer my sincere appreciation to Yeh Hsueh, Jie Zhang, and Lynn Paine not only for their help in organizing the focus group interviews in China but also for their helpful feedback on an earlier draft of the China chapter; Junko Hamaguchi, Hiroshi Usui, Lani Au, and Gaynel Buxton for their help in organizing the focus group interviews in Tokyo, Sapporo, and Hawaii; the anonymous reviewers for their thick feedback and intellectual contributions, which I have incorporated into my rewriting; my acquisitions editor, Elizabeth Branch Dyson, for her passion and commitment to this project; the editorial and design team at the University of Chicago Press, and especially to Mollie McFee for her support throughout the process; and John D. Moore for his copyediting. Finally, I want to give my heartfelt thanks to the directors, teachers, and experts who participated in this research project. Without you, this research project never would have been possible. Thank you for everything.

Notes

Chapter One

1. In their *Preschool in Three Cultures* study, Tobin, Wu, and Davidson (1989) invented the research method they call "video-cued multivocal ethnography." This is a research method in which researchers show participants videos when conducting interviews and use those videos as cues to provoke discussion.

2. A note on translation: In the Japan chapter, the word "teacher" is used to refer to practitioners because this is the most common term for early childhood education and care workers in North America, but while children and parents in Japan address and refer to them as "sensei," their job title is not "sensei" but *hoikusha*. This brings us to one of the words used most often by Japanese participants to describe their practice: *hoiku*. One common dictionary translation of this word is "childcare," which is consistent with translating *hoikuen* as "childcare center." But the meaning of the term *hoiku* when used by Japanese early childhood educators to describe their practice involves more than just caring for children. This is a word that combines the characters for "keep" and "develop." This meaning does not refer to keeping children from developing, but rather, just the opposite: to keep, in the sense of protect and support, a place for children's development. "Develop" here does not carry nearly as much of the feeling as it does in English of being a psychological concept. There is another Japanese term for children's psychological development: *hattatsu*. Therefore, in the Japan chapter, when I quote participants who used the term *hoiku*, because the term has no single English equivalent, I vary the translation according to the context, sometimes using "way of being with children," sometimes "way of supporting children's development," sometimes "work with young children," sometimes "teach," and most often and most simply, "approach."

Chapter Two

1. Portions of this chapter appeared, in a different form, in Chapter 5 in *Teaching Embodied* (Hayashi and Tobin 2015).

2. In 2015, Madoka added an all-day infant toddler program and extended care for the preschool aged children (Hayashi and Tobin 2017).

Chapter Four

1. Arizona's Early Childhood Block Grant is state funding that aims to promote student achievement by providing flexible additional funding for early childhood programs.

2. First Things First is Arizona's public funding source for supporting the healthy development and learning of young children from birth to age five.

3. Creative Curriculum is one of the most widely used curricula created by an educational company in the US.

4. Attila the Hun was the leader of Huns in the fifth century known for his harsh modes of control.

5. "Let It Go" is a song in the Disney movie *Frozen*, released in 2013. It was popular around the time the interviews were conducted.

6. "Mountain Dew" is a soda well known for its high caffeine content.

References

Alibali, Martha W., Mitchell J. Nathan, Matthew S. Wolfgram, R. Breckinridge Church, Steven A. Jacobs, Chelsea Johnson Martinez, and Eric J. Knuth. 2014. "How Teachers Link Ideas in Mathematics Instruction Using Speech and Gesture: A Corpus Analysis." *Cognition and Instruction* 32 (1): 65–100.

Azuma, Hiroshi. 1994. *Nihonjin no shitsuke to kyōiku* 日本人のしつけと教育 [Discipline and education in Japan]. Tokyo: Daigaku Shuppankai.

Bakhtin, Mikhail. 1981. *The Dialogic Imagination: Four Essays*. Austin: University of Texas Press.

Bakhtin, Mikhail. 1990. *Art and Answerability*. Translated by Vadim Liapunov and Kenneth Brostrom. Austin: University of Texas Press.

Bellenkes, Andrew H., Christopher D. Wickens, and Arthur F. Kramer. 1997. "Visual Scanning and Pilot Expertise: The Role of Attentional Flexibility and Mental Model Development." *Aviation, Space, and Environmental Medicine* 68, no. 7 (July): 569–79.

Bellm, Dan, Alice Burton, Marcy Whitebook, Linda Broatch, and Marci P. Young. 2002. *Inside the Pre-K Classroom: A Study of Staffing and Stability in state-funded prekindergarten programs*. Washington, DC: Center for the Child Care Workforce.

Benesse. 2009. "*Korekara no youjikyoiku*" *Hoikusya no shishitsu wo takameru ennai kensyu toha* 『これからの幼児教育』保育者の資質を高める園内研修とは [Future early childhood education and care: In-house training for improving a quality of early childhood practitioners].

Berliner, David C. 1986. "In Pursuit of the Expert Pedagogue." *Educational Researcher* 15 (7): 5–13.

Berliner, David C. 1988. *The Development of Expertise in Pedagogy*. Washington, DC: AACTE Publications.

Berliner, David C. 2004. "Describing the Behavior and Documenting the Accomplishments of Expert Teachers." *Bulletin of Science, Technology & Society* 24 (3): 200–212.

Bion, Winfred. 1967. "Notes on Memory and Desire." *The Psychoanalytic Forum* 2 (3): 243-256.

Bloch, Maurice. 1991. "Language, Anthropology and Cognitive Science." *Man*, n.s., 26 no. 2 (June): 183–98.

Bourdieu, Pierre. 2000. *Pascalian Mediations*. Palo Alto, CA: Stanford University Press.

Boyd, Margaret. 2013. "'I Love My Work But . . .' The Professionalization of Early Childhood Education." *Qualitative Report* 18 (36): 71, 1–20.

Buchanan, Rebecca. 2015. "Teacher Identity and Agency in an Era of Accountability." *Teachers and Teaching* 21 (6): 700–719.

Carter, Kathy, Donna Sabers, Katherine Cushing, Stefinee Pinnegar, and David C. Berliner. 1987. "Processing and Using Information about Students: A Study of Expert, Novice, and Postulant Teachers." *Teaching and Teacher Education* 3 (2): 147–57.

Che, Yi. 2010. "Preschool Teachers' Reactions to Early Childhood Education Reform in China." PhD diss., Arizona State University.

Chen, Xiangming. 2015. "Meaning-Making of Chinese Teachers in the Curriculum Reform." In *Autobiography and Teacher Development in China: Subjectivity and Culture in Curriculum Reform*, edited by Zhang Hua and William F. Pinar, 193–211. New York: Palgrave Macmillan.

Csikszentmihalyi, Mihaly. 1975. *Beyond Boredom and Anxiety: Experiencing Flow in Work and Play*. San Francisco: Josey-Bass.

de Certeau, Michel. 1984. *The Practice of Everyday Life*. Berkeley: University of California Press.

de Frietas, Elizabeth. 2013. "What Were You Thinking? A Deleuzian/Guattarian Analysis of Communication in the Mathematics Classroom." *Educational Philosophy and Theory* 45 (13): 287–300.

Doig, Brian, and Susie Groves. 2011. "Japanese Lesson Study: Teacher Professional Development through Communities of Inquiry." *Mathematics Teacher Education and Development* 13 (1): 77–93.

Dreyfus, Hubert, and Stuart Dreyfus. 1986. *Mind over Machine*. New York: Free Press.

Ericsson, K. Anders. 2004. "Deliberate Practice and the Acquisition and Maintenance of Expert Performance in Medicine and Related Domains." *Academic Medicine* 79 (10): S70–S81.

Ericsson, K. Anders, Ralf T. Krampe, and Clemens Tesch-Romer. 1993. "The Role of Deliberate Practice in the Acquisition of Expert Performance." *Psychological Review* 100 (3): 363–406.

Ericsson, K. Anders, and Robert Pool. 2016. *Peak: Secrets from the New Science of Expertise*. Boston: Houghton Mifflin Harcourt.

Feiman-Nemser, Sharon, Sharon Schwille, Cindy Carver, and Brian Yusko. 1999. *A Conceptual Review of Literature on New Teacher Induction*. Washington, DC: National Partnership for Excellence and Accountability in Teaching.

Feng, Xiao-xia. 2017. "An Overview of Early Childhood Education in the People's Republic of China." In *Early Childhood Education in Chinese Societies*, edited by Nirmala Rao, Jing Zhou, and Jin Sun, 55–70. Dordrecht: Springer.

Foundation for Child Development. 2018. "Power to the Profession Task Force's Decision Cycles 3–5." https://www.fcd-us.org/power-to-the-profession.

Gladwell, Malcolm. 2008. *Outliers: The Story of Success*. New York: Little, Brown.

Goffin, Stacie G. 2013. *Early Childhood Education for a New Era: Leading for Our Profession*. New York: Teachers College Press.

Hayashi, Akiko, and Joseph Tobin. 2011. "The Japanese Preschool's Pedagogy of Peripheral Participation." *Ethos* 39 (2): 139–64.

Hayashi, Akiko, and Joseph Tobin. 2014. "The Power of Implicit Teaching Practices:

Continuities and Discontinuities in Pedagogical Approaches of Deaf and Hearing Preschools in Japan." *Comparative Education Review* 58 (1): 24–46.

Hayashi, Akiko, and Joseph Tobin. 2015. *Teaching Embodied: Cultural Practice in Japanese Preschools*. Chicago: University of Chicago Press.

Hayashi, Akiko, and Joseph Tobin. 2017. "Reforming the Japanese Preschool System: An Ethnographic Case Study of Policy Implementation." *Education Policy Analysis Archives* 25 (100). http://epaa.asu.edu/ojs/article/view/3213.

Hiebert, James, and James W. Stigler. 2000. "A Proposal for Improving Classroom Teaching: Lessons from the TIMSS Video Study." *The Elementary School Journal* 101 (1): 3–20.

Hindmarsh, Jon, and Pilnick Alison. 2007. "Knowing Bodies at Work: Embodiment and Ephemeral Teamwork in Anaesthesia." *Organization Studies* 28 (9): 1395–416.

Hutchins, Edwin, and Tove Klausen. 1996. "Distributed Cognition in an Airline Cockpit." In *Cognition and Communication at Work*, edited by Yrjö Engeström and David Middleton, 15–34. Cambridge: Cambridge University Press.

Ingersoll, Richard M., and Michael Strong. 2011. "The Impact of Induction and Mentoring Programs for Beginning Teachers: A Critical Review of the Research." *Review of Educational Research* 81 (2): 201–33.

Jackson, Susan A., and Herbert W. Marsh. 1996. "Development and Validation of a Scale to Measure Optimal Experience: The Flow State Scale." *Journal of Sport and Exercise Psychology* 18 (1): 17–35.

Jiang, Yong, Li-juan Pang, and Jin Sun. 2017. "Early Childhood Teacher Education in China." In *Early Childhood Education in Chinese Societies*, edited by Nirmala Rao, Jing Zhou, and Jin Sun, 85–100. Dordrecht: Springer.

Ko, Bomna, Tristan Wallhead, and Phillip Ward. 2006. "Professional Development Workshops—What Do Teachers Learn and Use?" *Journal of Teaching in Physical Education* 25 (4): 397–412.

Kounin, Jacob S. 1970. *Discipline and Group Management in Classrooms*. New York: Holt, Rinehart & Winston.

Lave, Jean, and Etienne Wenger. 1991. *Situated Learning: Legitimate Peripheral Participation*. Cambridge: Cambridge University Press.

Lewis, Catherine. 1984. "Cooperation and Control in Japanese Nursery Schools." *Comparative Education Review* 28 (1): 69–84.

Lewis, Catherine. 1988. "Japanese First-Grade Classrooms: Implications for US Theory and Research." *Comparative Education Review* 32 (2): 159–72.

Lewis, Catherine. 1989. "From Indulgence to Internalization: Social Control in the Early School Years." *Journal of Japanese Studies* 15 (1): 139–57.

Lewis, Catherine. 2000. "Lesson Study: The Core of Japanese Professional Development." Paper presented at the Annual Meeting of the American Educational Research Association, New Orleans, LA, April 2000. https://files.eric.ed.gov/fulltext/ED444972.pdf.

Lewis, Catherine, Rebecca Perry, and Aki Murata. 2006. "How Should Research Contribute to Instruction Improvement? The Case of Lesson Study." *Educational Researcher* 35 (3): 3–14.

Lewis, Catherine, and Christine Lee. 2017. "The Global Spread of Lesson Study." In

International Handbook of Teacher Quality and Policy, edited by Motoko Akiba and Gerald K. LeTendre, 185–203. New York, NY: Routledge.

Li, Hui, and X. Christine Wang. 2017. "International Perspectives on Early Childhood Education in the Mainland China, Hong Kong, Macao and Taiwan." In *Early Childhood Education in Chinese Societies*, edited by Nirmala Rao, Jing Zhou, and Jin Sun, 235–50. Dordrecht: Springer.

Liu, Chang. 2017. "Living Together: The Bodily Life of Preschools in China and the United States." PhD diss., University of Georgia.

Luft, Julie. A, Gillian H. Roehrig, and Nancy C. Patterson. 2003. "Contrasting Landscapes: A Comparison of the Impact of Different Induction Programs on Beginning Secondary Science Teachers' Practices, Beliefs, and Experiences." *Journal of Research in Science Teaching* 40 (1): 77–97.

Mahmood, Sehba. 2013. "First-Year Preschool and Kindergarten teachers: Challenges of Working with Parents." *School Community Journal* 23 (2): 55–86.

Mead, Margaret. 1978. *Culture and Commitment: The New Relationships between the Generations in the 1970s*. Rev. ed. New York: Anchor Press/Doubleday.

MEXT (Ministry of Education, Culture, Sports, Science and Technology). 2019. *Youjikyoiku no jisen no sitsukoujyou ni kansuru kentoukai, youjikyoiku no genjyo* 幼児教育の実践の質向上に関する検討会, 幼児教育の現状 [The current situation of early childhood education: Discussion of improving a quality of practices in ECE].

National Research Council. 2015. *Transforming the Workforce for Children Birth through age 8: A Unifying Foundation*. Washington, DC: National Academies Press.

Parks, Amy Noelle, and Mardi Schmeichel. 2014. "Children, Mathematics, and Videotape: Using Multimodal Analysis to Bring Bodies into Early Childhood Assessment Interviews." *American Educational Research Journal* 51 (3): 505–37.

Phillips, Deborah, Lea J. E. Austin, and Marcy Whitebook. 2016. "The Early Care and Education Workforce." *The Future of Children* 26 (2): 139–58.

Polanyi, Michael. 1962. "Tacit Knowing: Its Bearing on Some Problems of Philosophy." *Reviews of Modern Physics* 34 (4): 601–15.

Polanyi, Michael. 1966. *The Tacit Dimension*. Chicago: University of Chicago Press.

Rappleye, Jeremy, and Hikaru Komatsu. 2017. "How to Make Lesson Study Work in America and Worldwide: A Japanese Perspective on the Onto-cultural Basis of (Teacher) Education." *Research in Comparative and International Education* 12 (4): 398–430.

Ryles, Gilbert. 1949. *The Concept of Mind*. Chicago: University of Chicago Press.

Schempp, Paul, Steven Tan, Dean Manross, and Matthew Fincher. 1998. "Differences in Novice and Competent Teachers' Knowledge." *Teachers and Teaching: Theory and Practice* 4 (1): 9–20.

Schreiber, Constantin, and Gustavo E. Fischman. 2016. "The Visual Turn in Comparative and International Education Research." In *Handbook on Comparative and International Studies in Education*, edited by Donald K. Sharpes, 127–51. Charlotte: Information Age Publishing.

Scopelitis, Stephanie Athene. 2013. "Interactive Explanations: The Functional Role of Gestural and Bodily Action for Explaining and Learning Scientific Concepts in Face-to-Face Arrangements." PhD diss., University of Washington.

Spiro, Rand J, Brian P. Collins, and Aparna R. Ramchandran. 2007. "Modes of Openness and Flexibility in Cognitive Flexibility Hypertext Learning Environments." In *Flexible Learning in an Information Society*, edited by Badrul Huda Khan, 18–25. Hershey, PA: Information Science Publishing.

Stevens, Reed. 2012. "The Missing Bodies of Mathematical Thinking and Learning Have Been Found." *Journal of the Learning Sciences* 21 (2): 337–46.

Tatto, Maria Teresa, and Sharon Senk. 2011. "The Mathematics Education of Future Primary and Secondary Teachers: Methods and Findings from the Teacher Education and Development Study in Mathematics." *Journal of Teacher Education* 62 (2): 121–37.

Tobin, Joseph. 2019. "The Origins of the Video-Cued Multivocal Ethnographic Method." *Anthropology & Education Quarterly* 50 (3): 255–69.

Tobin, Joseph, Yeh Hsueh, and Mayumi Karasawa. 2009. *Preschool in Three Cultures Revisited: China, Japan, and the United States.* Chicago: University of Chicago Press.

Tobin, Joseph, David Wu, and Dana Davidson. 1989. *Preschool in Three Cultures: Japan, China and the United States.* New Haven: Yale University Press.

van Manen, Max. 1995. "On the Epistemology of Reflective Practice." *Teachers and Teaching* 1 (1): 33–50.

Wagner, Brigid Daly, and Lucia French. 2010. "Motivation, Work Satisfaction, and Teacher Change among Early Childhood Teachers." *Journal of Research in Childhood Education* 24 (2): 152–71.

Walsh, Daniel. 2002. "The Development of Self in Japanese Preschools: Negotiating Space." *Counterpoints* 180:213–45.

Wang, Jian, Sandra J. Odell, and Sharon A. Schwille. 2008. "Effects of Teacher Induction on Beginning Teachers' Teaching: A Critical Review of the Literature." *Journal of Teacher Education* 59 (2): 132–52.

Whitebook, Marcy. 1999. "Child Care Workers: High Demand, Low Wages." *The Annals of the American Academy of Political and Social Science* 563 (1): 146–61.

Whitebook, Marcy, and Dan Bellm. 1999. *Taking on Turnover: An Action Guide for Child Care Center Teachers and Directors.* Washington, DC: Center for the Child Care Workforce.

Xiao, Bing, and Joseph Tobin. 2018. "The Use of Video as a Tool for Reflection with Preservice Teachers." *Journal of Early Childhood Teacher Education* 39 (4): 328–45.

Index

Page numbers in italics refer to figures and the letter t following a page number denotes a table.

Collins, Brian J., 3
commitment, 20, 111, 114, 118, 145, 161–62
communication, 37, 106, 154, 171, 178; with body, 32, 55, 56, 58, 60, 129; embodied, 63, 88; of trust, 17, 66
complexity, 29, 31, 32, 139, 152, 155
composure, 1, 23, 54, 56, 171; lack of, 12, 15, 16, 18, 19, 21, 28; retaining, 22, 183; sense of, 164, 175
conferences, 46, 47, 146, 158
confidence, 31, 35, 89, 122, 137, 156; in children, 64; gains in, 56, 114, 124–25, 142, 162; lack of, 21, 48, 51; loss of, 47, 60; of parents in teachers, 150
Confucian concepts, 8, 104
congrong (calm), 77, 165. *See also* calm
consciousness, 42, 43, 81, 167, 183
constructivist theory, 108
contextual factors, 103, 175–76
continuities, 50, 62, 111, 122
control, 122, 131; ability to, 75, 86, 124, 173; approaches to, 91; of daily routines, 26; establishing, 87; of groups, 116, 130; loss of, 22, 170, 171; *na xia*, 88; over bag of tricks, 148; over children, 53, 66, 158, 163; of professional growth, 144, 179; relinquishing, 31, 129, 135, 140; scaffolding vs., 113; of self, 159
coursework, 5, 98, 100, 118, 148, 150; preservice, 39, 85, 97, 145; professional growth and, 147, 180; salary tied to, 179
Creative Curriculum, 123, 188n3
creativity, children's, 20, 89, 90, 109, 113
creativity, teachers', 92
criticism, 8, 35, 46, 51, 119, 177, 178
critique, 5, 21, 35, 37, 104; self-, 39, 178
Csikszentmihalyi, Mihaly, 183
Cudiamat, Cheryl, 6t, 114
cultural factors, 81, 100, 109, 163, 175
culture, 9, 100, 145, 177, 182; Chinese, 81, 87, 101, 105, 108, 109; Confucian, 104; Japanese, 32, 38, 50

Daguan Kindergarten, 83, 88, 97, 98, 102, 106
Davidson, Dana, 82, 187n1
deaf children, 47, 48, 63, 181
decision making, 56, 84, 90, 184; composure and, 183; mindfulness in, 86; quick, 43
deliberative practice, 4, 67, 129, 148
demeanor, 58, 59, 62, 127, 130
Developmentally Appropriate Practice, 114, 148

directives, 92, 111, 158, 162; policy, 175, 182; from superiors, 91, 179
disposition, 3
Dresden, Janna, 128, 132, 140, 145
Dufault, Gwen, 126, 130, 138, 173; calmness of, 137, 139, 165; on parenting, 152; on professional growth, 125

Early Childhood Block Grant, 117, 188n1
early childhood educators, 4, 7, 76, 116, 155, 161; change with experience, 181, 183; Chinese, 83, 168, 176; Japanese, 8, 26, 63, 163, 169, 187n2; parenting and, 152; St. Timothy's founded by, 114; US, 123–25, 146, 148, 163, 172, 180; withitness and, 171
East China Normal University, 76, 86, 93, 96, 98, 108, 109, 168
economic factors, 95, 100
embodied pedagogy, 2, 64, 103, 131, 171; benefits of, 32, 91, 173; changes in, 54–56, 65, 67; continuity in, 62; expertise in, 129–30; empathy, 30, 55, 63, 129, 141
ennai kenshū (in-house study groups), 44, 45, 178
enthusiasm, 47, 139, 156, 161, 182; communicating, 55, 129
Ericsson, Anders, 4
evaluations, preschool, 78
evaluations, student, 175
evaluations, teacher, 78, 79; Chinese, 75, 81, 92, 93, 175, 177; US, 176, 179
evaluations, training, 105
experience and expertise, 2–4, 73, 78, 100, 181–82, 183
extrinsic motivators, 177, 179, 180
eye contact, 62, 130, 171

facial expressions, 19, 54, 62, 171, 172; anguished, 61; atmosphere created with, 33; children's, 25; communicating with, 64; gentle, 65; hard, 63; naturalness of, 21; restrained, 58
failure, 36, 37, 141, 164, 169, 170; fearing, 5; pedagogical value of, 12, 21, 39, 74, 89. *See also* mistakes, teachers
fangshou (letting go), 77, 88, 170, 173. *See also* letting go/let it go
feedback, 34, 35, 44, 104, 179; in Chinese professional development, 177, 178; from colleagues, 5, 45; learning from, 42; from mentors, 150

attending to children, 15, 27; changes in body use, 54; characteristic differences between, 124; finding oneself as a teacher, 41; initial, 2, 14, 143, 150, 162, 164; interacting with children, 62; learning from children, 39; ready to change, 179; self-reflection, 43

status, 69, 70, 93, 94, 125, 152, 175

Stevens, Reed, 56

strategies, 84, 91, 134, 143, 169; brainstorming, 104; changing, 168; competence in, 182; correct, 138; decisiveness, 88; development, 180; effective, 75; experience gives, 74; *mimamoru*, 37; repertoire of, 16, 18, 32, 84, 90, 116, 117, 127; tactics vs., 92, 148; teacherly restraint, 29; Teaching Strategies Gold, 160. *See also* tactics

strictness, 37, 66, 132, 173; in China, 87, 174; right time for, 17, 88, 99; teacher variations in, 77, 86

structural factors, 68, 163, 176

study groups, 44, 48, 70, 102–5, 106, 109, 178

Su, Guimin, 95

sui ji ying bian (change quickly), 168

Sun, Jin, 105

tacit knowledge, 3, 56, 183

tact, 54, 65, 86

tactics, 17, 91, 92, 148, 161. *See also* strategies

Tanaka, Mizuho, 24, 41–42, 63, 65, 181; crisis in confidence, 47, 48, 51

Taoism, 8, 91, 163, 167, 173

teacher-centered approach, 96, 98, 140, 166. *See also* child-centered pedagogy

theory, 56, 75, 92, 93; in China, 98–99; constructivist, 108; inexperienced teachers know, 73, 83, 97, 100

thoughtful thoughtlessness, 8, 90–91

tightness. *See* looseness and tightness

Tobin, Joseph, 12, 16, 68, 95, 97, 187n1; on curriculum change, 118; on embodied pedagogy, 129, 171; on physical care of children, 82; on teaching inexperienced teachers, 30

top-down directives, 123, 175, 182

top-down reforms, 7, 91, 92

touch, 64, 82, 171

training, 95, 102, 103, 140, 160; Child Development Associate (CDA), 117; Chinese vs. Western, 108; Creative Curriculum, 123; differences in, 98–99, 175; in-service, 96, 105, 108; practical experience vs., 97, 107; programs, 7, 127; trainers, 78, 95, 96, 105, 123

triage, 132–34

trial-and-error learning, 13, 14, 38, 39, 56

Umeda, Jannie, 2, 126, 133, 137, 143, 146; on being a parent, 151; bodily techniques, 130, 131, 132; calmness of, 138, 139; career trajectory, 112, 113, 145, 154; changes with experience, 1, 114; interventions, 135, 169; on letting go, 134; mentoring of, 115, 127, 150; rigidity, 116, 167; on scanning, 172; study participant, 6t, 111–13, 123, 161; talking, 136

urban vs. rural preschools, 93, 94, 105, 108; professional development, 100, 107; working conditions, 95–97

Usui, Hiroshi, 22, 167

Vail, Cindy, 120, 128, 154, 165

van Manen, Max, 3, 8, 60, 67, 84, 86, 168, 183; on silent knowledge, 55

video-cued multivocal ethnography, 1, 4, 6, 7, 9, 114, 187n1

Wang, Christine, 94

Wang, Jian, 100, 101, 102, 170; career trajectory, 69–72, 93–94, 107; on caring, 1, 82; expertise of, 75–80; looseness of, 86–87; study participant, 2, 6t, 68, 69

Watkins, Wayne, 147–48

Wenger, Etienne, 101

window schools, 70, 106, 107

wisdom, 25, 85, 104, 128, 139, 152, 162. *See also* practical wisdom

withitness, 56, 60, 81, 88, 171, 173, 183

Wright, Amelia, 167

Wu, David, 82, 187n1

wuwei (inaction), 8, 89, 91, 170

wuweierzhi (ruling by inaction), 89, 90, 170

Xiao, Bing, 170

Xie, Ping, 83, 84, 106

xueyizhiyong (put concepts into practice), 84

yōchien (kindergarten), 14, 43, 52, 178, 182; *hoikuen* vs., 44, 47, 48, 49

yohaku (empty space), 28, 29, 88, 89, 174

Yong, Jin, 91

Yoshizawa, Hidenori, 6t, 10, 50

Yoshizawa, Hironori, 6t, 10, 12, 21, 38, 50, 54, 166

Lightning Source UK Ltd.
Milton Keynes UK
UKHW010009090422
401309UK00002B/42